973
THE
D1803025

ENTERED APR 5 1991

PORTRAITS OF AMERICAN PRESIDENTS
VOLUME VIII

THE CARTER PRESIDENCY

FOURTEEN INTIMATE PERSPECTIVES OF JIMMY CARTER

Edited by
KENNETH W. THOMPSON

Miller Center of Public Affairs
University of Virginia

UNIVERSITY
PRESS OF
AMERICA

The Miller Center

University of Virginia

Lanham • New York • London

Copyright © 1990 by
University Press of America®, Inc.
4720 Boston Way
Lanham, Maryland 20706

3 Henrietta Street
London WC2E 8LU England

All rights reserved
Printed in the United States of America
British Cataloging in Publication Information Available

Co-published by arrangement with
The White Burkett Miller Center of Public Affairs,
University of Virginia

The views expressed by the author(s) of this publication do not necessarily
represent the opinions of the Miller Center. We hold to Jefferson's dictum that:
"Truth is the proper and sufficient antagonist to error, and has nothing to
fear from the conflict, unless by human interposition, disarmed of her
natural weapons, free argument and debate."

Library of Congress Cataloging-in-Publication Data

The Carter presidency : 14 intimate perspectives of Jimmy Carter /
edited by Kenneth W. Thompson.
    p.   cm.—(Portraits of American presidents ; v. 8)
  1. United States—Politics and government—1977-1981.
  2. Carter, Jimmy, 1924-. I. Thompson, Kenneth W., 1921-.
                    II. Series.
        E176.1.P83   1982 vol. 8   [E872]
    973'.0992 s—dc20   [973.926]   90–12387 CIP

ISBN 0–8191–7812–8 (alk. paper)
ISBN 0-8191-7813-6 (pbk. : alk. paper)

    The paper used in this publication meets the minimum requirements of
American National Standard for Information Sciences—Permanence
of Paper for Printed Library Materials, ANSI Z39.48–1984.

Dedicated

to

Jimmy and Rosalynn Carter

who gave every encouragement

to

the Miller Center Oral History

of

the Carter Presidency

TABLE OF CONTENTS

PREFACE · · · · · · · · · · · · · · · · · ix
    Kenneth W. Thompson

INTRODUCTION · · · · · · · · · · · · · · · xi
    Kenneth W. Thompson

PART ONE: A PRESIDENT'S FAITH

1. CONTEMPORARY NATIONAL AND INTER-
NATIONAL ISSUES, 1987 · · · · · · · · · · 3
President Jimmy Carter

PART TWO: GOVERNANCE AND THE CABINET

2. THE PRESIDENCY AND THE CABINET:
FORMING A NEW CABINET DEPARTMENT · 19
Judge Shirley Hufstedler

3. THE CABINET SYSTEM AND LABOR: TASKS
OF A MIDDLE-SIZED DEPARTMENT · · · · 39
Secretary of Labor Ray Marshall

4. CABINET GOVERNMENT AND PRESIDENT
CARTER: AN ALTERNATIVE FOR
ORGANIZING POLICYMAKING· · · · · · · 59
Attorney General Griffin Bell

TABLE OF CONTENTS

PART THREE: POLITICS AND ECONOMICS: THE TIMES, THE CRISES AND THE PEOPLE

5. THE TIMES, THE CRISES AND THE PEOPLE . . 85
   Secretary of Commerce Juanita Kreps

6. GOVERNMENT AND INDUSTRIAL COMPETITIVENESS VIEWED FROM THE CARTER PRESIDENCY 93
   Secretary of Commerce Philip M. Klutznick

7. POLITICS AND AGRICULTURE: LESSONS OF THE CARTER PRESIDENCY 115
   Secretary of Agriculture Bob S. Bergland

PART FOUR: THE CARTER FOREIGN POLICY

8. CARTER'S FOREIGN POLICY: THE SOURCE OF THE PROBLEM 135
   Secretary of State Cyrus Vance

9. CARTER'S FOREIGN POLICY: SUCCESS ABROAD, FAILURE AT HOME 145
   Director of the Policy Planning Staff
   Anthony Lake

10. THE CARTER PRESIDENCY AND THE UNITED NATIONS 159
    Ambassador Donald McHenry

11. THE CARTER PRESIDENCY AND AND FOREIGN POLICY 177
    Secretary of State Edmund Muskie

PART FIVE: THE CARTER PRESIDENCY: PUBLIC PHILOSOPHY AND PRESIDENTIAL STYLE

12. CARTER'S POLITICAL RHETORIC 199
    Professor Gaddis Smith

TABLE OF CONTENTS

PART SIX: THE FIRST LADY AND THE VICE PRESIDENT

13. THE PERSPECTIVE OF THE FIRST LADY . . . 217
    Rosalynn Carter

14. THE PERSPECTIVE OF THE VICE PRESIDENT 239
    Walter F. Mondale

PREFACE

A pattern has emerged in the course of organizing Miller Center forums which has led to the present volume. We have discovered that the leading authorities on particular presidents have helped the Center to draw others with common background to the University of Virginia. By "word of mouth advertising," they have encouraged their friends to come to Faulkner House. Their help has been of inestimable value to a fledgling public affairs center. It has enabled us to conduct further presidential studies through the contributions of distinguished visitors to the understanding of contemporary presidents.

Partly by accident and partly by design, we have discovered our guests were turning the spotlight on certain American presidents. They were viewing particular administrations with shared values but different perspectives. Their differing experiences each illuminated a dimension that otherwise might have remained obscured. They helped us to understand the President they knew best. The product is a portrait, not a photograph; it helps us see the character and spirit of a leader, not the more or less important details a photograph tends to convey. It tells us what was central to his life and works, not what was peripheral. The photograph reveals what can be seen with the naked eye. The portrait shows one thing the photograph cannot reveal: the human essence of the person portrayed.

With this volume, we continue a series of Miller Center publications, *Portraits of American Presidents*. We are grateful to the University Press of America for making volumes in this series available to a wide audience. We have embarked on similar inquiries into the presidency of Ronald Reagan. In the Introduction which follows, the editor traces the history of the Center's interest in the presidency of Jimmy Carter.

INTRODUCTION

What sets the Carter Presidential Portrait volume apart from other volumes in this series is its concentration on the President and First Lady, Cabinet level officials, certain intangibles such as the nature of the times, accidents and unforeseen events and presidential style and politics. No White House officials participated in the forums that led up to the publication of this oral history. For that, a word of explanation is perhaps required. This Portrait is a followup to an earlier substantial effort to build an historical record of the Carter presidency and in particular the Carter White House.

Almost immediately at the close of the Carter administration, the Miller Center inaugurated an extensive oral history project with leading officials in the Carter White House. Some sixty persons came to the Center at the University of Virginia for day-and-a-half long debriefings with Center staff and visiting presidential scholars from institutions such as Harvard, Princeton, Johns Hopkins, and Vanderbilt among others. Senior White House staff were accompanied by junior colleagues in groups of from two to seven in number. In the words of one Carter official, they were invited "to keep their seniors honest." In fact, they were extraordinarily helpful in reconstructing events when memories failed. Discussions were taped and each official edited and returned the text of his or her individual oral history. Each participant stipulated the basis on which a particular text could be made available to scholars and writers now or in the future. Some specified that the material from this oral history should be accessible to essentially any student or researcher immediately. Others chose to embargo their testimony for periods of up to fifteen years.

Upon the completion of the Miller Center's oral history of the Carter White House brilliantly directed by Professor James Sterling Young, it was clear that even so far-reaching an oral history left gaps in the story of the Carter presidency. This was particularly true because of the important roles played by senior Cabinet officers and their impressions of the years from 1976-

INTRODUCTION

80. Their absence from the table left important missing chairs in the dialogue. Accordingly, we invited respected members of the Carter Cabinet to come to Charlottesville much as members of the previous postwar administrations and cabinets had participated. What proved somewhat surprising is that the two postwar presidencies in which a larger number of Cabinet members declined invitations were the presidencies of Franklin D. Roosevelt and Jimmy Carter. In the former case the limited response can be attributed to leaders passing from the scene. With the Carter presidency, the reasons are more obscure. For some the history of the Carter presidency may be too recent and the experience too fresh and perhaps painful. Others may be reluctant to comment on the action of living political figures or enter into contentious debates with contemporaries. Others may connect their involvement in such a history with future career plans. Whatever the reasons, we hope to publish a second volume in which absent members of the administration join in the completion of the Carter history.

These absences should not detract, however, from the value of a volume that opens with a presentation by President Jimmy Carter and closes with a response by the First Lady, Rosalynn Carter. Significantly, the Carter Portrait volume is the only Miller Center presidential portrait in which the President and the First Lady graciously joined in its preparation. Much as the Carters have demonstrated dedication and resolve in making their retirements an occasion for worldwide service in the well-being of mankind, for the Miller Center they both became part of a serious effort "to set the record straight." President Carter's contribution in reviewing certain events in the 1980s can properly be called an expression of his political faith. It serves as an introduction to all that follows.

In the same spirit, Judge Shirley Hufstedler in the lead chapter in the section on "Governance and the Cabinet" seeks to help Americans understand what was involved in being the founding secretary of a new Department of Education. Not only is she representative of the outstanding women and minority leaders whom President Carter brought into government, but she began virtually from scratch in organizing a new department. Thus her picture of the Carter presidency is instructive regarding the President's enthusiasm for education. It lends an additional dimension to the story by tracing the steps that Cabinet members must take in making a place for a new institution within government.

Secretary of Labor Ray Marshall was already an internationally known labor economist and student of industrial

INTRODUCTION

relations when he joined the Carter administration. He praises Carter for his ability to comprehend difficult issues affecting labor and the economy. With problems of youth unemployment, drugs, homelessness and crime having reached crisis proportions, Marshall's description of programs he helped organize has an immediacy and relevance for the 1990s. Further, Marshall is one of the few Cabinet members who had some professional contact with Carter in Georgia and his perspective is therefore based on pre-presidential as well as presidential observations.

When President Carter announced the appointment of Griffin Bell as attorney general, he predicted Mr. Bell would leave office as one of the nation's greatest attorneys general. With all his affection and loyalty for Carter, however, Bell stands out among Carter intimates for being singularly objective about the President. He has been outspoken about the conflict between legal standards and political expediency. In the present reflections, he goes beyond the Carter presidency defending Cabinet government in general as an alternative to domination by White House staff. While never losing sight of certain weaknesses in the Carter presidency, he calls attention to a more universal tendency toward substituting an ever expanding staff both in the executive and legislative branch for responsible officials elected or empowered by the Congress.

In Part Three, the focus is on politics and economics and on the main currents of the times, the crises that arose and the people involved. The Carter presidency was shaped by the public's response to Watergate. Ironically, this was both its strength and its weakness. Mr. Carter as an outsider was seen as restoring righteousness and integrity to Washington. A succession of crises made the administration's tenure more difficult, however, especially the Iran hostage crisis and the failed rescue attempt. OPEC's decision to raise oil prices helped bring on double-digit inflation. Major staff people in the administration, some with little Washington experience or knowledge of Congress, may have increased the difficulties further and led to the creation of a public image of ineptness and internal division.

Juanita Kreps was secretary of commerce from January 1977 to November 1979. A distinguished educator and economist, she preceded Philip Klutznick in that position. She makes "The Times, the Crises and the People" the main focus of her discussion. She also reflects on presidential style and gives her own interpretation of President Carter's major strengths and weaknesses in governance. Thus her review not only catalogues the administration's greatest successes but also some of its main disappointments.

INTRODUCTION

Secretary of Commerce Philip M. Klutznick who succeeded Secretary Kreps had served in government in six or seven earlier administrations and is a highly successful business leader. He views the Carter presidency against this background and in a political and economic context. He praises the President for his courage and decisiveness. Klutznick captures the spirit of the Carter administration and the President's drive for prompt action by subordinates. He reviews the backgrounds of those whom he sought to recruit for his administration. Perhaps without intending, Klutznick tells a great deal about Carter the man.

Secretary of Agriculture Bob S. Bergland, like other Cabinet members, was a stranger to President Carter but not to the practice of politics. His political mentor in the state of Minnesota and in national politics was Hubert Humphrey but he and Carter soon discovered common ground in the needs and problems of agriculture. Because of his background in the populist midwest, Bergland was perhaps more attuned to the outsider reformist thinking of Carter. His admiration for the President never prevented him from recognizing the high price Carter paid for inexperience with the ways of Washington. As a former congressman, Bergland was especially appalled by glaring weaknesses in the Carter administration's congressional relations. He reflects on some of the unique aspects of the administration such as Mrs. Carter's attendance at Cabinet meetings. On this and other subjects, Bergland's account should be read alongside interpretations by the Carters themselves to obtain a full picture of appearances and reality in the Carter administration.

In Part Four, discussions turn to the most controversial and paradoxical dimensions of the Carter presidency. On the one hand, the achievements of President Carter in foreign policy were immense. In terms of goals and accomplishments, the Carter legacy is outstanding. Few administrations can match success stories such as the Camp David Accords, the Panama Canal Treaty, the strengthening of relations with mainland China and SALT II, the main provisions of which the Reagan administration accepted despite candidate Reagan's criticisms during and following presidential campaigns. Commitment to the search for viable negotiated settlements to outstanding disputes became the hallmark of the Carter presidency, especially of Carter and Secretary of State Vance. At Camp David, Carter and Vance showed themselves to be consummate negotiators. Beyond diplomacy, Carter took the lead in dealing with global problems of the future such as human rights and the environment.

Yet, on the other hand, a succession of foreign policy controversies led to Carter's undoing. It was a foreign policy

INTRODUCTION

crises that was perhaps the most significant factor in Mr. Carter's defeat in the 1980 election. The appearance of dissension and disarray within the administration was the focus of criticisms of the Carter presidency and centered largely in foreign policy. The nation's inflation seems to have resulted as much from the aftermath of the OPEC oil crisis as from any other single cause. Furthermore, those who were most critical of President Carter were disproportionately scholars and writers on foreign policy who should have been his defenders. To them the swings of the pendulum that marked Mr. Carter's statements on foreign policy were disturbing. In the beginning, he warned against inordinate fear and obsession with communism. At the end, he announced that one event had totally changed his conception of Soviet foreign policy intentions, the Soviet invasion of Afghanistan.

Cyrus Vance was Carter's secretary of state up to the abortive Iran hostage rescue operation. He brought to his task wide ranging experience in defense and foreign policy. In his oral history, he discusses relations with President Carter and his sense of Carter's approach to foreign policy. His respect and affection for Carter remained constant throughout their relationship, yet Vance evaluates Carter's strengths and weaknesses, including his style of leadership. He is critical of Carter's use of the White House staff and especially of Carter's failure to warn against empire building in his foreign policy group. But Vance remains to the end what he has been throughout his public service: a dedicated and responsible leader, skilled in negotiations and dedicated to the vision of a more peaceful world order.

Anthony Lake was the unusually able director of the Policy Planning Staff in the Carter administration. In his oral history, he goes over much of the same ground Secretary Vance covered but from the standpoint of a policy planner trying both to look to the future while not ignoring the urgent problems of the present. Lake finds that the much discussed Vance-Brzezinski conflict originated in the structure of the NSC system and the practice of having foreign policy articulated and explained by two voices. The President's failure to define clearly the respective roles of the secretary of state and the NSC adviser was part of the problem. The press was mischievous in accentuating the rivalry. However, the choice of chairmen, whether from the NSC or the State Department, for the two central committees for policy and security review under the NSC was an invitation to struggle. Personalities obviously affected relationships. President Carter somehow failed to inspire the bureaucracy and drive their action perhaps because he ran as an antigovernment

INTRODUCTION

candidate. The staffs of the two bodies helped fuel the fires of controversy. Thus Carter's foreign policies became an external success but probably a domestic politics failure. Nonetheless, Lake can recite an impressive array of foreign policy successes of the Carter administration. He concludes that historians are likely to elevate the standing of the Carter administration as, over the next ten or twenty years, they reexamine its history. As he provided an intellectual foundation for the Carter administration's foreign policy while he was a trusted member of Vance's staff, Lake in his oral history offers a remarkably objective and far-sighted estimate for the future.

Donald McHenry also throws the spotlight on relations between the national security adviser and the secretary of state, in particular Brzezinski and Vance. Clearly he considers this relationship to have been Carter's achilles heel. Throughout, McHenry is warmly sympathetic and personally supportive of President Carter while critical of some aspects of his approach. His major criticism is of the President's tendency to become overly absorbed in details. Overall, Ambassador McHenry confirms the picture of Carter as a highly intelligent president, sometimes overextending himself in concern for issues on which greater delegation of responsibility would have been more productive. The Iran hostage crisis was the ultimate example of the President allowing himself to be consumed and immobilized by the details of a problem. The President's blind spot was the Brzezinski-Vance conflict. McHenry joins Lake in leaving no doubt as to the person most responsible for the conflict. Inasmuch as the two viewed the making of foreign policy from different vantage points in the administration, the convergence of their viewpoints on the source of the conflict is significant.

Cyrus Vance resigned over the Iran hostages rescue operation and Edmund Muskie took his place. Carter and Muskie had met in Plains, Georgia when Carter was interviewing candidates for the vice presidency. The press reported that the two did not find themselves in immediate rapport during that meeting. After Vance's resignation, the two came together again and before that Muskie as a senator had successfully carried out several foreign policy missions for the President. Muskie describes his appointment, his relationship with the President and the way he handled relations with National Security Adviser Brzezinski. He gives some of his personal views on the conduct of foreign policy by Carter. He examines constitutional and foreign policy issues in which he played a part. His oral history is a full and measured account of his eight months of public service in an area for which he began preparing himself fifty

INTRODUCTION

years earlier. When he entered Cornell Law School during the depression, he said in his acceptance letter that he intended to prepare for a career in the Foreign Service. Years later that opportunity came and he more than met to the challenge.

Gaddis Smith, Larned Professor of History at Yale, reviews Carter's successes and failures as a communicator. With Ambassador McHenry, Professor Smith gives Carter high marks for the moral and political content of his presidential philosophy. However, he asks why his public speaking often fell short of the high purposes he sought to communicate. Smith offers examples of Carter both at his best and at his worst and tries to explain the reasons for the differences. For example, Smith finds too much self-reference in Carter's rhetoric and too little invoking of the ideas of others. Compared with his successor, President Carter had clear limitations as a communicator which Smith seeks to explain.

Mrs. Carter is sometimes described as politically the most influential First Lady since Eleanor Roosevelt. No one can miss her genuine interest in politics. She saw herself as a full-time partner in governance with President Carter. It has been well said that the two positions that have undergone the most far-reaching changes in recent presidencies are those of vice president and First Lady. Mrs. Carter confirms what other contributors to this volume have described: her keen political instincts. Like her husband, she also conveys deep concern for the well-being of mankind everywhere reflected in the projects she has embraced both within and since leaving the White House.

Walter Mondale like Robert Bergland began his political career as an associate of Hubert Humphrey and a member of the Democratic Farm Labor Party. He gained distinction as U.S. senator from Minnesota from 1964-77 and was President Carter's vice president from 1977-80. Their relationship was marked by an active partnership, unusual in the history of presidential-vice presidential relations. Mondale confirms some of the views others expressed on the Carter presidency, but adds several new dimensions to the understanding of Jimmy Carter.

The reader may wish on completing the volume to return to President Jimmy Carter's opening chapter. Having read the descriptions of President Carter's strengths and weaknesses by others, it is useful to reread Carter's own statements of his beliefs and policies. The contrast is striking between Carter's views on a few problem areas and those of friendly critics. An example is the Vance-Brzezinski relationship, but there are others. By placing such competing views alongside one another, we may be able to move closer to a more responsible evaluation of the Carter presidency.

PART ONE:

A PRESIDENT'S FAITH

CHAPTER 1

CONTEMPORARY NATIONAL AND INTERNATIONAL ISSUES, 1987

PRESIDENT JIMMY CARTER

MR. THOMPSON: President Carter, we have asked former University of Virginia President Edgar Shannon for a word of welcome on behalf of the University and the Miller Center Council on which he serves. It was President Shannon who was "present at the creation" in the earliest discussions with Mr. Burkett Miller that led to the establishment of the Center. President Shannon.

MR. SHANNON: Mr. Carter, it is certainly a great pleasure to welcome you here. I wish that Governor Linwood Holton, who is the chairman of our Council for the Miller Center, could be here. I'm standing in for him today, but as Ken Thompson has said, I've been involved with the Center from the very beginning, when it was just a notion in Mr. Miller's mind and a gleam in his eye. It's been a great pleasure to see the fruition of that idea and it is particularly heartwarming to welcome you here. You have worked with us extensively and we are so grateful for that. It's a very exciting and happy occasion to have you here at our Center in person to see the kind of work that's going on here. I'm sure all of these people have lots of questions that they'll want to ask you, and I think you'll have an enjoyable time in the interchange. So on behalf of the Miller Center, the University, and the Council, we thank you for coming and welcome you here.

MR. THOMPSON: Some nine years plus ago when James Sterling Young, the Bancroft Prize winning author of the Miller Center, came here, he spoke about the need for a new kind of oral history. He had observed at Columbia University the type of oral history which had been carried on, largely by people who, as Dean Rusk once remarked, thought it was no more difficult to interview a former President or secretary of state than it was to interview a retired second baseman from the New York Mets. That kind of oral history was valuable, but Mr. Young had in mind something a little different. Under his leadership, a remarkable new approach to the presidency, the first of its kind, was undertaken here. We embarked on an oral history of the Carter White House. Praiseworthy as this idea was, it would simply not have been possible without the cooperation of the thirty-ninth President and his staff. I think Mr. Young should tell us about that oral history or comment in any other way that he sees fit.

MR. YOUNG: I'll say a word very briefly. The presidency of Jimmy Carter was a first in many respects. Mr. Carter was the first president to be elected from the deep South since the Civil War—I say that as a fellow Georgian with some pride. He was the first true outsider to be elected president since Woodrow Wilson, and there were many firsts in policy and in operating style. However, the first that counts perhaps the most for us here at the Miller Center is that he was the first president to open his presidency to intense, sober and objective examination by scholars before his library was opened. President Carter and almost fifty members of his staff, with his support and cooperation, gave very generously of their time to sit down around this table and other tables to reflect on their experiences in office. So it is the first presidency that has left behind a record of its reflections in a study for future generations so that we all may learn from that experience. We put together a little photographic record of our project and I want to present this token of our appreciations to President Jimmy Carter from the scholars and staff of the Miller Center with appreciation for his contribution to the study of the American presidency.

PRESIDENT CARTER: Let me just say, since we have such a limited amount of time, how delighted and honored I am to come to the Miller Center.
    It has been not only gratifying but also exciting and enjoyable for me to see a definitive oral history of our administration recorded. We are looking forward to having the transcript of the interviews come to the Carter Presidential Library. I understand that there are twenty-two volumes with three thousand pages, which will be a wonderful resource for scholars, historians, biographers, and others who come to the Carter Presidential Library. I'd like also to invite all of you to come down and see what I think is one of the most remarkable

architectural developments of which I know, with the exception, of course, of what Thomas Jefferson did here. We used a lot of his ideas, and I think he would be pleased at the rapidity with which we are making our records available. We have already declassified and made available six million documents. Less than one-tenth of 1 percent have been withheld from public scrutiny. My direction to Don Schewe, our director, is to make available to the public everything possible outside the very narrow constraints of national security. So you are welcome to come down to the Carter Presidential Library.

I'm so sorry that Governor Holton couldn't be here. He was scheduled to meet me before the great snows of Virginia precluded my last visit. He was a very illustrious governor at the same time I was governor, a highly successful competitor with me in getting nice things to happen to Virginia when I wanted them to happen to Georgia. I hope you will tell him how much I missed him personally. Thank you very much.

QUESTION: Knowing your commitment to civil rights, especially as a southerner, could you comment on the Reagan administration's record—especially that of the attorney general's office and William Bradford Reynolds—in enforcing civil rights legislation and other matters, such as the march in Forsyth County.

PRESIDENT CARTER: I think the Reagan administration's record on civil rights is embarrassing for our nation and is a disgrace to the White House. President Reagan has gone into office and tried to put people who don't display a basic sympathy for civil and human rights into key positions in the State Department, such as the assistant secretary for human rights, and also in the Justice Department. The sympathy for civil and human rights was epitomized not only by me but by my Republican and Democratic predecessors, Ford, Nixon, Johnson, and Kennedy. His is a radical departure, but I think that President Reagan's policies would have been more devastating to the civil rights in this nation and human rights abroad had it not been for the restraints exercised by the Congress on one hand and by the Federal judiciary on the other. These policies create an atmosphere of racism in our nation that is troubling; they say it's okay now to forget about civil rights. I think most of the legal positions taken by the Justice Department under Reagan have been the opposite of what I would have had my attorney general take and what my Republican and Democratic predecessors would have taken.

In human rights, the so-called "constructive engagement" policy towards South Africa is typical. In this case the restraint of public opinion and the restraint of congressional action have modified the Reagan administration's natural inclination to condone this government of racism and apartheid. The attitude of people when aroused—as was demonstrated in our own country by the twenty thousand marchers in Forsyth County—is a positive counteractive force.

QUESTION: In light of recent events in the Reagan administration with respect to Iran, and in light of your own experience of disagreements between your national security adviser and the secretary of state, can you share with us any reflections on your view of the proper relationship among the National Security Council, the national security adviser, and secretary of state?

PRESIDENT CARTER: Yes. In a totally objective way, I think that the relationship that I had in my administration was the proper one. I made the decisions on foreign policy and defense policy when I was President. I don't think anybody would question that, including Secretary Vance, Secretary Muskie, or Mr. Brzezinski. Because of that fact, I wanted a very strong, evocative, and innovative national security adviser. When I was elected president, I had the whole nation from which to choose and Brzezinski, by the way, was the one that Secretary Vance recommended for national security adviser; Vance was the one that Brzezinski recommended, conversely for secretary of state. I would say that 95 percent of the time, or even more, they were completely harmonious in their policy recommendations, but there is an inclination within the press in Washington to exacerbate the differences that do exist. I did not deplore the differences.

Brzezinski had a tiny staff, relatively speaking, including thirty-five or so professionals. The State Department is an enormous bureaucracy by contrast and is extremely lethargic; the inertia of the State Department is almost overwhelming. Once it gets started going in one direction, you can't change it and when it stands still, you can't get it to move. I can't recall a single exciting or innovative idea that ever came out of the State Department during the four years that I was President. That's the nature of the State Department—it's an anchor.

Brzezinski and his staff, on the other hand, would come up every week with several innovative, bright ideas, 90 percent of which might ultimately have been discarded or modified. Whenever I made a decision, I would always have it thoroughly "vetted" (to use a State Department phrase) by the State Department, the Defense Department, and perhaps other departments. I never acted unilaterally on a recommendation by

Brzezinski that involved international policy. So I looked upon the national security staff as my own personal staff to give me ideas, but then I very carefully made sure that the National Security Council, in some form, helped me make the final judgment. I made the final decision and always took the responsibility for it.

We had a regular weekly meeting of at least two hours on Friday mornings with Brzezinski, Vance or Muskie, Brown, the Vice President, and sometimes others. We discussed every item that anyone could think of that might be pertinent during that week, and Brzezinski took notes. He submitted his notes to the Defense and State Departments to make sure that they were accurate and then the notes came to me for my files. On Wednesdays Brzezinski, Brown, and the secretary of state had a luncheon meeting where they discussed matters that didn't require my presence. So there was a "melding" of the group. There were some obvious differences of opinion between Brown and me or between Brzezinski and me, but I didn't deplore that. I thought it was okay.

One thing that ought to be done is to retain that core of ideas and that possibility of cooperation. The bad thing that has happened recently, of course, is the coalescence within the White House of a small operational group which actually carries out a decision contrary to the sound advice of the State Department and the Defense Department and apparently—though I don't know—without even the knowledge of the President. This is a horrible derogation of responsibility, and possibly laws have been violated in the process. The president needs a strong, vital national security staff without operational characteristics, unless the National Security Council itself specifically has a finding, signed by the president, and certified to be legal by the attorney general. Then, on rare occasions, they might carry out a mission, perhaps just one or two times in four years at the most.

QUESTION: Could I ask one question as a footnote? If this is the pattern, then is there any danger in that the role of the NSC adviser as custodian and coordinator is difficult to sustain? There are several forthcoming books, one of which we've been reviewing recently, that make the argument that it was very difficult for Brzezinski to be both advocate and custodian.

PRESIDENT CARTER: Brzezinski's advocacy role was strictly limited by me. Some of you know Brzezinski, and he is an evocative, outspoken person. He would like to be a lightening rod. Whenever anything went wrong, Brzezinski was eager to take the blame. I never knew him to duck and say, "Well, I didn't really want this; the President wanted it," if it were a mistake.

Secretary Vance, a fine, gentle person, had extreme loyalty to the State Department. He looked upon himself as a descendent of Thomas Jefferson, as a secretary of state more than he did as an aide or assistant to the President. Vance was very loyal to the State Department and he was very cautious about what he said. Sometimes I wanted a public statement to be made or I wanted a small group of key columnists in Washington to be briefed privately. For instance, I would sometimes request that Secretary Vance make a public statement concerning Cuba, Angola, or China; quite often he would not do it if it were controversial, or perhaps, if it violated what the State Department thought was best. There were no violent differences. He would absolutely refuse to let a small group of distinguished columnists like Scotty Reston and others enter his home or enter the State Department dining room. On occasions like that, after I waited a few days for this to be done, I would tell Brzezinski to go ahead and make the statement. I might tell Brzezinski, "It's okay for you one Sunday afternoon to be on 'Meet the Press,' if Secretary Vance continued to disagree with my decision. But when Brzezinski did anything of that kind, it was with my approval as an alternative to a precise, pointed, and perhaps pithy remark that I felt was needed to shape public opinion.

QUESTION: Mr. President, looking at the Defense Department, the fundamentals of the national defense, and the inter-service rivalry, for a moment, what are your views upon the growth of the Defense Department and the services today?

PRESIDENT CARTER: When I came into office we had had a dramatic reduction in defense budget expenditures in real terms over the previous eight years. This was not because Nixon or Ford wanted to see this done, but because the Congress was exercising restraint on budgetary allocations primarily as a reaction against the Vietnam experience. Therefore I decided quite early with Vance, Brzezinski, and others to have an inexorable and predictable increase in the defense budget every year. Our goal was a 3 percent increase above and beyond the inflation rate and we basically adhered to this. Every year when we prepared a defense budget, it was prepared by me, the secretary of defense, the joint chiefs of staff, the National Security Council, and the Office of Management and Budget. Also quite often, when there was a particular question to be answered, I would call in the key members of the House and the Senate Armed Forces Attention Committees to make sure that we had some degree of compatibility. It was an organic evolution of the budget. Whenever they wanted a new weapons system, I required Secretary Brown to decommission an obsolescent or obsolete system to stay within the budget restraints. We built up the rapid deployment force in this way. We had to build up our forces, as you know, in the Indian Ocean and the Persian Gulf region later on. But I felt that at that time the Defense Department was well under control.

When President Reagan ran against me in 1980, he repeatedly said that the Defense Department had been going to hell under my administration and that the budget had gone down; this was erroneous as I pointed out to him subsequently. He recommended something like a 13 percent increase above the inflation rate in the first year and an 11 percent increase above the inflation rate in the next year. The Congress went along with President Reagan's recommendation in the first two years. I think Weinberger has been eager to take any money he could get for the Defense Department and they've not decommissioned any old systems. Almost every new idea that came along about a weapons system has been endorsed heartily, and the public has been convinced that each was vital to our national security. The resurrection of the B1 bomber is the most vivid demonstration of absolute and total waste on a weapons system that will have no efficacy even after it's finished and which will not perform its putative duties.

The result has been a reaction in the Congress against this uncontrollable spending, and for the last two years, as you know, there has been a zero increase in the Defense Department budget, which means the budget is like a roller coaster. There is an outpouring of profligate spending for a couple of years and then no spending increase in the next year. There is no careful planning and no involvement (or very little involvement) of the joint chiefs of staff. Now we are seeing a Defense Department that is suffering because of these altercations over alterations in budgets.

QUESTION: Mr. President, one of your major achievements was the formalization of relations with China. Taiwan, of course, has remained an issue. Would you care to comment on Peking's demand for the U.S. to at least set a date for termination of its arms sales to Taiwan?

PRESIDENT CARTER: Yes. I covered this, fairly well I think, in my memoirs, *Keeping Faith*, which you might want to read. I must say Deng Xiaoping was a very tough negotiator. Even before I was inaugurated, but after I was elected, I made it clear to the members of the House and the Senate at a meeting at the Smithsonian Institution (about a hundred people were there) that I intended to normalize relations with the People's Republic as one of my major goals as president. I also discussed plans to conclude a Panama Canal Treaty, move towards peace in the Middle East, and certain other things at that gathering. But Deng Xiaoping insisted that we not provide any more military assistance to Taiwan. I would never agree to that. I insisted that he make a public announcement that the differences between the People's Republic of China and Taiwan would be resolved peacefully. He would never agree to that publicly. Those, then, were the two things on which we did not agree and, in effect, we just kept our own positions and went ahead with normalization. As you know, I continued to sell Taiwan military supplies of a basically defensive nature.

The treaty concluded between us and Taiwan was honored meticulously. It had a provision in it for a one-year notice prior to termination, and we honored that one-year notice of termination. In addition to that we agreed not to recognize Taiwan as an independent nation, but we established a trade mechanism within Taiwan based on the Japanese example. I would say that our commerce with and our visitation to Taiwan has probably increased dramatically ever since we recognized the People's Republic of China. So we reserved the right to continue to sell defensive weapons to Taiwan on my terms, but not including weapons with which they could attack the mainland of China from Taiwan. China insisted upon its right to call for and accomplish the termination of the difference with Taiwan in any way it saw fit. I wanted them to say, "We guarantee that it will be through peaceful means." Though they never would say that, I think China will never try to resolve the differences with Taiwan through other than peaceful means. I can't imagine a military effort.

I believe that China's present role in Hong Kong is being carefully orchestrated from Beijing to show the world and the people on Taiwan that there can be an area in China—that is Hong Kong—where the people can preserve their own way of life and have access to Western ways. As you may know, since then Deng Xiaoping has offered Taiwan its own independent army and a very large degree of autonomy. I don't know what will ultimately happen, but my presumption is that we will continue to make sure that Taiwan can defend itself. On the other hand, China will try to resolve its differences with Taiwan through peaceful means.

QUESTION: Mr. President, as we all know, this is the bicentennial of the Constitution and a prominent group in Washington came out with proposals two or three weeks ago on how to change the Constitution. I'm wondering how you would change the Constitution on the basis of your experience, if you had a free hand to do so? I'm thinking particularly of the relations between the Congress and the president and the question of terms of office.

PRESIDENT CARTER: First of all, I would hate to see us have a constitutional convention because I think it would be an uncontrollable body that might dramatically modify the existing Constitution, which, in general, is all right. There are two specific things that I would like to see changed if I could unilaterally change them.

First, I would prefer to see a single one-term, six-year presidency. This is the case, as you know, in a number of foreign countries, and it works very well. I could have done a better job in six years than I did in four years; I would have not been stigmatized when I did something of a dramatic nature that seemed to be politically oriented to get me re-elected. Also this would have precluded a lot of the public positions that President Reagan took, for instance, when he was basically running against other Republicans like Rockefeller, Nixon, and Ford. In his earlier life while seeking the Republican nomination, Reagan took positions on things like China, human rights, and arms agreements with the Soviets that later proved to be a great handicap for him. I don't think he would have done those things if the incumbent president could not have run for re-election. One six-year term is one change, then, that I would make.

Another thing I would change would be the two-thirds majority required of the Senate to confirm or to ratify a treaty. This seems illogical because a third of the members of the Senate can now block the legal implementation of an international agreement consummated by the president. Perhaps it ought to take a two-thirds majority of the Senate to override what a president has concluded by agreement with a foreign nation, or at least a majority ought to be adequate for ratification. Because about a third of the members of the Senate now, including Strom Thurmond and Jessie Helms and others, will hardly support anything that has international scope and especially anything that deals with the Soviet Union, it is difficult to ratify any treaty. There's a presumption that if something is good for the Soviet Union, if they agree to it, then it inherently is bad for us.

So those would be the two basic changes I would make. I would not recommend that we go to a parliamentary system of government or dramatically change our system, nor would I recommend that we change the basic relationship among the President, Congress, and the Supreme Court. I think that system has basically proven to be very well advised.

QUESTION: President Carter, having been in the Justice Department of your administration, I would assume that perhaps you are not totally in agreement with Attorney General Meese's policies. I would like to ask you what effect you think his policies are having on the country, and, assuming a Democratic victory in 1988, what would be necessary to rectify those policies for the next administration?

PRESIDENT CARTER: As you may know, when I was President I appointed more than 45 percent of all the federal judges in the nation in the brief period of just four years because it happened that we expanded the district and circuit courts. Over a period of eight years, President Reagan will probably appoint about half of the federal judges at the circuit and district court level and several Supreme Court justices. That gives a great deal of stability to the policies of our country. I've seen my own appointees, without any influences from me, carry out the basic principles of environmental quality, civil rights, and so forth in opposition to what the Reagan administration has proposed as the cases have been brought to them. I think, to answer your question then, President Reagan's remaining influence will carry over into the next administration, but will not exceed the influence that my own administration has had through my appointees to the district and circuit courts. Reagan's policies will have minimal adverse impact.

My guess is that the next administration will revert back to the basic progressive policies of the four or five previous administrations. For instance, on environmental quality, on civil rights and other matters of that kind, Gerald Ford's, Richard Nixon's, Johnson's, and Kennedy's policies were similar to mine. I look upon my policies on those matters as being quite compatible with those of my predecessors. The radical departure has been under the Reagan administration.

QUESTION: Mr. President, I think there is general agreement that Camp David was a very valuable achievement but that its aftermath has been quite disappointing. I wonder how much of the failure to follow up and expand on the Camp David agreement—to produce a full-fledged settlement in the Middle East—is attributable to the United States government and how much is attributable to Israel and to the Arab states?

PRESIDENT CARTER: I've written a book about this called *Blood of Abraham*, and I'm going back to the Middle East next month for another three weeks of quiet conversations. I'll see not only the incumbent and opposition leaders, but also the scholars in the great universities of Damascus, Cairo, Alexandria, Tel Aviv, Jerusalem, and so forth, just to bring myself up to date on it.

So that brings us down to the question of whom the Democrats will choose and I don't know the answer. There are some notable people whom the Democrats could choose that I would like to see in the White House. Someone like Senator Bill Bradley from New Jersey would be good, but I do not think he will run. Mario Cuomo might show some popularity in the South—it would surprise me if he did, but he might. He is an intellectual. He has proven to be a successful, tough Italian infighter in the street brawls of New York politics and he is an evocative speaker. Joe Biden is a candidate. There might be a governor somewhere that's as unknown as I was at an equivalent time who will come forward. Bruce Babbitt might very well show success.

My own personal choice, if I could select a nominee, would be Sam Nunn. First of all, I think Sam Nunn would be a good president. His credentials on social matters are very good. I would say they are compatible with mine which by definition makes them good! He is strong on defense but he's also very critical of wastefulness in the Defense Department, and he is looking now at overall defense policy, which is good. I think Sam Nunn could carry the South and mathematically it's almost impossible for a Democrat to win the presidency without the South. Nunn would be the most successful in insuring that the Democrats would sweep the South. So he would be my choice, but I'm not publicly endorsing him. I've talked to him about it and encouraged him to run and so have many other people. I have no idea whether he will run yet. So I think the Democrats have a good chance provided they choose the right person. That's where the winnowing process comes in with the long and tedious primary season, which I think is good. I don't deplore it; it's good for the candidates to learn about our nation and it's good for the nation to learn about the candidates.

The unpredictable element, which I'm sure some of you are studying, is the massive southern primary. We had "Super Tuesday" in 1984, which I helped to initiate before I went out of office as governor, but the impact of thirteen to fifteen states having a simultaneous, early primary in the South is still to be determined. Clearly it does escalate the importance of the South. So I feel good as a Democrat about our prospects in 1988, but a lot can happen between now and the election.

MR. THOMPSON: About a month ago, Senator Nunn spoke at this table and he promised to come back. More recently, a leading popular newspaper announced, "He's back," and then explained it was not Nixon but Jimmy Carter to whom it referred. Ray Price pointed out in an article recently that it took Nixon only ten years to come back, whereas it took Truman twenty and Hoover thirty. Well, it has taken Jimmy Carter only about six years, and we hope his coming back with a 55 percent popularity rating in the country, with three of his associates elected to statewide office, and with resurgence in many areas will symbolize a willingness to come back to the Miller Center and the University of Virginia.

PRESIDENT CARTER: I hope you will all remember my invitation to come to the Carter Library and Center if you are passing through Atlanta. I think you will be pleased with the time you might spend there, and I'm very grateful again, not only for a chance to come here, but for the very significant work you've done and the honor that you all have paid my administration by working on the oral history. Thank you again.

PART TWO:

GOVERNANCE AND THE CABINET

CHAPTER 2

THE PRESIDENCY AND THE CABINET: FORMING A NEW CABINET DEPARTMENT

JUDGE SHIRLEY HUFSTEDLER

NARRATOR: There are a number of breakthroughs in this Forum with Judge Hufstedler. We have not exactly broken the sound barrier in our introduction of leading women figures in the American political scene. As she explained to me, ten years from now this is going to be different, and as I look out on my classes at the University, I understand what she means. Half of the graduate students in certain departments are women. So far as I know we've never before had a Woman of the Year. Judge Hufstedler was picked by the *Ladies Home Journal* as "Woman of the Year" in 1976.

In a more serious vein, her visit represents one other breakthrough. We have not yet entertained Father Hesburgh, who must have the world record for honorary degrees. If he holds the record, Judge Hufstedler with fourteen or fifteen honorary degrees from Yale, Michigan, Rutgers, Pennsylvania, and a great many other distinguished institutions must be a close second. So in that respect, too, we are fortunate. She was secretary of education from 1979 to 1981. She is currently a partner of the law firm of Hufstedler, Miller, Carlson and Beardsley. She is a graduate of the University of New Mexico and of the Stanford Law School. She was admitted to the bar in 1950. She is a member of the Board of Trustees of Cal Tech, of Occidental College, of the Aspen Institute of Humanistic Studies, and other important bodies. She is a member of the American Law Institute and formerly of its council. She is a past president of the Association of Women Lawyers. She was on the Stanford Law Review. Now it is appropriate that a renowned judicial scholar tell you something about her achievements in the field of law. Professor Meador.

PROFESSOR DANIEL MEADOR: I will just add a few comments because we mainly want to hear from Judge Hufstedler. Ken has given the rundown of her many accomplishments. I would add a few things. It's fair to say that she is regarded as one of the leading judges and leading lawyers in the United States. One can say that without putting the adjective of woman before it. It goes unqualifiedly for both males and females.

She has one of the talents that I have always thought indispensable to the really first-rate lawyer and that's creative imagination. That's a sure earmark of a very good lawyer and without it you can have a competent lawyer but not a great lawyer. She has that talent to a high degree. It has been my pleasure to be associated with her over a period of a dozen years or so in a variety of projects dealing with improving the administration of justice and reforming the court system.

Rarely do we make much headway within one generation on court reform. Judge Arthur Vanderbilt said it was not a sport for the short-winded and that is true. But her ideas are out there and they are seriously debated. They have formed a large part of the agenda for discussion in the last dozen years or so when these problems have been worsening.

She was for many years a judge on the U.S. Court of Appeals for the Ninth Circuit which was one of our major appellate courts running all the way from Nevada to Hawaii and Alaska, a large part of the United States. I should add just another couple of items on the personal side. She is quite a mountain climber, among her many accomplishments, and has tackled the Himalayas more than once. As I recall from the past accounts, she has climbed up above 19,200 feet on foot, no mean achievement, I would say, along with her husband Seth. Seth Hufstedler is himself a very able lawyer. He was past president of the California state bar, past president of the American Bar Foundation, and has held many other positions.

JUDGE HUFSTEDLER: The truth is that a lot of the ideas that I have had, and that Dan Meador and I both worked on, probably should have been tried in a small way some place to find out if they work; if they failed they would be inconspicuous enough that at least they would not be identified with our names. It is true that these things are not for the short-winded. Indeed, you have to have the concepts of the long-distance runner in order to get anything accomplished in moving around judicial systems. I discovered that at least some of those qualities are essential when you are trying to do something as bizarre as setting up a new Cabinet-level department. I will talk to you briefly about what that process was about, what it was like working with Jimmy Carter and with Fritz Mondale during that time.

Dan Meador mentioned my enthusiasm about mountain climbing. It happened that I had just returned from a climbing expedition in Zanska, which if your Asian geography is momentarily shaky, is in Kashmir, an area slightly north and west of Tibet. It is a great set of ranges of mountains. After going over those, we went over a Himalayan range and dropped into a glorious place called the Valley of the Blue Sapphires because it is a place for the mining of blue sapphires. Until 1975 it was closed entirely; nobody was permitted to go there. It is entered by dropping over a 17,900 foot pass over a great glacier and then walking down 7,000 feet in a day to drop into this valley.

After this kind of top-of-the-world experience, I had been home recovering from jet lag and planning to plow into my case load when I got a telephone call from one of my former law clerks who said, "There are inquiries from the White House about you. Is it all right if I release some data about you?" I said, "Of course." After all, I have been in public life for so many years I don't suppose I have had a goose bump that wasn't reported by somebody. It is very difficult to have a sense of any personal privacy under these circumstances. I thought no more about it until she called me back again and said, "The White House wants more information." I thought, "I can't imagine what kind of committee or commission the White House is proposing for me." A third call came, it was Fritz Mondale who said that I was on a short list being considered as secretary for the new Department of Education and would I be willing to consider that? Since I am one to consider almost anything, I didn't really take it too seriously. He asked if I would come back to Washington, and the answer was "yes." This was on a Wednesday and I packed myself up and got to Washington on Thursday night. Friday, this routine began. By Saturday I had the eerie feeling that I wasn't just on the short list, I *was* the list. It gives you the feeling of confidence you would have if you thought you were just courting and all of a sudden you are marching down the aisle. I said to myself, "Now wait a minute, I'm not sure I really want to do this." I made a quick call and my husband flew out to Washington and we sat there and thought about it because, after all, this would turn our lives upside down and sidewise. But after talking it over I decided "yes," indeed—and my husband thought so too—I'd like to do that because not very many people have ever had a chance to set up a new Cabinet department.

The truth was that after nineteen years on the bench, although many days brought very interesting problems, not every day was the learning environment that it had been nineteen years before. That even happens, I am told, to professors. So I thought, here is a great opportunity. As you know, federal judges are appointed for life, on good behavior, and of course there is another little footnote. There is no pension for federal judges, you understand. You are salaried for the rest of your life, but when you leave you get nothing. If one is going to leave, one must leave in time to recover enough to be able to provide oneself the wherewithal before one totters into one's dotage. All things considered, I thought it was a very good idea.

After meeting with the various echelons, eventually on Sunday, I was told that the President wanted to meet with me in the Oval Office the next morning at 9:30. By this time I had developed one of those really one hundred percent ghastly colds, the kind in which your temperature is a hundred and two and all your joints are aching and I thought, "Boy, I'm going to do a lot for the country. I'm going to give the President of the United States one of the world's worst colds and he will be out of commission."

The first time I met Jimmy Carter, it was just the two of us. We went out to the very small garden outside the Oval Office where the chrysanthemums were in bloom. It was a lovely, golden fall day in Washington. Jimmy Carter told me what education meant to him, what it meant to him to serve on the school board, what it meant to him to see the turnaround in the education of blacks and whites, what it meant to him to see people left out of the educational structure. He spoke of how intensely he wanted the department to work, and what he hoped that I could do.

In the meantime there was a *leitmotiv* that was going through this very earnest conversation with the President. There was one of those bushy-tailed squirrels who, without the slightest qualms about stepping all over the President, would keep walking and running across the President's feet and back again. I thought, "Out of such moments, history is made." I hoped the President was not going to catch my cold and that the squirrel did not have any particular loathsome disease which was going to be communicable to either one of us.

After hearing him, I became convinced that I would have the total support of the President in trying to get that new department built. We did have a moment of disagreement thereafter, one of the few I ever had with the President. He wanted to call a press conference immediately and announce the decision with respect to the new secretary of education and I said, "Please don't do that, Mr. President. My court does not know I'm leaving. My son does not even know, and it would be nice for me to be able to tell my family and my court that all this was going to happen."

It was not the President's fault, but I had assumed I would have three weeks in which to wind up my judicial life and get myself moved. Well, I didn't have three weeks, I had about ten days because the rest of the time was spent running back and forth to Washington getting ready for the confirmation hearings and trying to find out what was in place for the department. The answer was nothing. It also happened that at the time of the birthing of the department we were in that stage of the federal budget process which is technically called the "passback." That is when the first round of figures had gone into the Office of Management and Budget and the Office of Management and Budget is giving the target dollars for every department and every agency. That starts the process of appeals for all the programs that any department runs. The process goes through levels of appeals in OMB and then the appeals go to the President. Among other things, I was not only going to have to wind up my judicial life and try to rearrange, reset and vacate cases, but I was also going to have to learn the entire budgetary process because I had no department. I was going to have to learn to carry that budget by myself. I had a couple of people who had been assigned to help me.

Learning a fourteen and a half billion dollar budget, which is about the size of a Manhattan telephone book, so that you know all the programs, all of the options, what the levels of funding are, what they have been, what every one of those programs does, and where I would target what priorities I wanted to have in the department immediately meant a good deal of quick study and homework. At the time I was doing that, lists were being developed for me to start interviewing candidates for all of the presidential appointments in building the department. There was a statutory deadline. I had one hundred and eighty days in which to organize the department. There had been a price tag estimate of ten million dollars set on building the department. I was determined that we were going to bring the department in before the due date and that we were going to bring it in for less money. I read resumes of over a hundred people from all over the United States for the sixteen presidential appointments and interviewed dozens. I learned the budget and carried it personally. The President in the meantime asked me to head up his task force for his major domestic initiative for 1980 which was the Youth Act of 1980. That was a joint venture between the Department of Labor and the Department of Education and involved identifying the people and working up the legislative specifications. Needless to say, sleeping was not very high on the list of my priorities.

There were some other jolts that had to do with the changing environment between the federal bench and the

Cabinet. While you cannot describe the federal bench as a monastery and certainly not as a nunnery—because there was only one woman on the federal appellate court at the time and that was me—you do have a significant amount of insulation from lots of things. No matter how much people might try, you cannot be approached on the subject of any case which is under consideration; you cannot be approached by the press or anyone with respect to the topics of the court while you're in it. You can engage in the liveliest kind of socratic debate with your colleagues and with your law clerks with conviction that what you say is in total confidence. It does not go out of the courtroom. It is very rare that there is a security break.

Coming out of that environment, I soon discovered to my astonishment and dismay that it takes twelve pages, single-spaced, just to list the number of organizations with lobbyists on education in Washington. It is the entire array. Anybody associated with higher education knows it isn't the happiest of all communities with total agreement on everything. There is more than one set of agencies that deal with the problems affecting higher education alone. But, there are legions of interest groups. There are different teachers' unions, there are parents' unions, there are Title III groups, there are Title I groups, there are school board associations—everybody's got an association, everybody's got a piece of turf and everybody's got an interest group that they want to have identified.

Needless to say, the birthing of the department was not greeted with waves of universal national acclaim. It had barely squeaked through in getting passed at all. There was intense suspicion, particularly in higher education, that the department was going to be a terrible mistake, because it was simply going to be a puppet of teachers' unions.

My problem was, how do I create a department from one hundred and sixty-five educational programs from six departments and two agencies? The best known was the "Education" in HEW; the other department educational programs were less well known. In trying to unify these programs, I had to figure out how to manage to squeeze out enough human being vacancies to get the staffing of the department going. Those programs came over with their appropriations and their legislation, but they also came over with the bodies who were attached to them. I had to try to negotiate with all of the departments, none of whom wanted to give up a single vacancy, because they wanted the vacancies under the existing hiring freezes just as much as I did. And I had to negotiate the space for my department. The department was scattered all over Washington. Nobody wanted to give up one square foot of space, not physically, not turf, not anything. And if you aren't able to go in there and fight on the determination orders, you are already branded a loser. Washington is power and turf, and if you don't know how to protect your turf, very quickly whatever you want to do you are not going to be able to do because the image of whether you are a "do it" person or not is all-important.

That kind of hardball was not the nicest thing that ever got dealt to me in life, but I had to do it. That problem would have been tough enough under a hiring freeze. When you're building a department, you not only have to have the people who run the programs in that department, but you have to build an Inspector General's Office.

I was going to have to figure out a way to operate the whole thing with fewer people than were available to run the department programs when they were elsewhere. One of the best kept secrets was that set of realities. Because there were lots of anxieties about building a Department of Education in the first place, the press was my best friend and worst enemy at the same time. The early reports all said, "What is this little old lady from Pasadena going to be doing with seventeen thousand employees and a fourteen and a half billion dollar budget?"

In the first place, eleven thousand plus of those employees were, in fact, school teachers in the military schools overseas for military dependents. They weren't bureaucrats at all. And in the next place, the department didn't get them for a period of some five years after their presumed transition from the Department of Defense.

The fourteen and a half billion dollars was thought to be sort of free-flow discretionary money, which was absolutely false. Every dollar was annexed to a specific program. If a secretary began to play with those dollars in any way, she not only would have had GAO wrapped around her neck; she would have had the specific congressmen and senators who were on the committees that oversee her department on her neck as well.

Congress had created not only a department; Congress created the departmental design, with trivial exceptions. You know all those organization charts with those little boxes? One can't do anything in Washington unless you can color-in little boxes. There are all these assistant secretaries because those were bargaining chips in getting the legislation passed. As you know from other environments, the name of the game is who has direct reporting to the secretary. Everybody wants direct reporting to the secretary. Those who didn't have direct reporting in the legislation itself were all trying to shape a little box that would have an arrow directing them to report to the secretary.

I would be criticized in the press because I had this crazy-looking organization and by people on the Hill who had forgotten entirely the fact that they drew that blueprint, I didn't. Many people on the Hill also believed that the opening of the department was the greatest possible bonanza for placing hard-to-place constituents, or others for whom they would like to find jobs, because they thought that the department was a vast employment enterprise.

I had few vacancies for anything; it was really cut and paste. The education community believed that one of the best things you could do with a displaced professor was to send him or her to one of the never-ending jobs in the department. They didn't realize that most of the people that I had anything to do with employing were accountants for the Inspector General's Office, or lawyers, whose problems were managing regulatory portions of the agency, and not program people at all. I was always trying to explain to people, "I haven't got all those employees!" and, "No, Senator Sidewash, I'm sorry I can't take care of George Schmo for you, because I don't have any job for him."

One problem I discovered somewhat to my astonishment. In the courts on which I sat, everybody was not in sweet agreement all the time, but my colleagues were not personally petulant. In dealing with the Hill, that was not always true. With respect to one man on the Hill, if I didn't call him up on Wednesday and wish him a happy Thursday, he would be petulant and would give me trouble on some aspects of departmental work. In terms of turf, there are projects that are protected either by staff or by a congressman or by a senator. They believe they own those programs and if you try to do something that you think is important to change the priorities of the department, they are all over you like a nest of bees. There are still others that give you different kinds of fits.

Senator Warren Magnuson was very helpful to me in many ways. Warren Magnuson cared a lot about education. But there were some elements of education that he was pushing very hard for historical reasons and for reasons of certain constituencies of his that I did not want to push. For instance, vocational education has more friends on the Hill than you know what to do with and that is without very close reexamination about what *voc ed* is doing across the United States. Some of these schools are very, very good and some of them are teaching buggy whip manufacture to young people, and still others are trying to teach farm wives how to put up produce that nobody has canned for twenty years. The structure is not moving in response to genuine needs. Moreover, I knew that no matter how much I shrunk the budget from the department with respect to *voc ed*, the people on the Hill would put the money back in. The state legislatures would do the same thing. I did not need to use the power of the department to try to maintain funding for *voc ed*. I could let other folks do that.

I needed to focus attention on various kinds of programs I wanted to prioritize for the country, to use the power and the pressure of that place at the Cabinet table, both for the President and the Vice President. Vice President Mondale was a key figure in this because Fritz Mondale himself was deeply interested in education. When he had been on the Hill he had been instrumental in getting many of the major educational bills passed. I could count on Fritz Mondale's help, and I got it when I was putting together the Youth Act of 1980. We didn't get the Youth Act passed. We got it through the House. We got it through the committees of the Senate, but before we could get it to the floor of the Senate, the time ran out. After all, that was an election year and a very short legislative year. The bill went down the tubes literally at the last minute.

That gives an idea of what the feeling and the pressures were of this job. All the Cabinet jobs are very hard work, but this one was a pip because of the timing, which was very difficult. I had made it an objective to show the nation that in education we could practice affirmative action without taking one tiny little nick on quality. It was extremely important for me to do that. Because if you can't do that in education, everything we are trying to do in education doesn't seem to be very meaningful. I did it. The people were superb. I didn't take one nick on quality. We had women, blacks, Hispanics, old-fashioned country-style white Protestant males. We had the whole scene and it started to work beautifully. But it takes a lot of time and a lot of energy. It doesn't make it easier when the number of screamers per square foot on single issues not only surrounded, but coagulated around the Department of Education for a variety of reasons.

The difficulty and the necessity for every department of managing the daily relationships with the Hill isn't a sometimes thing. A secretary is on the Hill, personally and regularly. I was testifying regularly before various committees and commissions. Once a department is built, there are times when one can send your undersecretary or a deputy to do certain aspects of testimony. But with the new department, I couldn't do that. I had to do it all myself. To put it mildly, that was the most intense education I've ever had in my life. There were disappointing things, and there were funny things. There were exciting things, and there were grimy things. But among other things, I learned indelibly that the career bureaucrats whom I gathered from various departments, some of whom I got lined-over from other departments, were incredibly dedicated, able, hard-working people. They had more brickbats thrown at them than anybody but school teachers, and they are paid almost on the same scale. They worked terribly hard and oftentimes utterly thanklessly.

It is true there were some people with tired blood but I found out that even geriatric distress can be alleviated by giving a person a sense of hope that they can really do something. It all began to bubble up and come together, and it was something that I thought was potentially great for this country. It was an opportunity I am absolutely delighted that I took. I don't think I can ever work that hard again in my life. In the entire time I had the job I managed to take off four days—the day before Christmas, one Christmas day, one Easter weekend, and one Sunday and that's all. My day began at four o'clock in the morning and I rarely got to bed until eleven o'clock at night, seven days a week.

So anybody who says to me, "Did you have fun?" has to have a rather bizarre idea about what's fun. But that is the wrong question. "Did you think you accomplished something? Did you think it was worth it?" The answer to that is overwhelmingly, "yes." I had the opportunity to work with Fritz Mondale on a number of programs that I thought were good for this country and the opportunity to work for some very able people on the Hill. True, there is an occasional person who is not one of the finest flowers in your rose garden, but whether they are or not, you've got to learn to deal with them. You have to learn what you can give away, what you can negotiate away, what you can bargain with, how you can compromise without losing a sense of virtue, how you can establish priorities so that you know what you can do, and how you can accomplish what you know must be done even when it is extremely unpopular.

Some of the things I had to do are some of the most emotionally and politically volatile things in the country. School desegregation—is that an easy issue? Bilingual education—an explosive issue. Gender equity—how would you like to deal with those congressmen in the Big Ten who get unglued about the idea that females may show up on the football team? Trying to tell them that wasn't necessarily so was not exactly what they wanted to hear. There were a lot of bubbling, bursting issues. And then there are always crises that you could not possibly foresee.

President Carter called me one day and said, "Shirley, we have two hundred and fifty thousand Cuban refugees about to land in Florida. Let's see what we can do about getting together teachers to educate them." It happened to be about ten days before the teachers break to go on summer vacation. I had to find in the department authorizing legislation which has an appropriation annexed to it. The chief state school officer from Florida called me and said, "What am I going to do? We don't have any money in the budget to take care of this." I said, "Well, let me try." I began an intense search to find any legislation in the department that had refugees attached to it with an appropriation. My mission—find six million dollars fast, in time to get it to Florida so that teachers could be paid not to take the summers off they had planned but to go teach the Cubans. The intense search finally revealed one piece of legislation that had really been designed to take care of Indo-Chinese. I could not simply take that piece of legislation without working with the Hill. If I had bent a piece of legislation out of shape without clearing it with the key people on the Hill, they would put my department under oversight immediately. That's what happens. Bless their hearts, everyone of them said "okay." So I got my six million dollars and we got it to Florida. The educational program, with tremendous support by the educators of Florida, began to make that happen. That is one of those things you cannot anticipate; you cannot put it in the budget. You have to deal with it, because it is there.

There were times of real fun, too. With the aid of a superb person, Liz Carpenter, my assistant secretary for public affairs who used to be Lady Bird Johnson's press secretary, we structured the opening of the department. The first ceremonies were in the White House, with a program that was called, "Thank you, Mrs. Brown." We got some of the greatest artists in the United States, to bring the teachers who were the most important to them in their careers. There was not one artist who refused, and the only persons who couldn't bring their teachers were those whose teachers were dead, but they spoke about them. It was a wonderful celebration of what it means to be a great artist and to have a debt to a great teacher.

We were fortunate to be able to do a scene at Colonial Williamsburg and at the College of William and Mary. When you are talking about education and what higher education means, you have to look at Virginia. We wanted to pay the historical debt.

We had another session in a small community to celebrate one of the last functioning one-room schoolhouses and also to launch the postage stamp which commemorated the opening of the department. All of these things had different kinds of symbolism for different sorts of reasons in order to give a sense of what education means in the United States and what the department can mean in helping people.

Some of those were genuinely fun. It was a chance to try to put the pieces together from many different ships and to try to make the thing sail on time for one-tenth of the cost that was estimated. I wouldn't have missed it for anything.

QUESTION: You've talked a lot about your relationships with the Hill, and you mentioned your initial conversation with the President and some later help from Mondale. I wonder if you could spell out a little bit more your experiences with the White House once you arrived and along the way until you left. What were the week-to-week, day-to-day experiences with the staff and in dealing with the President? Were there problems there?

JUDGE HUFSTEDLER: The process was very smooth indeed. I worked with quite a few people on the White House staff, Stu Eizenstat perhaps more than any of the others because he was head of domestic policy. I spent a good deal of time with other persons like Charlie Schultz and Ray Marshall because we were working on various economic aspects of the Youth Act. By the time I had arrived on the scene, the President had developed a practice of having fewer formal Cabinet meetings and more meetings with his secretary-level persons for breakfast. When we were working on a particular set of issues, there wasn't much point of my spending a lot of time with the Secretary of State, or he with me, although we were warm friends. We weren't working on the same kinds of projects. When we were trying to get some things together with the Department of Labor, it was more important for me to spend time with Ray Marshall, Secretary of Labor, and with some of his chief staff persons and some of my chief staff persons. We would spend a little time at breakfast or occasionally I would fly with the President on Air Force One to some kind of a national event, whether the signing of the higher education amendments or a series of meetings in California.

I knew that any time I really needed the President for something, he would do it. When I needed to have a couple of arms squeezed on the Hill with respect to the higher education amendments, I needed his help. With a person as busy as the President, one does not abuse the privilege. But it is very comforting to know it's there.

Jimmy Carter was accessible to his Cabinet. All members of the Cabinet had this nice red White House phone in our homes. I said, "nice," but sometimes it gets you up in the middle of the night and the news isn't always good. But in terms of accessibility, whether in my office, or in the furnished condominium I rented, all I needed to do was pick up the phone. The White House operator answered. One identifies oneself and asks to speak to the President. Sometimes the President would answer immediately. More often than not, he would call me back, somewhere between thirty minutes and two hours. The President was accessible.

Fritz Mondale was also accessible, but I rarely had to call him because we were seeing each other regularly anyway with respect to a series of projects. Sometimes it was just as useful to call a senior staffer because the information I needed hadn't been prepared as a memorandum to the President; there wasn't any sense in calling the President about something he had not seen before in a memorandum.

In this particular White House, the President and the Vice President took intense personal interest in all the steps of the budget process. Whether in Cabinet meetings or in these budget meetings, the President would sit on this side of the table, where I'm sitting now, and the Vice President would sit immediately across the table from him. There would then be White House staffers flanking them, and then my people. The object of this exercise is to go through the budget for the department—we are not talking about the little bitty items; we are talking about the biggies—and ironing out the differences between the Office of Management and Budget and what I wanted for the department. One limits the number of appeals one takes because the President can't be bothered about appeals about everything. I would save up about three items for which I really wanted the money, and I would make a personal appeal to the President for that money.

The fact is that President Carter wanted to know every detail about everything. He knew all the details about all the programs of all the departments, whether it was the Department of Defense, the Department of State or the Department of Education. He had studied them all, and, believe me, that is a chore.

There would be significant debates. I didn't win them all, but I will say I came close. It was that kind of relationship. Also, there were occasions, on an average of once every two weeks, when something was going on in the White House for which the Cabinet was supposed to appear. Some of these were created by social occasions in which foreign heads of state or state governors were being entertained. It is strange how quickly, instead of an awesome place, the White House becomes another office. It happens very quickly because Cabinet officers go there to work, not to sight-see.

Meetings of one sort or another were quite regular. There were times when the President would have several of us over for a glass of wine, a tiny reception in the home quarters of the White House. It is a very nice thing to sit up on the porch of the residential quarters looking out over that magnificent vista, sitting there on rocking chairs, talking about what one is going to do. Sometimes it was what's going on with the campaign, sometimes what's going on in other countries, and sometimes what kind of assistance the President wants to have in certain kinds of programs.

I don't mean to suggest, however, that there was informality in the White House. That is not so. The President of the United States, no matter who is the President of the United States, is indeed the President, and you never forget it.

Cabinet meetings open formally, as do conferences in the Supreme Court of the United States. The President comes in last. Everybody else is seated. Each Cabinet officer shakes hands with every other Cabinet officer at every meeting. And when the President comes in, you can almost hear the echoes of "Hail To the Chief." The President would make the rounds and shake hands with everybody in the Cabinet before the meetings would begin.

As a little postscript, there is a very nice tradition that those of you who know the presidency will no doubt have heard. It has existed for some time; when it started I don't know. The members of one's department buy the department chair that is seated at the Cabinet table. These chairs are made by Colonial Williamsburg. The members of your department buy the chair for you and it's got the designation at the back. It doesn't have your name on it, but it has the name of the office on the back. It is presented to you as you leave the department. I now have in my home the Cabinet chair from the Cabinet table when I was secretary of education. It is very nice. I never have figured out when or who orders the next set of chairs, but I'm sure somebody takes care of that.

QUESTION: All of what you have described sounds like the mechanics of policy administration. I wondered how much time you had to think about broad perspectives in education, in what direction you would like the country to move and how appropriate the institution that you occupied was to that sort of discussion?

JUDGE HUFSTEDLER: I've thought about it a great deal. The reason I talked to you about the budget process is because policy drives the budget, not the other way around. Within limits, you decide what the policy is going to be by deciding what kind of push you want to give on which elements of the budget. You are reviewing the quality of all the programs the department runs. An intense set of reviews were conducted by me and my undersecretary; every single solitary program of the department is reviewed. One looks not only at the level of funding, but also to the results. What are the studies that show effectiveness? Can we move the money in a way that will make a difference? That is the way many of the major policy decisions were made.

In addition, of course, I had a vision about the department. I thought about it a great deal, about what it could do within the boundaries of the legislation that created the department and what within the political environment could possibly avoid a veto within a particular span of time. Yes, I thought about that a lot, and I discussed it with people I had reason to trust. Early on, I found out that when I wanted to carry on a socratic debate with a group of people within the department, I'd ask a socratic question, and it would come out in the morning press that I had given the answer, which limits the ambience of a debate.

First, be clear that we were rolling a great deal of money under various kinds of formula grants. There is a complex system for doing that, not only with respect to how the grant and loan programs are managed, but how one wants to move monies, or how one can escalate monies that go through the federal government to state agencies for distribution to local schools and in local school districts.

A great deal of the work prescribed by that intense lobby by higher education groups had already gone on in terms of the reauthorization of the Higher Education Act before I stepped onto the scene. There were more provisions of various kinds in that legislation than those that came out in the later administration on a tax reform bill. Everybody had pieces put into that. It's a clumsy piece of legislation, but I figured it this way: I was determined to get the higher education reauthorization; if the President were re-elected, I could get the authorizing legislation fixed up a good deal by seeking amendments in the next Congress. If, on the other hand, the President lost, I was aware that the new administration by Mr. Reagan would not sign a higher education reauthorization bill. To me it was much more important to get the authorizing legislation through, than to make it beautiful. If one was going to attempt to run things on continuing resolutions, it is not going to work.

All of you know you cannot run an institution of higher education of any substance without having the opportunity for monies to pay the tuition and to help students through guaranteed student loans, direct students loans, supplemental education opportunity grants, basic educational opportunity grants. It wasn't a question to me. I didn't have to worry about the question, should the United States government be in the situation of attempting to provide student financial aid? I already knew the answer to that, "Yes."

It is beside the point whether or not it was a good idea. I happen to think it was. But the fact is that institutions in the United States of all kinds of higher education are absolutely dependent on that set of monies to make the situation go. The fact is that of the fourteen and a half billion dollars, 40 percent of that budget went for student aid in higher education. That is a lot of money. There was no way you could pull the plug on that without causing extreme dislocations in higher education.

My mission was very clear. I didn't have to spend acres of time thinking about it, but I did have to spend time thinking about how I was going to structure and create the strategy to get that authorizing legislation through. It took a lot of work because that legislation was about to go down the chutes about ten times. I couldn't fiddle with it too much, or I wouldn't have gotten it through. And yet the bill, that is the dollars and cents bill attached, was a larger one than I believed the President would support because the funding was so high. There was a lot of negotiating and horse-trading about how we were going to get that through. I still think I'm absolutely right, because the funding has been cut back. Without a piece of authorizing legislation, you are not worried about the funding because there isn't any legislation to fund.

There are other longer-range strategies about which I felt very strongly in terms of trying to improve the funding and opportunities for international education. I had longer-term strategies which I was working on to try to create a larger reservoir of foreign language work, because we are hideously impoverished on foreign language-fluent people, even though our country is as polyglot as any in the world, and perhaps more so. Yet, how do you develop the resources so we could do that? Any one of you in higher education knows what we went through in the spasms of the sixties and seventies, when people thought it was a dirty trick to require any student to take any language other than English. The result is we have a tremendous dearth of people who can manage the languages. Whether you are talking about diplomacy or business, the Japanese don't send their people over here to do business with us speaking only Japanese. We do that to them. The Russians don't send a bunch of people to negotiate Law of the Sea treaties or anything else with us who speak nothing but Russian, but we do that.

Now, the United States has $50 billion of annual business in the Spanish-speaking world; yet, an American automobile manufacturing business has sent cars to Central and South America, named "Nova," meaning "to go" in Spanish. The company wondered why it did not sell very well! The lack of a reservoir of language fluency has put us at a disadvantage at many levels. I had developed some strategies for that. I had a lot more plans than I had time to institute.

QUESTION: I'd like to frame a question having to do with the office of the president as you see it. One of the comments you made was that Mr. Carter was intimately familiar with details of

The Presidency and the Cabinet

the budget. It has been said by a number of people that he was deeply immersed in all aspects of every problem. In hindsight, do you think President Carter might have been well advised to follow the theory of delegation and allow his staff and the Cabinet officers to do many of these things which you indicated that he shouldn't possibly have been doing?

JUDGE HUFSTEDLER: I don't want to give an impression that Mr. Carter did not delegate a great deal. He did. But he wanted to know what all his folks were doing. What you need is a combination.

QUESTION: Isn't that undercutting the delegation immediately?

JUDGE HUFSTEDLER: Well, it depends upon whether or not you try to run the other person's affairs. He didn't do that; for example, I ran the Department of Education. It doesn't make any difference whether a President's style is the style of Mr. Carter in knowing more than he needed to know about what was going on, or whether it is the delegating style of Mr. Eisenhower. In terms of what government is like today, the success of a President depends much more on his ability to capture the media and use this facility. One could be a knucklehead, but if he looks fine on TV he will be perceived as doing well, and if that is not his metier, he is going to be perceived as doing poorly. Franklin Roosevelt would have done as superbly well with television as he did in radio. Abraham Lincoln would have flunked. His face is now beloved but he would not have been beloved on television. Can you imagine those debates or going out to talk on the circuit with this lanky figure with his pipe hat? Or can you imagine what it would be like with T. R. Roosevelt with his rather squeaky voice urging the troops up San Juan Hill? He wouldn't have been elected alderman if he had run on television.

We have not accommodated presidential style and approach to the demands of an extraordinarily complex system. I suppose if I could design "the perfect President" it would be a president whose mind worked liked a computer, who had the compassion of Florence Nightingale, and who had the stage presence before television of Mr. Reagan. How in the world you'll ever find anybody who has all of those things, I don't know. What it reminds me of—and I feel this way about the presidency—is what it's like to be on a search committee for the president of a university. Everybody wants to have a president who is a superb scholar, who is magnificent with the alumni, who knows every stone and furrow of the campus, who is marvelous in making presidential appointments of the finest people, and who presides at all meetings, is on various commissions, and who writes monographs. That's all the Committee wants. That's all we want for a person who is going to be president of the United States, with the additions that the person must be fluent in foreign policy and economics and military affairs.

I think that Jimmy Carter's presidency will be much, much better thought of a decade from now than during the time it happened, just as many of us remember Harry Truman's presidency fondly. To be a successor to Franklin Roosevelt would be tough in the first instance. Harry Truman could not have ended up with a successful presidency today in terms of his accent and presence on the stage. He was not a Shakespearean actor. He would have had problems. But notice how fond we have become retrospectively of Harry Truman. And I think we will be fond, retrospectively, of things that Jimmy Carter accomplished because some of those things are very well kept secrets.

The things that were the most important about Jimmy Carter's administration were more what didn't happen than what did. There were many provocations that could have turned into war, the invasion of Afghanistan being the most significant. People were angry about our not sending our athletes to the Olympics in Moscow, and the farmers were furious about not sending grain to the U.S.S.R. There would have been more immediate enthusiasm about sending troops, but despair if we had done so because of what would have happened.

The negotiation grounded in Carter's personality and born-again religious faith that brought about the Egyptian and the Israeli peace treaty was a remarkable bit of business. The saving of a million acres of land in Alaska for wilderness was not greeted by any applause in Alaska, but future generations will appreciate that it has been done. The energy that was saved contributed to the oil glut and the cracking of OPEC.

A lot of things were accomplished for which the President got almost no credit, but for which we will honor him ultimately. The style of the engineer has lots of pluses; it also has some minuses. It is difficult for me to say that a successful presidency should always be judged by whether or not you get a second term.

QUESTION: There has been a great deal of discussion early on in the Reagan administration about eliminating the Cabinet position of education and putting it back with HEW. I have two questions. How much would we save if we made that move of putting it back where it was? And secondly, how ineffective might it be to administer all these programs in the department of HEW compared with being on your own?

JUDGE HUFSTEDLER: In the first place, it saves nothing. It would be very costly to do. In the second place, nobody knows how to do it because it isn't just one program, it is all of them. For anybody who has even thought about the exercise of how to put the toothpaste back into the tube after it has been squeezed out, you can see that it is not a very efficient operation.

Secondly, it is extremely important to have education at the Cabinet table. Why? Because Washington runs on power and the perceptions of power, whether it is there or not. Whoever reports to the President is automatically deemed to have power and, by the way, usually does. And the farther you get pushed away, the less things happen. As a Cabinet secretary, I could get the media into the schools. As a commissioner of education, forget it. As a Cabinet member, I could get the support of the President on an education bill when I needed it, and senators and congressmen from either party would listen. Even if they don't always agree, you had your hearing.

Education in the United States is just too important not to have a seat at the Cabinet table. That does not mean that the federal government should dominate education. In the first place, it doesn't. In the second place, the amount of support to elementary and secondary education has always been too modest; even at the height of funding it was 9 percent. Who runs anything with 9 percent?

I think it would be a significant loss to the country. The department hasn't been able to do what I think it is capable of doing, the things I think could be very valuable to this country, because anytime you've got a Cabinet officer whose president told him that his mission is to get rid of the department he is trying to run, that department has a morale problem. The president is not going to go to bat for you when his mission is to bat the department out of existence. Dr. Terrel Bell has done the best he can under the circumstances which are unbelievably trying. It is going to take some time to rebuild the department financially and to build in morale, but I think these things can be done with dedication, support, and time.

QUESTION: Do you think the organization of higher education is convinced now about the department, that you generally have the support of higher education?

JUDGE HUFSTEDLER: I don't think I can put it that strongly. I can say the fears that were not rationally based, or some of them that were rationally based but didn't come true, have been replaced by a level of confidence that is essential to higher education. Higher education also recognized, or at least some of the leadership did, that without a Cabinet-level department in a presidential election year, there wouldn't have been any reauthorization of higher education.

What we've said is there is not a victory, but we have a treaty.

NARRATOR: About a former President it was said that whenever you were in his presence you sensed you were observing a mind at work. This afternoon we've certainly observed a mind but also a spirit, vision, and much energy. I hope from time to time that there will be many stopovers for Judge Hufstedler in Charlottesville to discuss presidents and education.

CHAPTER 3

THE CABINET SYSTEM AND LABOR: TASKS OF A MIDDLE-SIZED DEPARTMENT

SECRETARY OF LABOR RAY MARSHALL

NARRATOR: Former secretary of labor, Ray Marshall is a professor at the University of Texas well known for his contributions in the field of labor economics and industrial relations. He was secretary of labor in the Carter administration.
  Dr. Marshall was born in Oak Grove, Louisiana, and raised in a Baptist orphanage. At age fifteen he joined the Navy, served in World War II, and received his education through the GI Bill. He earned his bachelor's degree in economics at Millsaps College in Jackson, Mississippi, his master's degree in economics from Louisiana State University and his Ph.D. in economics from the University of California at Berkeley. He taught first at San Francisco State and then at the University of Mississippi. He was a Fulbright scholar in Finland and returned to teach for five years at Louisiana State University, becoming a full professor. In 1962 he assumed his duties as a professor at the University of Texas.
  Because of his substantial writings and research and his interest in rural poverty and rural manpower problems, he early came to the attention of President Carter who consulted him when he was governor of the state of Georgia. During his presidential campaign, Dr. Marshall wrote background papers for Carter's campaign speeches. Later he became a member of his Cabinet as secretary of labor.
  Dr. Marshall has been chairman of the Federal Committee on Apprenticeship, a member of the National Council of Unemployment Policy, president of the National Rural Center in

Washington, and president of the Industrial Relations Research Association. Professionally in economics, he's been chairman of the American Economic Association Committee on Political Discrimination and is author and co-author of a number of works, including *Rural Workers in Rural Labor Markets, Human Resources and Labor Markets, Labor Economics: Wages, Employment and Trade Unionism* and *The Role of Unions in the American Economy*. In our discussion of the Carter presidency, we have only begun to touch on the most important economic issues. Therefore we are pleased that someone with Ray Marshall's professional credentials would join in our oral history.

SECRETARY MARSHALL: Thank you. The secretary of labor has several different jobs. One is to administer the Department of Labor. The department was created to protect and promote the interests of the American workers. I think that's a good mandate. It's the only department in the government that has the explicit job of representing workers' interest. When I was there the department had about 29,000 employees. The budget was roughly $30 billion a year.

The department had several divisions. The largest one in my time was the Employment and Training Administration which was responsible for jobs and training. The Occupational Safety and Health Administration is responsible for administering the Occupational Safety and Health Act (OSHA). During the Carter administration we transferred into the Labor Department the Mine Safety and Health Act from the Department of Interior. We had the Labor Standards Administration which is responsible for wage and hour administration and similar activities; there was also a division dealing with labor-management relations.

There was also a fairly large law division, the Office of the Solicitor, employing some 750 lawyers. The Labor Department is relatively unique in that it does its own litigation; most departments do not. Labor law is sufficiently specialized that the Labor Department does its own litigation and therefore has a very large Office of the Solicitor. We also have one of the oldest and best statistical agencies in government—the Bureau of Labor Statistics. It has an extremely important function to perform and serves as a source for research on the economy. In addition, there's the Office of the Secretary where many kinds of specialized activities took place. For example, we had the office of the Federal Contract Compliance Programs which is responsible for the enforcement of the nondiscrimination provisions of government contracts. The Carter administration unified the nondiscrimination enforcement work in the Labor Department. Previously it had been done in each of the agencies.

There was also the Women's Bureau which I elevated and moved into my office and made into an independent agency. As the only women's bureau in government, it took the lead in many women's issues. It was mainly concerned with employment problems of women. One of the most important labor market develops of this century is the increased labor force participation of women. It is hard for most people to imagine that as recently as 1950, 70 percent of American households were headed by men whose income was the sole source of income. Today less than 10 percent of American households are headed by men whose income is the sole source of income. Therefore, the increased labor force participation of women is one of the most important labor market developments we face.

We also had within the department a specialized office, which I tried to strengthen, and which was headed by the assistant secretary for Policy Evaluation and Research. It was very clear that we were in a period of economic ferment, and that many of the traditional approaches to economic policy-making were inappropriate. I felt that in order to protect and promote the interest of the workers, we had to have better economic analysis. Therefore, I strengthened the assistant secretary for Policy Evaluation and Research. That office works closely with the Bureau of Statistics in doing research.

The main problem, of course, was that the American economy had become internationalized and that fundamentally changed the way we had to make economic policy. We were also undergoing substantial technological changes and significant demographic changes. All those things tended to change the fundamentals of economic policy. We can no longer make economic policy in the United States in isolation from other countries. We felt we had to work more closely with other countries in designing our economic policies.

Another agency of the department is the International Labor Affairs Bureau. We became very heavily involved in international affairs generally, specifically in trade negotiations but also in general foreign policy. It was my view that you could not represent the interests of American workers solely on the basis of domestic policy. You had to be heavily involved in trade negotiations. You also had to be heavily involved in labor standards work. The basic purpose of labor standards was to limit competition in the labor market below a certain level. The rationale for that was to protect our human resources, to avoid child labor, unsafe and unhealthful working conditions, and also to cause competition to improve management rather than reduce labor standards. It's been pretty well demonstrated that there is a "Greshham's Law" of labor standards: bad standards drive good standards out. If you want to protect labor, your basic resource, you have to have labor standards. Those labor standards ought to meet the same conditions as any other rules. They ought to be transparent, which means you can find out what they are. They ought to be negotiated, if that's possible. They ought to be based on consensus, and they ought to be enforceable.

One of the problems in an internationalized environment is that you can no longer enforce your labor standards because you don't control what happens in Korea, Brazil or Mexico. For example, I had employers tell me that if we enforced the OSHA standards, they would go to Mexico. My response was that I was no more interested in seeing Mexican workers get cancer than American workers. But if they could go to Mexico and ship their goods back into the United States, it would be more difficult for us to protect American workers from cancer. Therefore, we needed to be concerned about international labor standards. We became fairly active in the International Labor Organization for that reason.

Before we took office, Secretary Kissinger had issued a letter saying that unless changes were made in ILO, we would withdraw. One of our first decisions was to honor the Kissinger letter, which was preceded by some debate. There was some disagreement within the administration whether we ought to withdraw. I felt that we should honor it because when you negotiate and threaten to walk out if changes aren't made, and the other party won't respond, you lose your credibility in a hurry if you say you were just joking. I think one of the most serious problems in American government is lack of continuity from administration to administration. Therefore it was important for us to honor the Kissinger letter. I also believed very strongly that the ILO could and should be a much more effective organization in protecting workers' standards. So we left and then rejoined the ILO which I think had some effect on improving it.

In addition, I was responsible for the foreign policy office of the Labor Department. We established a program to administer activities between the United States and a number of other governments, always at their request, to work on common problems. It became very clear that the State Department could not work on labor problems because it did not understand labor problems, just as it didn't understand agriculture problems. The best way to deal with those matters is from department to department rather than through the State Department. I think we had about eighteen of those agreements with other countries— some developed and some developing countries. We had a pretty good relationship with Brazil, for example, and a very good relationship with Mexico. It was clear to me that one of the most important relationships the United States has with another country in the world is with Mexico and that we should pay a lot more attention to that. We had a good relationship with Israel, Egypt and most of the European and OECD countries.

When a country would come to us with a problem, it might concern occupational safety and health, for example, a technical problem in how to deal with cancer requiring some epidemiological work; or a statistical problem having to do with labor market surveys, and the best way to put together labor market information systems. This task would require the Bureau of Labor Statistic's assistance. We helped Brazil with labor/management relations. We worked with the Chinese on taking a census which they hadn't done for many years. They didn't know if they had 800 million people or 1.2 billion. Their error was bigger than our population! The Chinese were also very interested in my rural work. In fact, I had been invited to China before I got to be secretary of labor. One of the big issues they wanted us to pursue was a labor incentive system. They were trying to develop a more rational system to allocate labor and how to give workers more incentives to work. Thus they hoped to improve labor productivity. These programs within the International Labor Affairs Bureau received a lot of attention.

I think that's enough on the Labor Department. You can see that it's a kind of middle-sized government department, not as big as HEW nor as small as the Department of Education.

In addition to being chief executive officer in the Department of Labor, the secretary of labor is the president's chief adviser on labor matters. That's a separate role from being secretary of labor. In that capacity the secretary of labor ordinarily advises the president on the appointment to the independent agencies, like the National Labor Relations Board, which is not a part of the Department of Labor. The secretary of labor ordinarily is responsible for recommending the appointments of the members of the NLRB, and also the members of the National Mediation Board which administers the Railway Labor Act, which is responsible for airlines and railroads. The secretary of labor makes recommendations for the Federal Mediation and Conciliation Service, which again is a separate agency.

In that capacity the secretary of labor is also a political adviser to the president. The secretary of labor is in fact one of the more overtly political Cabinet officers in our system. You have a constituency, and you campaign actively for your friends while trying to defeat your enemies. I took great relish in that because I think that's the way it ought to work. While I wasn't as partisan as some, I nevertheless felt that it was important to strengthen our activity.

One of the lessons I learned while I was in Washington was that there are Republicans you can get along with. If you grew up where I did you would still remember the first Republican you ever saw! The way that ordinarily happened was if you would be going down the street with your daddy, he'd punch you and say, "Look at the man but don't stare." That was my first definition of a Republican. I asked him what a Republican was and he said, "A Republican is somebody who lives here among the Democrats. And if the Republicans get the White House, they'll get the local post office." I overcame that type of preconception because I had very strong Republican support in the work at the Labor Department.

But basically, as a political Cabinet officer you campaigned. You went out and campaigned for members of Congress in trying to get support and you gave the president advice about how to relate to the constituencies with which you had the strongest relationships. Now the labor department's strongest constituency were the state and local government officials because the largest program in the Labor Department was the employment training programs which requires the close cooperation of state and local officials. So they looked to us for work. We also had constituencies in minority communities because they were interested in those same employment training programs. I made a special effort to establish a constituency of women. As women were growing politically more important, we established a relationship with women's groups—the League of Women Voters, Girl Scouts, Campfire Girls, NOW, and others. We made a special effort to respond to their invitations to speak and draw them into our programs. We were particularly responsive to Veterans because we had the Veterans' Employment Program, and they became another important constituency.

In my role as a political officer, I tried to get these constituencies to support the President's programs across the board. I'd advise the President on how to proceed if a policy affected one of these groups. We'd write him a memorandum and call him or talk with him if he was going to make a speech to some group. We'd explain our relationship with that group, the kinds of things they were interested in and what we had done.

The third set of responsibilities of the secretary of labor involves certain congressional mandates that deal with activities that are not necessarily within the department. For example, the secretary of labor is chairman of the board of the PBGC (Pension Benefits Guaranty Corporation), which is created to insure private pension plans. Within the Department of Labor you have the responsibility for enforcing ERISA (Employee Retirement Income Security Act) to protect their pension rights while the PBGC's responsibility was similar to the insurance programs of the FDIC and FSLIC for banks. The secretary of labor is also one of the trustees of the social security system. In the same capacity we also served on various interagency committees for trade and for economic policy. We created what we called the Economic Policy Group, on which I served. But different administrations do different things with respect to the economic policy-making process.

In addition to these kinds of responsibilities, the Labor Department had to be particularly concerned about the media. I had a group of people dealing with that because it was not an area that I knew much about. It was an area about which I learned a lot. As an academic, I had a very negative attitude about the media. I considered it to be superficial, and in a lot of ways dangerous, because it trivialized issues that I thought were very important. But I overcame that and learned that it performs a terribly important function. I learned that there are significant differences between the wire services, regional media, and the New York and Washington-based media, as well as between the electronic and print media. You need to know how to deal with the media or they could cause great trouble.

My basic policy was never to go off the record with any reporter. During my whole time as secretary of labor, I didn't do that because I don't believe in it. I think you ought to name names so that people can check it out. I don't like referring to what "some highly placed person" said. If there are leaks you can be sure that they have a purpose and very few of them are good. Therefore, if there is something that you want said, you ought to have the courage to come out and say it and be prepared to be called wrong. Consequently, my press conferences were frequently like seminars, so the reporters said, because I felt an obligation to go into a fair amount of depth. I found them to be very profitable because the reporters, while they did not always agree with me, were frequently useful when they criticized me. I could find out about things going wrong in the department a lot better by reading the press than I could by asking the people who did it! I learned to appreciate that function of the press, and I tried to have my own independent information system out there.

The other main function I initiated was a lobbying activity, but not just in federal government. I created a deputy undersecretary for intergovernmental relations to run the lobbying office up on the Hill. He was also our representative for all regions and had to relate to the governors, mayors and voluntary organizations. That too, I found to be very valuable because, as Lyndon Johnson used to say, things don't look the same from the banks of the Pedernales as they do from the banks of the Potomac. You need to have people reporting what's happening in the areas where the programs are really supposed to take effect—in the local communities.

QUESTION: We would be extremely interested in knowing how you established your connection with President Carter. When did you make the first contact? What were the circumstances? What were your impressions of him as governor? What were your impressions of him as a leader? Did your impressions change as time went on? How would you appraise him as political leader?

SECRETARY MARSHALL: I met him when he was governor but that was not a very lengthy or important involvement. He was there when I was director of the task force on southern rural development. He also served on that task force. He would read things that we'd write and respond and seemed to take a strong interest in rural development.

During the campaign I was asked to supply material for his speeches, write background papers, and brief him on economic, social policy, and labor issues. The impression I gained then was that Jimmy Carter was a very bright person. I was amazed that I could come and brief him on a subject that I had dealt with all my life and he could walk out on the porch of the pondhouse in Plains, have a press conference and give you the impression that he had dealt with it all his life, too. He was very quick to learn.

I thought too he was a good politician in putting together a strategy to be elected President of the United States. He had a good plan based on the assumption, which I thought was correct, that any good Southerner that year could get elected president of the United States. The strategy basically was to deny the Republicans the South, or at least deny them the solid South. Lyndon Johnson was the last democratic nominee to get a majority of the white southern vote, despite the Civil Rights Act. In fact, Lyndon Johnson understood that. When he signed the Civil Rights Act, he said to Bill Moyers that he had probably done a lot to give the Republicans the White House for the rest of his life. Partly because of the 1965 Voting Rights Act, which strengthened the black vote, Jimmy Carter was able to upset that balance. He didn't get a majority of the white southern vote but with overwhelming black support got enough to deny the Republicans the South. That was a fundamental part of the strategy and it paid off.

I thought he was particularly good in dealing with relatively small groups. He'd come to a meeting like this and captivate people. He was a lot better at that than he was with television. I often thought that when the television came on, the Baptist stood up. He got a lot stiffer than he really was. He was a warm, sensitive, witty person but his wit never came out on the television. He had a spontaneous wit in relatively small groups. For example, he said to us, "Well, I see we're getting a lot more popular." "How so?" somebody asked, because we had had a particularly bad day. Carter said, "I notice that when people wave at me now they use all their fingers." He was a lot better speaking extemporaneously than he was speaking from a prepared text. Another problem was that Jimmy Carter had a lot of trouble doing the small things a politician has to do, like giving people the pens he used in signing bills. He didn't believe in broadcasting his feelings. Johnson would give you a thousand pens.

I think, frequently, he did not really consider the political implications of what he was doing. We lost votes on the Panama Canal and I think we lost a lot on SALT II. Of course, the Russians helped make that worse when they invaded Afghanistan. On the other hand, there was not much political mileage in the energy program, which took up a lot of time. So many of the things he tried to do were truly good for the country but not necessarily good politics.

Nevertheless, I think he'll go down in history as a great president because of the things he did and tried to do. The big political mistake was that he tried to do too much which caused him to lose a sense of priorities. A president has to get his agenda established in the first couple of years. I think it was Harry Hopkins who said: "*The only way to protect the public interest is to get the public interest tied down before the vested interests get their vests on.*" Otherwise you try to do more than you're able to do. That was clearly our mistake to attempt so much that there was not a sense of priorities. But on the whole, he did what I thought was good for the country and I was proud to be a part of the process.

QUESTION: I think that the secretary's views with reference to the relationship between labor standards and trade would be of considerable interest. How do you see our trade policies helping in the securing of workers' rights around the world and in reducing the competitive advantage that other countries have?

SECRETARY MARSHALL: I see it as critical partly because the ILO standards are mainly enforced by moral power. And my experience with moral power is it works mainly with moral people. That's not the kind you are trying to change. Therefore, you need something else. I believe the way to enforce it is through trade. Every trade bill since 1980 has included labor standards, as in the Caribbean Base Initiative, the OPIC reauthorization, and the generalized system of preferences. I think we have developed an enforcement mechanism that works.

I'm president of the International Labor Rights Research and Education Fund which is trying to monitor labor rights. Somebody has to do that because the ILO can't really do it. It doesn't have the resources, and its operation lacks continuity. What you need is a sense of direction of what you want to do in Chile, Korea, and in other countries. I think it is terribly important to be clear about the objective. For example, it would be a huge mistake for us to try to use trade rules to protect incompetent trade practices in the United States. I don't believe in that. You ought to get rid of the incompetent industries. In fact, that's the reason I believe in labor standards. If you can't meet the minimum labor standards accepted worldwide, you ought not to be in business in my judgment. Why should workers subsidize incompetent companies? You strengthen management with labor standards. That's the reason IBM had their so-called full employment policies. Tom Watson saw that if managers could shift the cost of their incompetence to workers, they had no real motivation to manage. Therefore, IBM established lifetime employment long before the Japanese.

What we ought to be trying to do is to strengthen an open and expanding international trade system from which we all have a lot to gain, and not to restrict it. I believe that properly constituted international labor standards will do that for a variety of reasons. First, you need to be able to assure that the workers in those countries benefit from the economic development and trade taking place. In the absence of freedom of association, the ability of workers to organize and protect their own interests is limited and therefore they are unlikely to benefit. Instead the multinational corporations in league with those governments compete not to become more efficient but to reduce labor standards and reduce wages.

I believe that Keynesian-type economic policy has been, if not fatally crippled by internationalization, at least seriously damaged because we cannot stimulate the American economy in an open system when the rest of the world is stagnant. That's what happened with the 1981 tax cut. The higher incomes simply increased imports, and the trade deficit became unsustainable. But I still believe Keynesian-type, demand stimulus policies can be very effective in the global economy. It should help to remove the international deadlock. If we could get growth to resume in this hemisphere, in Mexico and Brazil, that process would help the United States a lot. These would be the places where we would be able to sell a lot of the things we make if the workers in those countries had the money to buy them. The only way they are going to get the money to buy our goods is by participating and benefiting from economic development. What's been happening though, is a disproportionate part of the benefits of growth and trade has been going to the elites. Then you get a flight of capital because the elites deposit the money in Switzerland or in the United States and it doesn't really help those countries to grow at all. For most of the people, conditions are getting worse. For a rather small elite, conditions are getting better. They frequently have very limited attachment to their own country; they'll ship that money out of there in a hurry. In fact, a large part of the loans that went to the Third World—at least half—was flight capital. So it didn't stimulate a lot of growth in those countries.

I believe labor standards that create an independent free labor movement in countries like Korea, Brazil and Mexico can help. I think it would be a mistake to assume that we could equalize wages. That is out of the question because wage differentials between the United States and other countries are too great for that. I'm talking about wage differentials for reasonably educated people; we are not talking about illiterates in Korea. The Korean literacy rate is higher, and their dropout rate is lower, than ours. In one project I was involved in we looked at the results from a VCR plant near Seoul. The IBM chairman of that committee told me that their best educated workers in the world were in Korea. In that VCR plant they worked twelve hours a day seven days a week, they had two days off a year, and they made $3,000 a year in 1985.

You are not going to be able to equalize their wages and ours. But what you can do is to see to it that those workers have freedom of association and can participate in the making of rules that improve their conditions within that system. I think trade-linked labor rules is the way to do it. I say to those people who are against it that the original plan for the GATT was to have an International Trade Organization (which didn't work out) and it had a social clause. My view is that labor standards are at least as important as commercial rules, and probably more important. But if somebody wants to argue about it I'll say it's at *least* as important to protect the safety and health of workers and let people develop their human resources. I just don't believe that protecting commercial rights is more important than protecting worker rights. They are no harder to enforce. I'd much rather enforce a labor standard which is straightforward. You can easily see whether they've got such a law on their books or not. That's not hard to find out. But are they dumping? That's one of the most difficult things to figure out, whether somebody is dumping. As an economist, I can tell you that the economists haven't got the foggiest idea about what anything costs. That is a matter of policy. That's not a matter of science. It costs whatever your accountants say it costs. If you get imaginative and creative accountants, they can make it come out the way you want it to come out.

The other thing we need to do is to overcome the resistance of workers in the developed countries to an open and expanding trading system. I don't think the international trading system ought to mainly protect our workers, though that is an important part of it. If you do that you create suspicions. Other countries will say that it's just a guise to protect our companies which are not world class. If the steel industry can't compete, too bad; it ought to go out of business. To compete, you've only got two options. One is to cut your standard of living and the other is to improve your productivity. When you've said that, you've exhausted the categories. If you forget wages then there is no competitiveness problem. You can sell your strategy if you're willing to cut your costs.

QUESTION: One of the things that we've been interested in is the extent to which a president is directly accessible to his Cabinet members. From what you said, it seems as if President Carter was. Would you care to comment on that?

SECRETARY MARSHALL: Yes, I think that is the case. I've known most of my predecessors in that office, going back to Jim Mitchell under President Eisenhower. My sense of it is I had a lot more freedom to run the department than any of them had. You can interpret that several ways. One is that the President was busier with other things and didn't want to fool with it. But I think he really believed that you ought to put those people in whom you had confidence in charge and let them run it. He believed in the Cabinet system. I set the policies and hired the people. All the political appointees were people I had personally interviewed and selected. None of them were hired by the White House. They sent me a list of some people that worked in the campaign and recommended that if I could find a place for these people I should try to do it. We had general guidelines. The president had told us all to make a special effort to hire minorities and women, and I did. What I did was simply enlarge the scope of the group from which we recruited.

I decided earlier, having been around the Labor Department as an adviser for some years, that one of the most important decisions a cabinet officer could make is how to deal with the civil service. My view was that whatever we got done during our time, they would do it. So half of my political appointees were civil servants. I tried to get them on our side. Beyond that, the President gave us general guidelines and then we operated within those general guidelines.

Anytime that I wanted to see him or get him on the phone I could do so. He insisted on being told anything he needed to know. He'd get you too, wherever you were. Rosalynn, too, would get us wherever we were. She'd be out making speeches somewhere and I'd get a call from her saying that she had some fellow in the other room proposing something; what do you think? She was very good at that. I campaigned with her some. She had a strong interest in things that were going on in the departments. So we got a lot of requests to look into things and do things.

The President, for example, was terribly concerned about some aspects of the Labor Department. He gave me special instructions to look into those. One was OSHA. During the 1976 campaign he heard all kinds of criticisms on the Occupational Safety and Health Act. I wasn't a politician, but I learned pretty fast that if you do what the president wants you to do, you'll be all right. *You've only got one constituent if you are an American cabinet officer, and that's the president.* So I got to be an expert on OSHA in a hurry. We tried to straighten it out and I think we did. We mainly improved the management of it; the Employment and Training section had serious management problems. He had told me in advance that he would like me to pay heavy attention to that and develop a strategy to deal with it, and that if I needed help from OMB or anybody to call on them.

He felt free to call us any time and we could get back to him. But the nature of the contacts tended to change through time partly because we got encumbered with a lot of work going on. The dates of the Cabinet meetings changed several times. A lot of the communications took place during or after Cabinet meetings. I learned to know his schedule and what problems he had. I only called him when I thought it was terribly important, ordinarily when we had inter-departmental conflicts that we couldn't resolve, say with OMB or the Council of Economic Advisers, which I frequently had. We sometimes had to take these kinds of issues to the President.

QUESTION: Did you have to go through a chief of staff to get to the President?

SECRETARY MARSHALL: No.

QUESTION: How could the President divide his time with everybody coming from all different directions? It would seem almost necessary that his chief of staff would have some decision-making power as to who sees the President and when.

SECRETARY MARSHALL: A good bit of the time it wasn't clear that there was a chief of staff; therefore I'd have to schedule it. I'd call a scheduler and say, "I need to get on the President's schedule." Or I'd get the White House switchboard and say, "I want to speak to the President." But you would do that only if it was really important. The fact that people knew you could do that made your relationship with everybody else better because you had the President's authority. If you lost that then you'd lost your effectiveness in our system. You either have access or you don't. If you're a Cabinet officer and you don't have the ability to take matters to the president, I don't see how you can do your work. The President didn't either. "Call me if you need me," is what he used to say. Very often that was the last thing he would say to you after discussing an issue.

QUESTION: I have a small technical question plus a general policy one. In working with a task force that the President set up on the bargaining rights of public employees in the federal service, our group was rather cautious. It had a background of executive orders that set up rights for the federal employees and we sought to improve it. But by the time it got to the White House, you somehow felt that you could get legislation that would do the same thing and put it into the law in a firm way. The first question is how did you do that?

The second question is what were your relations with the employer community? On the National Labor Relations Board we never established a firm degree of confidence with the employer community on the desirability of freedom of association for American workers. There was opposition to the Wagner Act, to the Taft-Hartley Act. The employers made us feel that we were not as effective as we wanted to be. Did you have a policy problem with respect to the management community and in respect particularly to the rights of workers to organize?

SECRETARY MARSHALL: We did. That's obviously one of the problems we had with the labor law reform. In 1977-78, we worked on labor law reform. I'm a strong believer in consensus building, and we tried to build consensus with employers on that legislation. The relationships were mixed. With the major employers in the country, the members of the Business Roundtable, I had very good relationships. I had known Jack Post, the executive director from Houston, Texas, and we had good relations with the chairman of General Motors, Tom Murphy of General Electric, and with Dupont. We could not, however, get them to support labor law reform, even though I think they believed in it.

One of the problems at that juncture was that it got to be political and ideological. As you know, American employers are more hostile to unions than any other group of employers in the industrialized world. I think it is a huge mistake for them to be that way. I told Heath Larry, when he organized the Council for a Union-Free Environment, that the only thing standing between him and a really militant labor movement was the AFL-CIO. Here we've got the only labor movement in the world that embraces capitalism and he was trying to destroy it. That didn't make any sense to me at all. You're not going to have a free and democratic society in Poland or the United States if you don't have free and democratic labor movements. It seems to me that our basic policy is sound. Workers ought to make the choice of whether or not they want to be organized. I don't think we ought to be pro-union or pro-employer. We ought to be pro-worker. Unions don't really have effective rights now because the penalty for the violation of the National Labor Relations Act is too weak.

It became fashionable to be anti-union in the 1970s for a whole host of reasons. You couldn't have gotten by with that, say, in the 1950s and 1960s. Part of it was the unions' fault in not being responsive to changing conditions. Part of it was that public opinion with respect to unions had declined and employers knew that. But the people who were the most difficult to deal with were not the major employers. Most of them dealt with unions, even though their relationships then were not as good as now. General Motors' relationship with the UAW is much better now. Why? General Motors does not believe it can survive without the UAW, nor does the Ford Motor Company. They began to see the benefits of the whole worker involvement system we had started working on. Why did they see it? They saw it because the Swedes and the Japanese put together a system that was very competitive and emphasized quality and employee involvement. Phil Caldwell, chairman of the board of Ford, said 80 percent of Ford's turnaround—the reason they earned more profits in the last two years than General Motors—was their employee involvement system. You will not have an effective employee involvement system without the workers having an independent source of power to represent their interests. It doesn't mean they have to be members of a union, but it does mean workers have to have an effective right to organize and bargain collectively. If you've got a union-free environment then you don't have an effective right to do that. I think that's a mistake.

The people we had trouble with were the small employers who were easily stampeded into believing that if you pass an innocuous piece of legislation—which is all it was, the law strengthened the penalties and streamlined the procedures—it would put them out of business. Not many small employers are going to be put out of business. In fact, I tried to make a deal: "You support the law, and I'll try to get an exemption for small employers." That's probably where I made a tactical mistake in being truthful. I said if I were organizing you, I'd hope you weren't covered by the National Labor Relations Act. I wouldn't organize your workers! I'd organize the small employers. That would be a lot more effective. The law does more to protect small employers than it does to protect their workers, even though it's the National Labor Relations Act.

With respect to the Civil Service Reform where we attached Title VII, yes, we needed the legislation. We need to improve the collective bargaining system within the federal government. I don't think it's a very good system the way it works now, but I think the legislation moved it forward. There were some things I wanted in the legislation but couldn't get. I think we should have the same kind of provision in the Federal Labor Relations Act that we have in the National Labor Relations Act, namely that it would be an unfair labor practice for you to bargain with an organization that didn't represent a majority of your employees. I believe in collective bargaining. In the federal government they would have 600 or 700 people represent 14,000; I think that is wrong. So I had them around picketing me for a while.

A final point I want to make is that most of the major American employers recognize that it would not be good for the country for the labor movement to go away. The labor movement has been weakened, and I don't think that's good for the country. I think most of the major employers agree to that.

QUESTION: It's a little late in the discussion to bring this up perhaps. Years and years ago I had the title of chief economist with the American Youth Commission just before the war. I was in charge of youth employment studies and eventually published two little books after Pearl Harbor. One was called *Post-war Youth Employment* and the other, *Barriers to Youth Employment*. That got me involved in the discussion for minimum wage as it affected young people. I discovered that in England they did not have a serious youth employment problem, apparently because they have a graded wage system in which the wages for youngsters between 16 and 18 and between 18 and 20, were definitely below the adult wage. I became convinced that the existing minimum wage system in this country, which does not differentiate between adults and youth, was the major cause of youth unemployment. The drafts of those chapters made various people in the Labor Department unhappy. In the Children's Bureau, generations of staff have been working on child labor problems; they disagreed with me. Ever since, as far as I can see, it's been the policy of organized labor in this country to concentrate unemployment among young people. In the American Youth Commission we did not believe in that. Did you get involved in that argument?

SECRETARY MARSHALL: Yes, I did. We passed the Youth Employment and Demonstration Projects Act. What we did there was good legislation. Regarding Great Britain, they have industry minimum wage standards. That makes a lot of difference. We also have youth differentials for the minimum wage. We passed the Target Jobs Tax Credit which has done a lot more for employers than relief on a minimum wage. What we did with TJTC was to give you up to $3,000 the first year you would hire young people and $1,500 the second year. The most they would have gotten for the youth differential on a minimum wage was $400-$500. We had another program where we had a 100 percent wage subsidy to employers. That's what YEDPA did, the Youth Employment and Demonstration Project Act. If young people agreed to stay in school, then we'd provide a job. We tried to get it in the private sector. When we had 100 percent wage subsidy, 18 percent of the employers we called on said they would hire the people if we paid all the wages. Then we asked them how many would still do it if we paid half? Five percent said they would do it.

I came away believing that we do have a serious youth employment problem in this country. To some degree the youth employment problem in the 1970s was demographic. It was caused by the aging of the post-war baby boom generation entering the work force. We did a lot to absorb them. But there are several other serious problems with youth employment, and I don't think they have a lot to do with the minimum wage. One of the most serious, I think, is basic competence and skills. I was astounded to learn that almost 20 percent of the high school graduates coming into the Job Corps were illiterate. At first people got deluded by that. They'd say if you correlate schooling with all kinds of social pathologies—unemployment, teen pregnancy, drugs, trouble with the law—you don't find much correlation. The trouble with that was that they weren't correlating education with all those things. There's a big difference between schooling and education or we wouldn't have 18 percent of those high school graduates coming into the job corps illiterate.

Recently we put all that together. Gordon Berlin of the Ford Foundation and Andrew Sum recently published a study following up on all that we had learned. What they found was there is almost a perfect correlation between your standing on the AFQT (Armed Forces Qualification Test) and other achievement tests and things like unemployment and all the rest (teen pregnancy, trouble with the law, etc.). It seems to me, therefore, that we need such programs as the Job Corps—minimum wage is not going to help the kids who need the Job Corps because they aren't going to get a job anyway. That's what I learned from subsidizing 100 percent of youngster's wages.

Four years later, I was chair of the State Job Training Coordinating Council for the state of Texas. What we finally hit on was that if we wanted to help young people, we should concentrate on basic education. The group most endangered in our society are young minority males. What we found is that the lower your scores on AFQT, the more likely you were to have several problems, that is to be a drop out, in trouble with the law, and a drug addict, perhaps all at the same time. The higher your score on the AFQT, the less likely you were to have those problems. What are we going to do with these people that are illiterate after being in school for twelve years? You obviously don't send them back to the schools that made them illiterate. So we developed a learning system using the armed forces simulation and computerized techniques. Building on that, we had Control Data Corporation work on a computerized learning system. The consequence of that in 1980 was that with ninety hours of instruction we could move people two grade levels. People have continued to work on that and now with twenty-eight hours of instruction, they could move you 1.4 grades in mathematics and one grade in reading. That's astounding.

My view is to take those programs that you know will work, like the Job Corps, and expand them. In other areas where you don't know what will work, experiment with wage subsidies and such.

One of the most important things we have learned, besides the importance of these basic skills, which they were not getting in school at all, was the "summer loss" phenomenon. The recent finding is that the lack of education achievement of seriously at risk young people apparently is due in part to the summer loss phenomenon. Most middle-income kids and higher-income kids don't have as much summer loss. They test you at the end of the school year, and test you at the beginning of the next year, and everybody has lost a little. But the lower income people have lost a lot. Eighty percent of the difference according to a recent study in Atlanta, between the advantaged kids and the disadvantaged kids was accounted for by summer loss. If that's the case, then we ought to do something about it. We ought to have summer youth programs with basic education attached. That's one of our mistakes in the jobs program. There was no education; we just put them to work.

The lesson I learned was that different groups of young people have different needs. Some of them need counseling. Those who need the Job Corps are among the most disadvantaged. They come from urban ghettos, and are already at a critical stage. Young people go through stages. They look for a job and if they can't find a job, then they adjust to unemployment. They come to have associates who condemn work. They say you're stupid to take a job if you can make money selling drugs or prostituting or robbing people. When they are at that stage, they are the toughest to deal with. That's the reason we ought to work in this country on school-to-work transition. For those kids who have adjusted to unemployment and work in the underground economy, the Job Corps constitutes what we call the "last chance syndrome." It is self-governing. If you've never been to a Job Corps program, you ought to visit one. It will do you a lot of good to sit and listen to those people. Ordinarily they elect as governor the meanest, toughest looking character in the whole operation. When the young recruit comes into the Job Corps swaggering and saying, "I've been a member of this gang," the governor will listen and say, "Look, don't tell us how tough you are. We know that what you're facing is the grave, jail, or skid row. We've been there. This is your last chance. If you don't want it, let us know because we have a lot of people who want it. And this is the only chance you are going to have to make it back into the mainstream of this society." Ordinarily it works.

The Job Corps has helped us learn a lot with learning and schooling. For example, they have a Job Corps graduation every Friday. Why should you have a graduation once a year? People now can learn at their own pace. You have all kinds of people in the same class at different levels. The way they teach algebra is for you to work on a problem and the machine says, "You missed. Try again." You work at it again, and it says, "You missed it again. Let me show you what you did wrong." There's no way you can bluff the machine. It's color-blind and non-judgmental.

I think we need a National Youth Service in the country. The last unifying experience the United States had was World War II. We're getting more and more fragmented and there are not many situations where young people have a chance to work together with people from different backgrounds. That's the kind of thing the Youth Service Corps could do.

NARRATOR: I think we all would like to continue this discussion. We've learned a lot about the Carter presidency and about substantive problems as well. If it were not for the fact that Secretary Marshall has another meeting with another group, we would continue. Thank you very much for a most educational Forum.

CHAPTER 4

CABINET GOVERNMENT AND PRESIDENT CARTER: AN ALTERNATIVE FOR ORGANIZING POLICYMAKING

ATTORNEY GENERAL GRIFFIN BELL

NARRATOR: I would like to welcome you to a Forum with Griffin Bell this morning on a subject that is of continuing interest to the Miller Center, the question of Cabinet government. It is a subject to which, in one sense, we were introduced a couple of years ago when Judge Bell took part in a conference of former attorneys general at the Miller Center. It is an issue that has recurred in many discussions since that time. It is a subject that almost every text writer comments on, including a recent one saying, "Of all the advisory bodies to which the President can turn for advice, the Cabinet consisting of the government's ten department heads is the oldest and most prestigious."

Many Presidents have also regarded it as of the least useful. Mentioned nowhere in the Constitution, the Cabinet was invented by George Washington who noted that Article II, Section 2 of the Constitution provided that "the President may require the opinion in writing of the principal officer in each of the executive departments upon any subject relating to the duties of their respective office." When Washington first met with these principal officers in 1789 there were only three departments of government: State, War and Treasury. By the end of his first term these department heads were known as his "Cabinet" and the term has stuck as more than seven other government offices have been elevated to departmental status. Nothing in the law requires the President to meet with his Cabinet or listen to its members' advice, nor is Cabinet approval required for any action he may take. And then there is a long discussion of the different uses that have been made of the Cabinet by different Presidents.

All of you know of Judge Bell's achievements and record. He was attorney general from 1977 and 1979; active in Atlanta affairs; a graduate of Mercer; he has an ongoing concern in questions of civil rights as well as questions of maintenance of order within society. We are fortunate that in a busy schedule at the University of Virginia he would take time to meet with us and discuss this subject. I think he may want to kick it off briefly but I know he hopes very much that you will raise questions following his presentation.

ATTORNEY GENERAL BELL: I was testifying in the House Judiciary Committee on Tuesday morning on an aspect of the antitrust laws. It had to do with a law that was passed in 1944 and the chairman of the committee read some letters that President Roosevelt wrote about this law urging that it not be passed. He commented that probably no President would ever write a letter now to the chairman of the House Judiciary Committee about a law. He would send some fourth-level aide over to speak to somebody, maybe the committee staff. He remarked on what a change had come over the government just in those years since 1944.

I begin by using that as something of a text because it may be that it was certainly no later than the Johnson administration that the White House staff has become so large that it has really subsumed the Cabinet. There is some doubt that Cabinets are any more useful, although George Washington set the system up and it has served us well over the years. There is hardly any Cabinet post now that does not have a parallel over in the bowels of the White House somewhere, some person who has never been confirmed and whose name might not even be known to the public. So let's go back to the beginning when Washington didn't have a Cabinet. There were those three departments that you mentioned, State, Treasury and War, and then there was the attorney general and the attorney general was a part-time post. But under the Constitution the President is charged with faithfully executing the laws and he can hardly do that without having some agent. So the attorney general was the President's agent.

Washington started out by letting the Cabinet vote on policy issues. Jefferson and Randolph and Couzens would usually take the same side and take issue with Hamilton and Jay and that's generally the way it started. I was surprised in doing some studying on the Civil War to know that President Lincoln let his Cabinet vote, particularly after Alexander Stevens, once president of the Confederacy, met with President Lincoln at Fort Monroe in February of 1865 to negotiate an end to the war—that was several months before the war ended. Lincoln and Stevens had served in the Congress together. They were Whigs. They sat beside each other so they knew each other. They could have ended the war after the conference but Lincoln got back to Washington and let his Cabinet vote on it and didn't get a single vote in favor of ending the war on the basis under discussions.

Stevens reported to Jefferson Davis and his ego was so great that he was not able to bring himself to end it unless he was made commander of all the armed forces of both sides on the pretext that they were having trouble with the French in Mexico. That was the end of that.

But the Cabinet has played a big role. President Franklin Roosevelt used his Cabinet greatly, some members moreso than others but they were big men in the government during the Roosevelt years. When World War II started Roosevelt changed some of his Cabinet members to put some Republicans in because he wanted to have the Cabinet more bipartisan.

In those days the White House staff was always very small. We didn't have a National Security Council director then and when you think about it perhaps we don't need one or maybe we don't need a secretary of state. If we have a President who is not capable of being his own secretary of state we are in bad shape. We are in trouble to begin with. We had a governor who set out to reform the prisons of Georgia. He announced one day that he had done the best that he could do until we were able to get a better class of prisoners. It may be that we are going to have to get a better class of Presidents, surely someone that knows enough about foreign affairs to be his own secretary of state. The same would have to be true about the Defense Department given the change in defense, and the sophisticated no-miss weapons that are being developed. The President just has to know something about all of this or he has to have an aide who knows something about it and an aide who is someone that the American people would have confidence in. I don't know that the secretary of the treasury is needed anymore other than as a part of the State Department foreign policy—world currency problems and those sort of things. There are others who are duplicating the functions of the secretary of the treasury. The secretary may be more like a corporate comptroller, certainly given the fact that the President's got an economic adviser over at the White House who does all the things the secretary used to do. I don't think you can get by without an attorney general. After that I'm not saying that there is any post in the Cabinet that is any more than an agency head.

I don't know how we could have Cabinet government now. I used to sit in the Cabinet and President Carter would ask every member of the Cabinet their views about something when many of the members of the Cabinet had only the foggiest notion about the questioning. But somehow most would give their views. Finally, after about a year and a half, two different members of the Cabinet said to the President that the "show and tell" style meetings were no longer fruitful. That is how Cabinet government ended up.

Now it's worse than ever because as I understand the Reagan system, they have truly done away with Cabinet government. They have groups that study various things and reach a composite view, not necessarily in a Cabinet. On antitrust questions I notice that the secretary of commerce is the dominant person involved although the attorney general and others are in that group. There are groups to study everything, so I don't know that Cabinet officers are playing much of a role. At least that is the system that is public, the structure that the American people know about through the media.

In the Carter administration we didn't have that. We had a counterpart for everyone. I don't think I had a counterpart, although the White House counsel was to some extent. I know that Brzezinski was Secretary Vance's counterpart and was often in command. He had a very narrow area as compared to the wide ranging duties of the secretary of state. He saw the President every morning and usually Secretary Vance was in the air somewhere, going to conferences or to funerals and those sort of things.

Mr. Brzezinski never appeared a single time in the Senate or before a committee of the Congress. He never had to appear—no one at the White House, think of this, ever appears in the Congress. They don't have to appear. They've never been confirmed and they tend to or at least try to dominate the Cabinet out of the White House but they don't have any responsibility to the Congress.

This has a lot to do, I think, with the breakdown—and that's all you can call it—between particularly the House and the President right now in the area of foreign affairs. Never in the history of our nation have we had committees of the Congress who wanted to have authority to decide whether we will have an intelligence operation, for example. The House Select Committee on Foreign Intelligence says now that President Reagan cannot carry on any kind of foreign intelligence operation without their concurrence in advance. This is a breakdown because it is contrary to the Constitution, the express terms of the Constitution, and the decisions of the Supreme Court that the President can make foreign policy subject to the power of the Congress of oversight to see if new legislation is needed or to control the appropriations.

As I now see it, we have co-Cabinet people in the White House and we've got a committee of the House trying to be the co-equal to the President in foreign affairs. I don't believe we can get our government in much worse shape than it is in now, structurally. We will have to come out of this. I think this Center can render a signal service by getting into this area and letting the American people know what has happened to their government and how different it is now from what the Founding Fathers and the early Congresses had in mind, particularly the first Congress in 1791, and how they structured the government at that time.

I don't think the world is any more complex now other than scientifically. Political science has not changed that much but we do need to insist that the White House staff be greatly reduced. We'll get a President eventually who will do that and who will go back to Cabinet government. When he goes back, however, he's going to have to eliminate almost half the Cabinet posts. They are just not needed. They are really agency heads. Some of the positions should be combined. I've never understood why we had a secretary of commerce and a secretary of labor. That creates a tension to begin with. You ought to have the same person worrying about that.

DUMAS MALONE: They did originally, you know.

ATTORNEY GENERAL BELL: They did?

MR. MALONE: Yes, commerce and labor together.

ATTORNEY GENERAL BELL: Well, they ought to go back to that. That is my general approach to the matter. I'll be glad to answer questions. I told Ken about how the Carter administration was set up. You can hardly speak on this subject generally because you would have to know the inside of the operation of every administration, just how they are doing it. All I know about the Reagan administration is what I read in the newspapers of how it is set up. I am in antitrust law so I'm interested in that and I was struck by the idea that Secretary of Commerce Baldridge was very outspoken about the antitrust ruling in the recent steel merger questions and finally backed the Justice Department off. He started out criticizing the assistant attorney general, something I would not ever have condoned. You would have to take me on rather than one of my people. And finally William French Smith, the attorney general, did rise to the occasion in answer to Secretary Baldridge but the opinion was changed. Having said that I don't mean the opinions should not have been changed. I think it was a bad opinion in the beginning. Sometimes the antitrust division seems to operate separate and apart from the government in policy matters.

NARRATOR: We are also privileged today to have our greatest historian with us, Dumas Malone. Do you want to ask the first or the last question?

MR. MALONE: All I know about what is going on now is what I read in the papers and see on TV. When did this business of having the National Security Council in the White House start?

ATTORNEY GENERAL BELL: In the Truman administration. We were doing a lot of things after the war. That's a bad time, I guess, in a country. After the war you tend to be reformers and most reforms are bad. You have to beware of the reformers.

MR. MALONE: I don't know. I just wish you would tell us what we ought to do.

ATTORNEY GENERAL BELL: I once told President Carter what to do about the National Security Council. Just transfer the post to the State Department and leave everybody in place, right where they are, but have on the table of organization that the chairman of the NSC reports to the secretary of state, and just put it on his chart and leave everything else alone. And then Brzezinski would know that he was reporting to Secretary Vance. That would have ended it. Kissinger would have known that he was reporting to Bill Rogers. In Washington, status is status and that's it. Now he might never have reported, in which event he would have to go.

MR. MALONE: Would it do to require the confirmation of these people who surround the President?

ATTORNEY GENERAL BELL: That would be the second thing I would do. I would say if you are going to have these people over there who are exercising the authority of the Cabinet, let's have a list of them and they are going to have to be confirmed. The Senate is going to have to go into their attitudes and backgrounds. And it is a dangerous thing, actually, not to do that. Can you imagine what disaster may loom over our country when you have these people there who are not accountable to anyone except the President and he hardly knows most of them? They are put in there on the recommendation of somebody usually. I know that in the Carter White House a lot of the people in there were Mondale people, who in turn were McGovern people. And they were not the people that President Carter knew. He knew Brzezinski in advance, I don't mean that, but he probably did not know David Aaron, Brzezinski's deputy. He knew Stuart Eizenstat, who was head of the Domestic Council, but he would not have known Mr. Karp, his deputy, and so forth.

People have a right to have the Congress see these people. They have a right to see them and know who they are, what sort of people we have working at the White House, doing all these things. They are exercising great power.

QUESTION: How do you think historians will evaluate the profile of the Carter administration's personnel and staff compared with Reagan's personnel or that of other postwar administrations?

ATTORNEY GENERAL BELL: I don't know how they will go about it, whether they will just evaluate President Carter or go off into different areas. I think many parts of President Carter's government were excellent; some were not that good. The perception of President Carter as a weak man has been wrong all along. I introduced him to the Atlanta Rotary Club about two years ago and made the startling announcement that when he was President, he had increased spending for defense more than anybody had done in many years. In real dollars Carter increased the allocation for defense spending more than Reagan has, but people didn't believe that.

COMMENT: He did so mostly in the last two years.

ATTORNEY GENERAL BELL: But nobody believed that; they thought he wanted to surrender everything. He's not like that at all. He is very strong in his views, and sometimes you can have a hard time convincing him of something. He is almost too rough with personnel. I was in the room when he fired Andy Young, and it was terrible to have him talk to Andy the way he did about meeting with the PLO. President Carter was big on using the word "disgrace," and he accused Andy Young of bringing disgrace on him when he met with the PLO.

Andy responded, "Well, Mr. President, you are right to fire me. You have to do what you have to do; I had to do what I had to do." That's the way they left the matter, but within thirty days Andy was out campaigning for President Carter. That's one thing that caused me to have admiration for Andy Young. He didn't carry any bitterness or rancor about his dismissal.

QUESTION: Why would he have been so sensitive to the press criticism of that, yet seemingly absolutely convinced in all the interviews we've had with him that there was no political problem with the Vance-Brzezinski rivalry? To this day when you raise that question, he will say that the problem was greatly exaggerated.

ATTORNEY GENERAL BELL: I know. That's why he got upset with me about a chapter in my book called, *What Went Wrong?* He doesn't agree that Mondale was ever anything but a paragon of perfection. You are never going to convince him otherwise. He made his mind up about that and that's it. He will never admit that there was any problem between Vance and Brzezinski. Of course, everybody around them knew there was a problem, but he is not going to admit that. I don't know if President Carter ever sat down to rethink all these things in his administration. Maybe a president ought to wait about ten years and then write what he thinks about his administration.

COMMENT: But he might change his mind if he waited that long.

ATTORNEY GENERAL BELL: Yes, he might.

COMMENT: Not many presidents write their own memoirs.

ATTORNEY GENERAL BELL: No, most of them are usually pretty old when they get out of the office. Anyway, he has very strong opinions about things, and you can't change them.

NARRATOR: But Carter had a rationale for keeping Vance and Brzezinski. The rationale was that Vance, who was not good at public presentation, needed to be complemented by Brzezinski, who was. Carter felt that he needed to have both sides of every argument. He just didn't seem conscious of the effect that would have on public perception.

ATTORNEY GENERAL BELL: Well, it didn't add up either. When I was getting ready to leave, I recommended two people to succeed me as attorney general. One was Warren Christopher, and the other was Ben Civiletti. I had told President Carter that I wanted to leave within a few months. I asked him what he was going to do about my successor, and he said, "Well, I've been thinking about it. I like Warren very much, he is a very fine man, but I can't spare him. I need him as deputy in the State Department." I told him that I thought it was a shame for Warren to lose out on being attorney general because he was needed at state as a deputy. It seemed to me that either Vance or Brzezinski could do Warren's job, but President Carter insisted that he couldn't spare him, so Warren missed out on being attorney general. Of course he did a great job at the State

Department. He did all the negotiating toward the end of the Iranian crisis. The President may have been right and I'm probably wrong. He knew a lot more about them than I did since he worked with them every day. Maybe he had it figured out that Brzezinski had strength of one kind and Vance of another. Yet the fact remained that they didn't get along. There was tension between them or it seemed so to me.

QUESTION: Don't you think the American public's perception of both Kissinger and Brzezinski was such that they weren't truly happy with either one of them?

ATTORNEY GENERAL BELL: Yes, they were too strong in the office.

COMMENT: Too strong in the office and also they weren't born in the United States. That played a role in the public's perception, I think.

ATTORNEY GENERAL BELL: Kissinger was born in Germany, but I thought Brzezinski was born in the United States.

COMMENT: No, he came from Poland. He was a Canadian citizen when I first knew him, then he changed to American citizenship. He has had three citizenships.

ATTORNEY GENERAL BELL: Kissinger said it keeps him from being president.

COMMENT: Yes, he wants to amend the Constitution!

ATTORNEY GENERAL BELL: No, he said he figured out how he could do it—he could be king. I actually heard him say that; it was a joke of course, but he said that there was no provision against having a king born in another country.

COMMENT: A lot of his jokes are half serious.

ATTORNEY GENERAL BELL: How many times have you had President Carter here?

COMMENT: He's only been here once, but we went to Plains on another occasion.

NARRATOR: He was a great success when he was here.

ATTORNEY GENERAL BELL: He's better in a small group.

COMMENT: He was very impressive at this table.

ATTORNEY GENERAL BELL: Yes, that's his greatest strength. If you have three or four people in a room talking, he is really super, but when he gets on television its another story. Vernon Jordan asked me one day if I couldn't get the President under control. He said, "We can't have our President carrying his own bags. That's terrible. This being humble isn't getting him anywhere. Nobody wants a president who is humble." Then later he had that fireside chat with the sweater on which didn't go over, either.

COMMENT: But that's what I think he was worst at, talking to a mass audience. He needed a live audience. Reagan, on the other hand, is quite good at talking to an audience through a camera.

ATTORNEY GENERAL BELL: When President Carter was running for governor the first time, his adviser Charles Kirbo represented a leading television adviser in some media work. He had started out as a radio adviser to Roosevelt, and then for other democratic presidents. He would get candidates and try them out on television to see how they would do. Kirbo arranged for Carter to take a test. The adviser told Kirbo that anything more than five minutes for Carter was a waste. When Kirbo asked what could be done to improve his TV performance he answered, "There is no way."

COMMENT: He also smiled in the wrong places. That was a very bad trait.

COMMENT: But this is with a television speech. If you look at him on television at a news conference, you don't see that. He is very much in command when he has real people in the room to deal with.

ATTORNEY GENERAL BELL: He could have a five minute statement and then answer questions. If he could do that once a week, he'd have everybody in the country in favor of it.

QUESTION: You outlined the history of the establishment of the first Cabinet under Washington. What are the historical precedents of the constitutional guidelines about confirmation?

ATTORNEY GENERAL BELL: It's statutory for most offices. It began with the first Congress because you confirm judges, ambassadors, Cabinet officers, and I think it has been expanded over the years. There is no constitutional precedent for it except for those officers who must be appointed with the advice and consent of the Senate.

QUESTION: You suggested in a way that a President should at least be knowledgeable enough to be his own secretary of state. You are not suggesting that he be his own secretary of state in practice, are you? Because it troubles me a great deal that you could have a President who is Commander and Chief of the Armed Forces and virtually secretary of state who could almost become a rogue elephant.

ATTORNEY GENERAL BELL: No, he couldn't. It would be impossible. He would not have any money. President Ford had to withdraw from Angola. No money. Congress has absolutely shut the government down, many Presidents down, by no funds. They are getting ready to do it now in Nicaragua. There may not be funds there for the CIA. We may leave the ammunition and guns on the ground for the Sandinistas. That's the way we came out of Vietnam. No money. We left two or more billion dollars worth of weapons and equipment there that are being used all over the world now when we came out of there in such disorder.

There are so many checks and balances in the Constitution that that wouldn't be a problem. I think we've had Presidents who were their own secretary of state. Can you imagine anything more dangerous than having General Marshall and Truman running the foreign affairs of the nation? But we did well.

QUESTION: Franklin Roosevelt was his own secretary of state.

ATTORNEY GENERAL BELL: Yes and John Kennedy aspired to be his own secretary of state. He said he was. Most people now would think Dean Rusk was a pretty good secretary of state, keeping a balance. But Kennedy had a somebody over there as head of the National Security Council who was doing a lot but he was really doing it in Kennedy's name. I think Kissinger was the first time we saw the dual secretary of state system. That was solved by making him secretary of state. He finally got the best of Secretary Rogers and took over. I've forgotten but I think that he was very careful about who followed him as head of National Security Council. No one probably can remember who that was. It was General Scowcroft who was a very much respected person.

QUESTION: I'm puzzled a bit by life in general and about Senator Moynihan on the Hill. His office criticized his own legislative body for proliferating staff and building the big new office buildings all the time, thereby continuing, as with the presidency, in proliferating staff and so on.

In the same article, I also read that Moynihan said some of the staff knew more than the senators did, actually, on facts of policy and assignments. In the *New York Times* on the 25th of this month there was buried on page ten a story about Moynihan searching for a middle ground. It seems that he didn't seem to remember that there may have been a briefing in which this covert mining had been mentioned, but that Smith, his aide, seemed to remember far more clearly than he did himself. And that's the gist of this story which is a fascinating piece and I left a copy, Ken, in case you haven't seen it. But at the end of all of this you find Moynihan sitting in his office and being asked questions about where does he now stand. He was looking to find the middle ground in terms of various positions in this matter and he said, "I don't know if it does square with adherence to international law—I don't know that it doesn't. I don't know that it does and I don't know that it doesn't. I did not think that this is an easy thing." He's showing, I think, an honest kind of puzzlement about this matter. He was asked if he still supported the aid program that he helped to fund and voted for last week and Mr. Moynihan said, "I am sitting wondering what is really going on." He is one of the brightest and best informed people on the Hill. But it staggers the imagination if there is that much confusion there and that much confusion in the White House. You wonder what is going on. You were talking about public knowledge and having confidence in people on the White House staff. It used to be under FDR that they were supposed to have a passion for anonymity. Now they have a passion for all sorts of things but not anonymity.

ATTORNEY GENERAL BELL: That puzzles me because Senator Moynihan is not only very intelligent, but he is and has been on the Senate Select Committee on Foreign Intelligence. Without being there it would stagger my imagination to believe that any of that went on without his committee being briefed. If he didn't get the briefing it's because his own staff member apparently didn't tell him. Usually we didn't brief staffs on certain matters, we would only brief senators and we would brief the members of the committee but it would not be unusual to brief staff members in some instances.

What happened is that members of the Congress have gotten such a large staff now that they are now just like the White House. They have a staff member who is the liaison to every committee they are on. They can call this staff member in and ask what's going on about such and such a matter. They don't need to know anything other than that. Congress has not always been organized like this. After Watergate and all the reforms, when the Church committee went after the CIA and the counterintelligence of the FBI, something had to be done to restore the confidence of the people. Ed Levi, the attorney general ahead of me, had arranged to get this Select Committee on Foreign Intelligence set up in the Senate. That meant that you didn't have to report all these matters to seven or eight different committees, just to that one committee. I then got the same thing done in the House. That's what I was complaining about earlier. The committee I got set up in the House, the House's Select Committee on Intelligence, is a committee that is now claiming co-equal authority with the President, which bothers me a great deal. At the time we got that done, however, we were having to report to many committees and subcommittees about these matters. It was just unworkable.

During the time I was there we never had a leak out of either committee, the Senate or the House. There were no times when we didn't brief them on anything of any importance and we would also brief the speaker and the majority and minority leaders in the House and the Senate. The system was working well. I don't know just what's going on right now, why it is in the shape it's in. I believe that the situation will stabilize. I know that we kept a very tight rein on the intelligence and counterintelligence agencies. I would imagine that there may be some politicians putting distance between themselves and the mines right now. That may be part of this.

It strikes me that the mining operation was not a good thing from the inception. But there must have been some people who thought it was or we wouldn't have been doing it, if we were doing it. My own view about that is that I would not put people around one of these places. I'd let somebody else do it. We don't need to get in these fracases, as I call them, ourselves. If there are really two sides, there are ways to help one side without being there and we would be better off if we followed that policy. But you have a lot of people in the government. There are all kinds of views going to those in authority. It's not like in the old days where you just had a few people and everybody knew each other and you sat around and reflected over things. Now you have position papers flying all over the place and the President gets something with seven different views on it. Each person has checked off on what their views are. It has something to do with technological progress, the xerox machines and what not.

This is a staff problem, though. Most of the staffs in government have quadrupled in fifteen years.

QUESTION: Isn't there any way of simplifying this governmental devastation?

ATTORNEY GENERAL BELL: Not with so many people.

QUESTION: I mean isn't there a way that from the President down they could accomplish the simplification of government back to where it was?

ATTORNEY GENERAL BELL: If you've got a President who has an innovative mind like that, he would start doing it and then he would drive the Congress into doing it. It has now infected the courts. You may have seen where Justice John Paul Stevens let two of his law clerks go, two of them out of four, year before last and said he just couldn't manage that many law clerks. The Justices ought to be doing their own work. He quoted Justice Brandeis who said the reason the public had confidence in the Court was, as he said, "We do our own." When I was a judge I had to start out with one law clerk, then I had two and then three. When I got to two I would not take the third law clerk. At that point I became a manager. It was hard to keep up with everything they could write. Could you imagine what a judge would be doing with four law clerks? Can you imagine having four assistants writing things up for you? And every sentence may be something that is very important. And stuck in there somewhere is something that ought not to be there, not dishonestly but through lack of experience. This is not good. It's in all three branches of the government. You'd have to have a leader who wanted to cut back and that leader would have to be the President.

QUESTION: For a good many years there was a tradition of appointing one Cabinet member who had been the campaign manager for the President. If this is going to be continued which one of the Cabinet posts would be the least detrimental to the country to follow this practice?

ATTORNEY GENERAL BELL: I wouldn't favor doing that. You know the Republican party and the Democratic party headquarters are both in Washington and if you want to have your campaign manager around so you can have dinner with him every night, put him over there at one of the political parties, because that's what his business is or he wouldn't be campaign manager. We no longer have a Post Office spot and I don't know just where you would put him, certainly not at the CIA. There are too many political decisions made in all these departments and everyone who was helping in the campaign knows the campaign manager and they are calling on him for something and it's bad.

Cabinet Government and President Carter

We have an ambivalent system. You want everyone to help you while you're running, then you don't want to see them anymore once you get in office. And if you do see them too often you'll get into trouble. They will be calling up about some friend that's being investigated or they will be wanting to get a defense contract and so forth. There is no end to it. I'm not certain that there is any place left for a campaign manager.

QUESTION: I'd like to know the function of the attorney general in the following situation realistically. The Twenty-fifth Amendment says the vice president has the power to declare the president unable to serve. During the Reagan fiasco Bush did not do this which I personally think was wrong. The President was in surgery. The President was five days recuperating. We don't know who was running the government. Could the attorney general get in there any way other than to advice the vice president? In other words, my point is the Constitution was not being carried out.

ATTORNEY GENERAL BELL: I'll have to disagree with that because when that happened I was on the ABC program that night at 11:00. I was asked that question. I said I thought it was being carried out because vice president Bush, although in the air, was in communication with the other Cabinet officers. He was in charge.

QUESTION: But he didn't declare himself acting President.

ATTORNEY GENERAL BELL: He didn't have to because there was nothing to be done during that time. If something had to be done such as using some part of the intelligence operation or an attack of some sort, he could have done it. But by the next day the President was talking.

QUESTION: The President was incompetent for at least ten days.

ATTORNEY GENERAL BELL: I think maybe ten hours.

COMMENT: Oh, no, he was under high doses of morphine.

ATTORNEY GENERAL BELL: Every time the President gets sick or falls off a horse, if he has to take something for pain are you going to put the vice president in? This has to be carefully done. We have to have stability in the government and I thought they probably handled it right. The only sign I saw of anything untoward was Secretary Haig making that statement and being so out of breath and all from walking up a few stairs. But I glossed over that issue that night on that program because I have confidence in this particular vice president, Bush, and I thought he was in charge and could have taken over.

QUESTION: Do you know if he was? Do you know where the black box was?

ATTORNEY GENERAL BELL: I don't know where it was, no.

QUESTION: You don't know who had it?

ATTORNEY GENERAL BELL: No, I don't. It could have been Ed Meese, for all I know. But I know Bush got on the ground as fast as he could.

QUESTION: That will be a slogan like, "Where's the beef," "Where's the black box?"

ATTORNEY GENERAL BELL: I don't know what we'll do about using the Twenty-fifth Amendment. It could be far worse now than when Wilson was President with all the different people in the White House. Who was the man there then? Colonel House was running the government and Mrs. Wilson.

COMMENT: I think there are powerful reasons for wishing staff away but I don't really think it's going to go away. I think this is a full employment program for young professionals. Everywhere you look. You see it in the courts. You see it in the White House and executive offices. You see it in Congress and for all I know you see the same phenomenon in corporate life. I don't think we have really decided how this affects our accountability and responsibility for decisions.

ATTORNEY GENERAL BELL: It will go away. You can depend on that. We may not be living when it goes away, but it will go away when we get the deficit so large that we're bankrupt and we've changed the form of government. It will then go away. It seems to me we ought to be intelligent enough or have managerial ability enough to let it go away before that. But it will go away. We'll get to where we are ungovernable at the rate we're going. This is quite a serious matter in the long range. We don't have to worry about it now. But look how it's changed just in thirty or forty years.

  I don't know what you are doing in your studies but you should check one fact. President Carter never got a piece of major legislation through the House under normal procedures. It was always necessary to set up an ad hoc procedure to get something through. That tells me the House is unworkable and if you were just keeping up with legislation a little bit you would know that. The Senate is not unworkable but the House at the present time is unworkable.

QUESTION: I was a great admirer of President Carter's and was state campaign chairman in 1980 and so all my comments and reflections are made with affection but also with disturbance. We've seen Meese recently and the sleeze factor and the teflon coating around Reagan and so on. I felt the pendulum swing against Carter with the Bert Lance affair because he appeared to vacillate when it appeared to be a question of morality and integrity and the things that he had talked about so much during his campaign. He was just unable to come to grips with the case in a decisive sort of way and I don't think he ever really recovered as President from the way that situation was handled. Could you give us your reflections, both factual and your own personal views, on the way that situation was handled and how it was permitted to do as much damage to the President as it was?

ATTORNEY GENERAL BELL: The President and I are friends. They had dinner with us last Friday night. The President is very high on Lance, they are close friends. And besides the emotional attachment there was poor staff work. It was allowed to go on too long. Lance, after he was asked to leave, didn't leave for more than a month. Several people had to ask him and urge him to leave. At one point the President came back from Camp David and embraced him, if you remember. That was after a member of his staff told him he had read the comptroller's report and there was nothing in there bad about Lance. The next day when others read it, it was terrible. The President had already come back and embraced him. After that, it became obvious that he had to leave and it was a month before he left. You are right, that damaged the President greatly. That was the beginning of what you would call a "sleeze factor." A President has to demand that his people leave immediately, before the office of the presidency is damaged. You ought to think enough of your President, if you are there serving him, to leave your own image out of it. You naturally want to protect your good name but you can't do that. That's one of the things you give up when you decide you're going to work for a President.

We seem to have lost sight of that kind of obligation in this country. We've got to get back to those days. You ought to leave immediately if something is wrong. You have to protect the President.

QUESTION: Why are we tolerating things that way? Repeatedly in case after case after case.

ATTORNEY GENERAL BELL: I do not understand it. I would not have let anybody stay at the Justice Department an hour if something like that came up. If they didn't leave I would say you just have to leave. And every President is being brought down by the same thing. It is difficult to stay longer than four years anymore. President Reagan may get re-elected but it will be almost an accident of history, an accident of politics because they are not getting a strong person to run against him. These staff problems keep happening over and over. No one can say how much harm it's doing President Reagan. He's had a way of being detached from his own problems. The public sees him as not being connected to these people, which is remarkable in itself but that seems to be the way it's going.

President Carter was never able to do that. We were talking last Friday night, not about any particular person but about his trouble with the press. The reason we were having dinner was that Jody Powell's book came out and there was a book party for Jody. He and his wife in Atlanta and several of us had dinner together. We were talking about the trouble. President Carter said that he had gone back and studied the presidencies of eight or ten Presidents. He said the press was very kind to Roosevelt. I've not studied that. I was just a small boy then. I'm not saying that that was altogether true. I think there was not anything like the present White House press corps which is post-Watergate and just operates with a vengeance, although they do not seem to do so against President Reagan.

President Carter says they were easy on President Kennedy but Kennedy wasn't President long enough for us to know if that would have lasted. They never told anything about any of the outside activities of Kennedy. And they were hard on Nixon, hard on Ford, hard on Carter, hard on Johnson, hard on Truman, but they skipped Roosevelt and Kennedy and Reagan. He was just giving the facts, not giving an answer to it but that is essentially so. They (the media) drove President Johnson into not running for re-election, although the basis was of course the Vietnam War and the fact that he was thought to be sleazy. They made Ford out to be a stumblebum. He'd fall out of the airplane, that is, off the stairway coming down. He would hit somebody with a golf ball. Yet he was probably the finest athlete we've had in the White House. They made him out to be just a person who couldn't walk. They can do you in like that. But that's all the more reason, though, why your people have to be prepared to leave.

I didn't buy a house in Washington. I figured my job was one day long. I rented an apartment. I told the press I had to be prepared to leave on just an hour's notice. That's the attitude you ought to have when you are working for a President.

QUESTION: I wonder if President Carter is right in his generalization about those three Presidents. It seems plausible that he is. I wonder if that is an indication of the press's real preference for entertainment. It does seem to me that those three Presidents were more entertaining as interlocutors in press conferences than the others mentioned. Certainly President Carter had every bit as much if not more intellectual skill and acquaintance with issues than the other people we're talking about. If the press wanted an interlocutor who really knew his stuff it seems to me they would have done much better by Carter and much less well than they do by Reagan. But Reagan surely is more entertaining than Carter was. Kennedy was much more entertaining than Reagan. Roosevelt was very entertaining as a press conference man.

ATTORNEY GENERAL BELL: I'll answer the question, not to make a statement, but did it ever occur to you that the press may be anti-intellectual?

QUESTION: Oh, many times.

MR. MALONE: I think there is too much of it. It's too open. You can't live life in quite such an open way and how any President can stand the sort of exposure, the degree of exposure that they now get—I don't think Reagan would do it for four more years. I think sooner or later that they would get him. It's just too much and I don't know what the answer could possibly be. But now this present campaign for the Democratic nomination is overcovered, it's over-reported, it's terribly overdone, and one result of it is that these men are so exposed that they are all going to say things that they really should not have said and that they really didn't mean to say about how they come and everybody knows about it. That's the trouble with our age. I sometimes think that this is the *de trop* age. There is just too much of everything. Too many people, too much publicity. Too much money, not well distributed, but too much. Just too much of everything. How Reagan has gotten away with it so far is amazing.

ATTORNEY GENERAL BELL: I've been twice or three times to public functions where President Reagan was, and I'll give you my view of how he gets by with it.

He is a person that people like. He's a person you enjoy being around and the press looks at it in that way. They genuinely like him. He's a hail-fellow-well-met type and he's not getting into details about anything. He's just sort of enjoying his job. I think they rather like that. You know they looked down on President Carter because he understood how the MX operated and all these different weapon systems and he studied the B1 bomber and studied the Stealth bomber and decided we didn't need both and he cut out the B1. He knew about all those things and had people briefing him on them. Well, that's too much for the press. You can't write all that. How would it sound? That's sort of the way it is. Reagan is very much like the prototype of the American male right now. He was a good athlete, he is a nice looking fellow and has been a performer. He is a good speaker. He has a laid-back style about him and that appeals to people and it seems to appeal to the press. They don't blame him much for anything that these people do. That won't last. You are right.

MR. MALONE: I don't see how it could for eight years. If it hadn't been for the war, Franklin Roosevelt couldn't have done it. Generally a President lasts about six years, and the last two are always bad.

ATTORNEY GENERAL BELL: That's the reason I favor a single six-year term.

QUESTION: Regardless of the press's attitude toward him, it seems to me that the picture of Reagan that comes across is that he is not too bright. I agree with everything you say but at the same time I think there is this impression that the job is just a little beyond him.

ATTORNEY GENERAL BELL: You know what people think about him? I've talked to a lot of people about this. They think he is like Truman. He's not that bright, but he is tough. They want a tough man, somebody who will make a decision. A lot of people equate him with Truman. Of course Truman had training as a senator, a lot of training during World War II as a senator during what they called the Truman Commission where they were studying defense contracts and that sort of thing. Now, as we look back we think of Truman as a person who was always direct and could make a decision no matter how tough it was. People think of Reagan the same way. We were embarrassed greatly as a nation by Iran, by the hostage situation. I don't know what any other President would do if he had the same crisis.

MR. MALONE: Oh, that would ruin anybody.

ATTORNEY GENERAL BELL: It made President Carter into a weak person. His image became one of weakness. I had some lawyer friends out in Texas I happened to see the next year after the election of 1980 and they asked me how President Carter was. I told them and they asked, is he still wringing his hands and it turned out they voted for Reagan. They were Democrats who voted for Reagan and they had voted for Carter in 1976 and they called him a hand-wringer. I said, "Why would you say that about him?" They said, "Well, he never did anything about the hostages in Iran." I said, "Well, he tried, and it happened to be a failure and if it had not been a failure he would have been a great hero." But it was a difficult problem. It would have been for any President and would probably have brought any President down.

The other thing President Carter did that Reagan would not have done is he let those Cubans from Mariel in on the boats. Reagan has since turned the boats back. People really got upset with President Carter about that. What he did, he let the South Indo-Chinese people in, the legacy of the Vietnam War, because we owed them something. Then Castro wanted to get rid of the undesirables and saw us let those people in on boats. He put his undesirables on boats. We only had one choice, to turn them back, and President Carter didn't turn them back.

I know a lot about that because Castro had 25,000 people he wanted to release. He said they were political prisoners. The attorney general was then in charge of immigration, not the President. Congress has plenary power over immigration and they gave the power to the attorney general to let people in on an emergency basis. Secretary Vance wanted to let those people in. I said we would let them in if we screened them. He said in what way? I said we would send the FBI to Havana. If Castro would agree to that, then I would agree to it. He wouldn't agree at first but finally did agree and we sent the FBI to Havana and screened out about a third of them. His argument was and the State Department's was that they ought to be screened in Florida and I asked how we would get them back? Castro got very upset about that because we beat him at his own game. Then when he saw the boat people coming out of South Indochina he put his people on boats and we didn't turn them back.

Those two things hurt President Carter as much as anything I can imagine. One of them he could control and one he could not. He couldn't do anything about Iran.

QUESTION: Your analysis of your experiences is absolutely fascinating but in summary everything you say indicates a very dim prognosis for government in our country. The only possible alternative that might lead to corrective measures of significance or setting things right, if that is possible, is bankruptcy which doesn't involve any public vote. Is this the only alternative that you see? Are you in effect saying in your skillful, articulate way that we have now progressed to the point where our democracy is indeed and in fact ungovernable?

ATTORNEY GENERAL BELL: No. There is a very easy cure. The problem is that everything is too politicized and the cure is to elect a President for one six-year term which would free the President from politics and he would then become the kind of leader we need and you would see a remarkable change. We need a stronger President but we don't need one too strong. This would do it.

If we follow the present system where the President is wearing two hats, one, he is head of his party and the other is he is supposed to be the President, he's never going to be much good the first four years and probably won't be re-elected. Eisenhower was the last President that served two four-year terms. Nixon was re-elected but he didn't get to serve. That is what I say. No. There are cures. There are answers to all these things.

COMMENT: But the term of the president has no relation whatsoever to the function of the Congress and many of the things that you are talking about have involved Congress.

ATTORNEY GENERAL BELL: But if the president got in there and got away from politics he would be telling us what was wrong with Congress.

COMMENT: Our present President is trying to do that.

ATTORNEY GENERAL BELL: He's trying to do that. We might give some thought to improving the Congress.

NARRATOR: Do you think that people have already begun a revisionist view of Carter?

ATTORNEY GENERAL BELL: I don't see any signs of it, and the reason for it is his continuing political activity. He is always taking a position. During the first three or four years Reagan was in office President Carter kept fairly quiet. But since then he has been speaking out, taking a position on most everything, and it is hard for the revision to set in as long as he is as active as he is. I have heard people that are dissatisfied with President Reagan make statements like, "Carter sure is looking better how," and that sort of thing. But I've never heard anybody quantify it.

Cabinet Government and President Carter

But, then, I never thought that he would be treated that badly by historians. I thought he had a good chance of being re-elected, had it not been for the hostage situation. The fact that he couldn't do anything about it was frustrating to the American people, and that convinced them that what had been said about him was true, that he couldn't manage anything and he wasn't a good executive. No one recognized that at a certain point, and perhaps down to the present, there was little anyone could do about the hostages.

NARRATOR: I think as much as we'd like to continue this, Judge Bell has a busy schedule. The last time he was here, Mr. Bell gave us ideas that we are still talking about and today he has repeated that performance. Thank you so much.

PART THREE:

POLITICS AND ECONOMICS: THE TIMES, THE CRISES, AND THE PEOPLE

CHAPTER 5

THE TIMES, THE CRISES AND THE PEOPLE

SECRETARY OF COMMERCE JUANITA KREPS

INTRODUCTION: Juanita Kreps is one of Duke University's most respected economists and educators having served as James B. Duke professor and assistant provost and vice president. She is the recipient of numerous honorary degrees and has held directorships in an impressive list of corporations. She is the author of important treatises in economics and has been president of the Southern Economic Association. In the following oral history, she discusses the times and the crises of the Carter presidency and the people who constituted the *dramatis personnae*.

JUANITA KREPS: The questions posed call for an assessment of the Carter presidency based on his leadership and administrative style; his relationships with the Congress, his staff and the Cabinet as well as the public and the media; and his achievements, particularly in comparison with those of other presidents. Also raised is the question of how future historians will judge his performance and how I now judge it.

THE TIMES

The answers are of course subjective and will vary from one member of the administration to another. Historians, too, will surely differ in their appraisal. What all of us take as a common base for evaluation, however, is the political scene at the time of Mr. Carter's election—in particular, the Watergate scandal that brought down President Nixon and was never quite forgotten during President Ford's short term in office. This episode and other extremes displayed by the Nixon staff—the secrecy, the cultivation of an aura of a "Royal Presidency," dishonesty among White House aides—shattered public trust in presidents and their chief advisers. The 1976 election of Mr. Carter reflected, perhaps more than any other sentiment, a strong distaste for power and its misuse and support for an outsider of unquestioned integrity.

There is nothing new in the observation that the times dictate the vote. In this case (and clearly, as well, in the 1980 election) we must remember that the qualities sought were those actually gained. Jimmy Carter is a man of simple tastes, a bit embarrassed by pomp and circumstance; hence, the sweater for fireside chats, the garment bag over the shoulder, etc. He is genuinely modest; he often remarked that he hoped to be a President worthy of the American people. He is religious, committed to human rights here and abroad, and since leaving Washington has spent his time promoting the economic well-being of persons in need and building an educational center for furthering world peace.

To some degree President Carter's defeat in 1980 may have reflected a rejection of the qualities sought four years earlier. The Nixon days were no longer an issue. Modesty in presidential lifestyle is not appealing to all voters. The pursuit of human rights abroad has been roundly denounced when it interfered with trade. The President's malaise speech was a major mistake. Voters do not like to be told that there are problems; they like to hear that the man in charge has things under control so they need not worry.

THE CHALLENGES

President's Carter's administration faced major challenges, quite apart from matters of style and communication. When he came into office he and his advisers viewed unemployment as a major problem; economists in the administration, academia, and business were paying little attention to inflation. When midway into the Carter term OPEC restrained oil output, leading to an escalation in its price and then to wage and price increases throughout the economy, the nation was caught up in a dilemma we should have foreseen but did not.

Economists' response to the inflationary spiral was slow, both in and out of government, since no one had adequate answers to the problem. Voluntary restraints on wages and prices were no more effective than Nixon's earlier price controls had been. By the end of the decade we faced double-digit inflation with no end in sight. This critical problem plagued the administration to the end and contributed to the President's political decline.

But much more significant was the hostage crisis. The nation's preoccupation with the plight of the captive Americans pushed all other issues off the front pages and television news. And the administration, after failing in its rescue attempt, could do little except try to bargain with the captors. The President pledged not to campaign for re-election under these circumstances and for some time left the field to his opponents.

AND THE PRESIDENTS

Public humiliation of the captives and the constant fear that they would be massacred reinforced the image of a weak administration. By contrast, the Reagan administration's later attempts to protect American interests abroad, which resulted in massive loss of military lives and eventually to attempts to trade arms for hostages, seem to have taken no toll on President Reagan. Nor has there been any political fall-out for President Bush, who directs attention to other problems.

What future students of the presidency will have to explain is the difference in public attitude toward President Carter's attempts to rescue the hostages and the subsequent actions taken by President Reagan. Was a bungled rescue attempt followed by constant efforts to bargain with irrational forces less statesmanlike than a glaring military failure and a naive offer of money for American lives? Was it a difference in media coverage, or better White House handling in the second case? Or had the American people at last lost any hope of dealing with Khomeni and thus had more sympathy than disdain with President Reagan's failures? Did it reflect an already firm view of the two men—a supposed weakness in one case and perceived strength in the other—that was not to be shaken by subsequent events?

SPECIFIC QUESTIONS: A GENERAL RESPONSE

Administrative style would seem to be of much less significance than the decisions made on critical issues before the President. Nevertheless, in an attempt to answer some of your specific questions, I offer the following comments.

President Carter's somewhat informal handling of administrative issues and their delegation to various departments, and between the departments and the White House, was generally effective. I seldom had any doubt as to what the President expected of me. Nor was it difficult to reach him by phone when new problems suddenly surfaced. Since we were both in our offices very early, I sometimes called him about seven a.m.; at that time he was almost always accessible.

His administrative style has been criticized primarily on two grounds. One, he was overly concerned with details, which should have been delegated to others; and two, he was indecisive. As to his worry with detail, I saw no evidence that such was the case; on the contrary, he seemed to have a better grasp of the big picture than I had, even when the problem was in my area. Unfortunately, the bureaucracy thrives on minutia, and often it is necessary to delegate an important problem to several departments or agencies, each of which tend to study it endlessly and report at great length. Once the reports and recommendations come into the White House, the staff has to summarize the findings and specify the options open to the President.

At this point in the process indecisiveness becomes an issue if the President fails to come to a conclusion in a reasonable time. But one may argue that only if he takes the time to understand the issues and assess the consequences of his decision is he acting with full knowledge. Remember, the questions put before the President are highly significant; otherwise, they would have been handled at the staff or Secretarial level. Moreover, the complexity of the issues he needs to resolve requires not only a reasonable understanding of the question, but also a grasp of their relation to a broad range of public policy issues before him. In my view, President Carter managed both quite well and in good time.

His relations with Congress were uneven, however, in part because he lacked a background in the legislative branch. Nevertheless, he did eventually get an energy policy. He did gain bipartisan support for his Mideast peace initiative. His budgets were conservative by all subsequent standards (ending with a deficit of about $50 billion), and there was relatively little wrangling in Congress on fiscal matters. The Panama Canal decision was close, but it carried. His human rights philosophy is now widely endorsed by both Republicans and Democrats. On the issues of great importance to him he had to work very hard to carry the day, but he was eventually successful.

President Carter's relation with the Cabinet was good, though as is the case of all presidents, I'm sure, he found it necessary to turn for advice more often to those secretaries heading certain departments: State, Treasury, Justice, OMB. He also relied heavily on the young men who had campaigned with him or worked for him in Georgia: Hamilton Jordan, Jack Watson, and Stuart Eizenstat, in particular.

The President's personal warmth and friendliness shown through in his conversations with individuals and small groups, particularly those of us who worked closely with him. In Cabinet meetings he spend at least as much time responding to the questions raised as he gave to laying out his own agenda. He was considerate of the Cabinet members' views—so much so that in Cabinet meetings he seldom resolved a disagreement among us by giving explicit instructions. Those would come later, usually from Stuart Eizenstat or another White House staff member.

With his staff he was even closer; these were men whom he had known for a long time. They in turn had good relations with the Cabinet and for the most part kept peace among us, despite the usual jurisdictional disputes. After a few months we came to expect a degree of wrangling over turf, and most of the Cabinet members seemed to have genuine respect for each other. Departmental staff members were very protective of their individual roles, which they often managed to push up to the secretarial level.

Soon after he took office President Carter grouped several Cabinet members into an economic policy group, chaired by Treasury Secretary Blumenthal, which met frequently. Whether a secretary attended a meeting depended on the agenda; usually it included Treasury, State, OMB, Labor and Commerce, the chairman of the Council of Economic Advisers, and the President's chief domestic policy adviser. These meetings became particularly important as prices rose sharply and the administration struggled to develop anti-inflation policies.

I never understood the rationale for the Cabinet housecleaning which occurred about halfway through the President's term. For each dismissal (the secretaries of treasury, energy, transportation and health, education and welfare) there was perhaps a different reason. The action followed a Camp David retreat at which a number of outside advisers were said to have recommended that the Cabinet needed a shakeup; that some secretaries were pursuing their own agendas rather than that of the President. Clearly, the President's staff and his advisers were looking for ways to improve the administration's image. But in retrospect, one can argue that the change in Cabinet officers had little effect on public perceptions.

As I have noted earlier, President Carter usually turned to his White House staff and to a lesser degree to the Cabinet as a group for advice on the issues before him. On many problems, however, he needed to reach beyond his own appointees for expertise. Later in his term he brought Lloyd Cutler into the White House and on many occasions he sought advice from experienced diplomats such as Sol Linowitz. In the fields of industry and commerce, where my department's responsibilities lay, business leaders and their organizations were particularly helpful to me and directly to the President. They gave frequent briefings to the President on the state of business, advised on tax measures—indeed, persuaded the administration to favor corporate income tax credit reduction over investment tax credits—and gave congressional testimony on the Arab Boycott law. In many instances, differences of view within the business groups or between business and the administration were too wide to bridge. But during my three years as secretary, I cannot remember a significant issue for industry on which the views of the corporate leaders were not asked for and taken into account.

In summary, the major disappointments of the Carter administration had to do with our failure to slow the pace of inflation following OPEC's increase in oil prices; our inability to free the hostages taken by the Iranians; some ineptness in dealing with the Congress; and poor public relations that gave an impression that the President lacked strength and decisiveness. To my knowledge, no one in the nation has suggested ways we could have avoided the fate we suffered in the first two cases, which together doomed the President to failure in the 1982 election.

Significant world progress was achieved through the Camp David accord; the Human Rights effort worldwide; restoration of trade and diplomatic relations with China; and domestic programs which further deregulated industry, provided strong programs of job training and economic development, and increased housing and urban development grants to the poor.

WHAT DO FORMER PRESIDENTS DO?

One concluding comment is appropriate, given recent press comments on Mr. Carter's post-White House activities.

After the humiliating defeat of 1982 and a series of deaths in the Carter family, a withdrawal from public life and from their commitments to serve the people might have been expected of President and Mrs. Carter. But not by people who have worked with the Carters. They have written for the record in painstaking detail. They have used their time to plant corn in Ghana, build houses for the poor throughout the United States, and attack political corruption in Panama. When he lectures to college audiences he demands that they give something of themselves to such endeavors; he is not advising them on how to make money.

His few criticisms of President Reagan have been justified, even in the eyes of many Republicans. Yet he must be appalled at the revelations from HUD, the Pentagon scandals, the financial excesses of the past eight years. How will the record read a decade from now? If we believe what the cynics say—that history is not what happened, but what historians say happened—there is little merit in speculating. But a careful documentation of the Reagan administration's eight years should make his predecessor's record, albeit short, look very good. The dignity and dedication Mr. Carter has shown since leaving office is further evidence of the sharp differences in the two men—differences that will be increasingly difficult for historians to ignore.

CHAPTER 6

GOVERNMENT AND INDUSTRIAL COMPETITIVENESS VIEWED FROM THE CARTER PRESIDENCY

SECRETARY OF COMMERCE PHILIP M. KLUTZNICK

NARRATOR: Philip Klutznick is among a handful of distinguished Americans who in the early years of the Miller Center lent their names and encouragement to the Miller Center. Andy Goodpaster, Dean Rusk and a few others joined Philip Klutznick in betting on a horse they had no idea would finish the race. They gave us encouragement. Such a generous gesture is by no means unusual for Phil Klutznick. He has done the same for other organizations.

Philip Klutznick was born in Kansas City and educated at the University of Kansas and the University of Nebraska. He received his law degree at Creighton University and numerous honorary degrees from his alma mater, from Brandeis and a host of other distinguished American universities. He served in the Roosevelt administration as commissioner of the Federal Public Housing Authority. In 1957, 1961 and 1962, he was a member of the United States delegation to the United Nations with the rank of Ambassador. He was closely affiliated with Adlai Stevenson and other political leaders in Illinois, including Richard Daley. He was a link at one point between President Carter and Mayor Daley in some of the discussions they held. He has played a prominent role in higher education and in religious activities. He's past international president of B'nai B'rith and of the World Jewish Congress. He was the leader of an interfaith organization called the Council on Religion and International Affairs. He's been active in social and economic activities too numerous to mention.

MR. KLUTZNICK: As I understand my assignment today, I'm not here to glorify Jimmy Carter or his past. I will tell you what I know from personal experience and you can judge for yourself. I shall be brief in my introduction in the hope that the essence of what I have to say may be drawn out by questions or observations.

Let me say I think the work that is being done here to record what may become history or has been history is extremely important. I don't accept Hegel's notion that we learn nothing from history; we learn from history if we want to learn from it. It is surprising how many historical events have guided people, preventing them from repeating past mistakes. Therefore, recording what presidents have done is vital to this country. It is only in recent years that we've had the instrumentality to do some of this and I applaud the leadership of this institution. I want to say that what I am about to make is a very modest contribution to the great work being done at the Miller Center. I hope you continue it in prosperity and in depth for many years to come so that my children and grandchildren will have a benefit that was denied me during my lifetime.

I know I'm not the best person to tell the whole story of Jimmy Carter's presidency. I can tell it in two respects, one, from outside the administration, and, two, from inside the administration. There is a decided difference between these two perspectives. To pursue my discussion, you have given me a series of questions.

When did I first meet Jimmy Carter? I received a call from Cyrus Vance saying that I must join the team. I replied, "Wait a minute, let me think about it." This was before the Ohio primary, when there was still considerable doubt about the outcome. He said, "I'm going to Italy and I'll be back in a few weeks, will you give me your answer?" I said, "When you come back, I'll give you my answer."

In between, I attended a meeting with the then mayor of Chicago, Richard Daley. Three of us were present, the head of Commonwealth Edison, the head of one of our financial institutions and myself. We were discussing the replanning and rebuilding of the Dearborn Street Station area. In the midst of the meeting there was a telephone call and the Mayor said to his secretary, "Tell him to wait awhile." He continued talking. About ten minutes later the secretary rang again and Mayor Daley replied, "All right, but he's going to have to meet some other people too, just wait a minute." He turned to us and said, "There's a fellow outside who thinks he's going to be President of the United States. He's coming here to see me, and I don't want to keep him waiting any longer. I'm sure you people would like to meet him; he's Jimmy Carter."

That was the first time I actually met Jimmy Carter. I'd known of him, and I respected his work as governor of Georgia. The mayor introduced us and then he left after a short talk. I turned to the mayor and said, "You know, I promised Cy Vance that I would give him an answer when he gets back from Italy. I like the looks of this man." He seemed so much like a lot of people I knew and I think that's important for a person who wants to be President of the United States.

Dick Daley turned to me and said, "Phil, why don't you wait until after the Ohio primary?" I said, "I don't think I'll wait. When Cy gets back I'll tell him." A few days later when I was at my office, my phone rang. It was Governor Carter. He said, "I need your help." I've heard that from a lot of candidates. Even when they're ahead they need help. I said, "You know, I've talked to Cy and I told him that when he gets back from Italy, I will tell him my decision." Obviously the help he was talking about at that point was not my moral support. He apparently needed something more. He said, "Well can't you help me now?" This was the first time any presidential candidate ever pleaded with me on the telephone. I said, "You don't want me to disappoint Cy do you?" He said no, he didn't think I should.

After all that, I did disappoint Cy. I joined them during the campaign. I was not at all disappointed in having made that decision, especially after he had won so overwhelmingly in the Ohio primary. I think he represented a type of person that should be a candidate. I started knowing politicians when I was a youngster in Kansas City. I first met Harry Truman when he was running for office as county judge. I met others as the years went on, and certainly up to then I had already served a few presidents. Carter struck me as being a kind of novel and unusual person to undertake this task with the energy that he did.

To make a long story short, he was elected and suggestions were made that I should come into the government. I had reached the age where I thought it was foolish for me to go back into government. I had been there six times before and when I got some feelers I just stayed away from them. Instead, I worked with him informally for a couple of years. I was especially impressed by his approach to the problem of the Middle East, an area in which I have a very deep interest. When he began what eventually became the Camp David Accords, he convinced me that he was a man who doesn't give up easily. Anyone who would have wagered that he would ultimately bring together the two forces would have gotten fifty to one odds at that time. Yet there were a few times when he looked like he was making it. I remember one occasion when he called about eight of us together and said, "Look, I think I've got it made with Sadat. I'm not sure about Begin. What can you suggest to us about getting him on board?" We did make a few suggestions, and he followed some of them and it did work out.

I was in Rome leading a Jewish delegation to meet with the Pope when we got the message that the President was coming back from his trip. He had gone to Cairo and to Jerusalem. He was a traveling salesman on this; he just didn't leave it alone. When it looked like the process was dead, he went back and gave it some more life. When I arrived in New York, my office was trying to reach me. The President was landing in Washington and they wanted me there to receive him. I said I couldn't make that connection since I had just gotten there and was due back that night in Chicago. I asked why he was having a celebration. His secretary said, "It looks like it's all in the bag." I had some doubts so I went home and went back to see him afterwards.

The thing that I found out and saw time after time when I went into the government was exemplified in 1978 when this man made up his mind and put his own hands and strengths to work on it. One of the problems that I've observed is that often the ideas are great, but the energy is poor. If a president has any great ideas, he better put some of his own energy behind them. Nobody in the government of the United States, and we've had the finest example of it the last few years, possesses the ability to get things done in the way that the president does. No matter how competent he is, the President of the United States has a priority as far as the people are concerned. They will follow a president while they disdain a member of the Cabinet or somebody else. We have seen a lot of evidence of that in recent years. The trouble comes when they don't carry out what they have committed themselves to do. Then we're let down.

The one thing I found most striking about this man was that he was willing to risk his presidency. He was willing to risk it in order to achieve an objective he believed in. I think that is true of Jimmy Carter to this day. I think that up to the present he has been underestimated by the people. History will give him a much better place than he's been given by the present population.

When he wanted me to come in and see him, I got a call from his right-hand man. I was in Omaha, Nebraska to receive my university's medal of honor and to attend a banquet. The caller said that the President had to see me the next morning. I said, "I can't be there." "Well it's very important to you that you be there." "How important is it if it takes another day?" "We'll call you back." This was typical of Carter. He would make up his mind on something and he wouldn't want to wait. I found that out several times during my presence in the Cabinet.

Well, they did wait. I didn't know what it was about. I heard a lot of rumors, but I don't pay attention to rumors anymore. When I came there the first person that met me was Stuart Eisenstat, his economic assistant and his right-hand man on other matters. He asked me if I knew what this was about. I said, "No, I hear rumors but I don't pay attention to them." He said, "First you've got to talk to Fritz Mondale, then Juanita Kreps, and third you talk to the President. I said, "That's a fine schedule, but what is it all about?" He said, "You're smart enough to guess." I said, "I'll wait until I talk to the others. But I suspect that you want me to go back into the government in some capacity." He said, "That's right." That's how I got back into government at a time when I made up my mind that I would never go back under any circumstances. By the next morning I was aboard.

President Carter is a very convincing person. Man to man, man to woman. He does it in a way that is so simple. The first question he asked me was, "Do you like administration?" I said, "Mr. President, what are you talking about?" He said, "I'm talking about a position in the Cabinet." I said, "Well, I've been here a few times at lower levels; I think an ambassador is higher in your recognition but he doesn't have the responsibility. I don't know anybody that really likes the drudgery of administration. But I know if you don't like it you better not take a government post, whatever it is, because there is a lot of administrative responsibility." Then he disclosed his own concern about it. He said, "You know the first year and a half I was here I didn't let a single detail escape." This was true. He wanted to know everything that was going on. He said, "I suddenly learned that I had to rely on other people to do things and I found it much easier that way." Well, I said, "Mr. President, that's a part of administration and not something apart from it."

In any event we finished a delightful discussion and he said, "Look, you're not to listen to anybody except me or Fritz Mondale from now on. Pay no attention to what anybody tells you." I got back that night to Chicago. At eight o'clock in the morning, which was seven o'clock their time, Fritz Mondale was on the phone. Fortunately, I was in the office and I accepted the call. I talked to my wife the night before and she said ok. So I went back into government.

I went back on the eve of Afghanistan. Before I had been sworn in, I had been cleared so that we could spend nights and days deciding what the President had to do in response to the Soviet involvement in Afghanistan. The result was the embargo. Everybody is acquainted with it. I shall never forget the criticism that Chancellor Schmidt gave me when I met him while I was still secretary. He didn't like economic embargoes, he being an economist. I said I didn't like them either but I couldn't see what that had to do with what we were talking about. He said, "I think it was a mistake to impose the embargo." I said, "What would you have done? They are a respectable group of people. I was with the people that labored far into the night, three nights in succession trying to figure out how we should respond to something like that. The Straits were involved, potentially, you need your oil, so does France, so do others and there were only three suggestions. One was to pick up the hotline. That's been done a half a dozen times and proved exactly nothing. The other extreme was to go to war. In between you have to exercise what little pressure is available by showing the other side that you are serious. As a consequence we elected that which is going to cause a lot of domestic political trouble, but I think the Russians will get the message."

That was the beginning of the relationship with Carter when he made that decision and then, characteristic of him, having made the decision, he went out to make the announcement. Enforcing an embargo is easy conversationally but it's a very complicated administrative job. There were a minimum of seven government departments that were involved in one way or another. The President announced that now that he had made the decision, he would appoint an interdepartmental committee that would, in forty-five days, write all of the regulations and do everything else needed to enforce the embargo. Then he looked around and said, "Phil, you are going to be the chairman of that committee." I walked into the office with him afterwards and said I couldn't say no but I was a new boy on the block. Why had he asked me to be chairman of a venture involving the State Department, the Defense Department, the Security Council, Agriculture, and I went on down the list. He said, "Precisely because you're a new person. They aren't mad at you yet. Maybe things will work out better if they've got a fellow there they haven't had a chance to get mad at." He proved to be very wise. Not only weren't they mad at me, but I was a little more careful in keeping peace than others might have been given their past struggles.

We met the deadline and had understandable trouble with Congress, the farmers, and the business community. There was more talk than real damage and I spent my first three months back trying to arbitrate between conflicting views. I don't know how many meetings we had with the representatives of the Warsaw Pact powers because we decided to exclude them as long as it paid to do so. The embargo wasn't directed towards anything but the Soviet aggression against Afghanistan. It brought us a whole array of problems. I think the fact that we were able to survive them and ultimately get the decision that we got out of the United Nations was a result of the patience and the willingness of the President to take guarded risks.

One thing I've learned in government is that there is no difference between being prepared to take some risk in government and being prepared to take some risk in the private sector. You can't win by playing it safe all the time. Historically, the embargo marked a change in our relationship with the other superpower. Shortly after the position had been taken that we were going to embargo critical materials and grain in excess of the contracted amount we were committed to deliver, the President called some 350 leaders from the business and non-profit community to the White House and announced that he changed his mind. He now questioned Soviet intentions and he was going to ask for an increase in the defense budget.

I go through this whole story so that the historical record can be corrected and that President Jimmy Carter can be recognized for starting the increase in the defense potential of the United States. Having said this, there are many other aspects of the presidency I got involved with, such as dealing with the first signs of the breakdown of our competitiveness in the world markets. That's a story all its own. I don't think we ought to go around saying it's everybody's fault but our own. We made some very serious mistakes early on as far as our production is concerned. It was not started in the Carter administration by any means. We let others get ahead of us using our technology, which they borrowed or took from us. We didn't have the courage to try to catch up. We kept talking about the history of the United States when we were an agrarian community and when markets were domestic and foreign. We forgot that international markets today involve the equivalent of what it was to sell products from Nebraska to the East Coast in earlier days. We can get overnight deliveries from all over the world. We have more unused technology than any nation in the world and we haven't applied it competitively for a number of reasons.

I got involved specifically with the steel industry. As a result of the President's initiative, Congress passed what was an international trade act, that transferred all the responsibilities for foreign trade from the State Department to the Department of Commerce and from the Treasury Department to the Department of Commerce. We wanted to give them the job of trying to develop a national approach to competitiveness and modernization. All this started under Carter. I'm not trying to be negative or partisan in what I'm about to say, because I don't see any evidence now of any change since we left office. There's been a feeling that the only way our free enterprise economy can be competitive is to free it completely. Take the government off our backs. Well, Ken has talked about interfaith—let me give you something from my faith. There's an old saying that goes back many years: "Pray for the stability of the government or else man will tear man apart." There cannot be freedom in the world, a free society where you don't have responsible government. There is a role for government. It is not to be on the backs of people, it is rather to help conciliate and to help cooperate with those parts of a society that are so essential to providing the things that our people need and other people need.

We were experimenting with this approach in the last years of the Carter administration. We experimented with it in steel and started to in automobiles in which we had the government at the Cabinet level involved with the producers, the industry, and labor. We managed to work things out, for which others are not claiming credit. We managed to come to a mutual understanding about a lot of things.

Let me cite an example. The first thing we did was to set up task forces to cover certain areas. There was so much complaint about how onerous the environmental regulations were and the industry was getting nowhere in making its case. We studied it impartially and together. They had a proper complaint. It was not a complaint against the objective. No one can complain against getting clear air and clean water. Even an entrepreneur who is suffering from it finds it difficult to complain about it. But he can complain that his company cannot afford to do what has to be done to bring it about. And that was just a complaint. They couldn't do in the time allotted what the law required, with the anticipated cash flow from the steel business. The solutions were very logical: extend the time. Don't change the objective. Make it possible or, in the alternative, help pay for it. And since we weren't going to help pay for it, one of the last things that Jimmy Carter did was to recommend a three year extension. And it was justified, completely justified.

The second thing we went to was technology. We had a subcommittee on technology. We live under a kind of an illusion that our job is to catch up with our competition. Anyone who has been in business long enough knows that by the time you catch up, your competition is ahead of you. So the assignment we gave to our technology was going to be to make steel like you make chemicals under a roof, in a continuous operation. You get away from all the environmental problems that are involved and on top of it you produce it at less cost than even the Japanese, who have become the standard for the most efficient operation.

When we agreed that that was the right thing to do we asked how much would it cost to produce one plant like that. This gives you an example of the kind of problem you run into. We all agreed it would cost a minimum of $750 million to produce that plant. The technology was all there except for one or two

Government and Industrial Competitiveness 101

things that they felt could be handled. But if you took a look at the financial statements of the biggest steel companies of America they couldn't afford to take that risk. It was going to take several years and it could be that at the end of the run it might not be as successful as all the estimates indicated. It was a logical proposition for government/business cooperation to do the technology, produce the result, and then turn it over to the private sector where it belonged for operation. And that was a program that we had recommended but it never got to Congress because time ran out for our administration.

It is problems like this that require the collective interest of the society and not just the industry alone. I believe with all my heart there are some things that free enterprise can't do by itself. So take that as one example.

Let me give you another one. This country has had the largest free market in the world. As a result everybody's come to us and sold to us. On the other hand, with all of our ingenuity and our ability, aside from the big companies that could afford it, small and medium-size businesses were not exporting in keeping with their strength. As a result, even though we maintained a surplus in the current account which included everything, in exports we were running a deficit right along. In a large measure this was attributable to our import of energy. On the current account we were constantly in surplus. The current account includes services as well as manufactured goods and products. And for a long while now (how long it will last I don't know) we have had an enormous surplus in our export of services whether it is computer service, lawyers, or architects. And on the current account we were saved.

The Congress was alert to this problem. There must have been at least nine bills to help create export trading companies. If others copy from us there's no reason why we shouldn't copy from them as well. Japan's great success is due in part to its unique type of trading company. Those bills were laying around when I became secretary of commerce. By accident the chairman of the subcommittee in the Senate was one of my senators. He called me one day shortly after I took office and said, "Look, I'm calling this bill up for hearing. It has been laying around for too long and you people have got to come up here so we can start creating export trading companies." I said, "Adlai, take it easy. I've only been here long enough to get my feet under the desk. All my reports are that everybody in the government is against it except you and a few senators. Give me a few weeks to work on it."

We worked on it. What were the problems? Again, this points up one of the problems as far as the world economy is concerned. You see it today in a minor way in connection with the Russian pipeline case—our antitrust laws. I don't make a case for all the people who think they ought to be kicked out the window. On the other hand, I get a little sick of those who have made of it an ideology or a religion. I was trained as a lawyer and I believe in what Brandeis used to say: "Law must follow social development. It cannot stay away from social and economic development." In one of the most important cases I ever handled in the Supreme Court of my home state of Nebraska, I used the Brandeis briefing technique in order to get that conservative Supreme Court to approve public housing in the state of Nebraska.

We could not have an export trading company where eight or ten companies got together and were ready to have a joint venture because it could violate antitrust laws in one way or another. Not only that, these ventures cannot succeed too well, if there are small companies involved, without the love and affection of the banking system. And the federal reserve and the controller of currency said, "Look, they can borrow from them, but the banks can't invest in them." We had long hours in which I pointed to the fact that our banks had established themselves in foreign countries all over the world. They had branches all over the world. They were the best source for business. Yet these people were saying the banks couldn't even take a 10 or 15 percent interest in a small trading company in order that we might be competitive? We finally worked it out, except for House action, then the Congress adjourned. Maybe this month or next it will be enacted. With this power we will put to work the strongest force that this economy has, the small and medium-sized businessman, a sector that has added more employees to the economy than any other.

Therefore, all of these barriers which are in place created of necessity a situation where our influence in the nation's and the world's economy was declining. But there is another factor we cannot escape. The markets in the world are changing enormously. The Third World is a hope of the future for industrial countries if they develop those markets. Those markets can only be developed if we make it possible by the right kind of public assistance, multilaterally or bilaterally, for those countries to create the income levels where they can afford to pay for the products they buy.

I ought to stop now and answer any questions that you might have.

QUESTION: I would like to ask you about the importance or unimportance of the Cabinet in the Carter administration. Most of us who have paid attention to such things remember that this was a President who started out singing the praises of what was called, I think mistakenly, Cabinet government. He is also reputed to be a President who left office with substantially revised views and practices of Cabinet government. What about Carter's approach to the Cabinet as an advisory instrument in his White House?

MR. KLUTZNICK: I think one must understand that the Cabinet acts as an adviser to the President. Individual members of the Cabinet also have statutory responsibilities. With respect to the latter, there is a crossover one can't clearly define. No one could ever charge Carter with interfering in what were their statutory responsibilities. There were some practices that he inherited from the past and continued which had been bad in the past and equally bad in his administration.

Let me give you an example. I was in the Roosevelt administration trying to spend three billion 1944-45 dollars for public housing in concert with our war production efforts. We didn't have an Office of Management and Budget. We had only a budget office. Having a budget office gave Cabinet officers and junior Cabinet officers much more authority and much more discretion. Since that time we've tried to simplify things by creating a massive Office of Management and Budget.

For years, the President would decide the coming year's goals with the Office of Management and Budget. Then they would ask the heads of the independent agencies and the heads of the Cabinet to come in with their budgets after they had set the goals. If you got into hearings pretty late as we did in 1980 and you had a budget that tried to innovate and the President heard about that innovation, you would be told that they were impressed with the ideas that you were proposing, but you'd have to come back next year because they'd fixed the top figure and there was no room under that top to adjust.

This happened to us in the Department of Commerce at a time when industry was suffering and when we were being beaten time after time with our own technology. We looked over the field and studied everything that we could and we concluded there was a gap. The gap was in basic research which everybody loved and which went on the shelf.

Some of you may know, we have a wonderful campus in Gaithersburg where the Bureau of Standards has its offices. I spent considerable time with them. We tried to figure out what contributions we could make to industry. We concluded that we were being beaten in the time between the completion of research and implementation of results. That's what MITI in Japan had done so effectively with some of our research. We proposed measures which didn't require any additional budget, small operations to test how various centers of industry could work with the government to improve productivity. For example, we were losing out in women's shoes. We were being beaten by the Italians and later by others simply because they could change their lasts over night and get into the market with something ahead of the shoe industry here. No one had paid attention to the U.S. shoe industry and it was dying. We set up an institute in Philadelphia based on cooperation between the industry and the government to determine what it was that we had in the way of technology that they could use.

Here's a second example. We made a study of waste in the manufacturing process and came up with a sum of about two billion dollars a year that the public was paying for unnecessary waste. A good part of it arose from the shaping of metal and plastic pieces that went into the manufacturing process. We put the Bureau of Standards to work on it, and they came to the conclusion that all you had to do was to change some of the mechanisms that were used in computer shaping. To do that, some testing had to be done before major commitments were made. We organized a project in Detroit where a lot of this waste was centered. Seventeen industries contributed their share. The city government made a contribution. My recollection is that we made a contribution of five million dollars to establish a testing area to see how effective we could be in the use of computer shaping and how we could eliminate that two billion dollars.

That wasn't enough. It was clear from these studies that there was tremendous room for something else. I called in the director of the Bureau of Standards and I asked "Why don't you give us a few examples of how we can improve productivity without any major changes?" They came in with one basic improvement. For the average instrument driven by an individual or by improving the power plant, you could improve output by 60 percent.

Armed with that, and with space provided by the Bureau of Standards, we requested an allotment to establish a quasi-university controlled by industry, government, and labor to test our ability to improve productivity. The institution was to try out new ideas and get them into the market place as fast as possible instead of keeping them on the shelf. That was included in our budget request. It was rejected out of hand almost immediately because there was no funding by this time. The ceiling had been fixed and there wasn't room for an additional $150 million.

Frankly, if I had been told that at the beginning, I could have found $150 million in my own $4.5 billion budget. I would have given productivity a higher priority and we wouldn't have made other commitments. It would have been there. Then the President decided to try to reduce federal spending. I had to reduce the budget by $450 million. I had no love or affection for the proposed budget because I was new on the job, and so I was successful. That's not so difficult if you really have to do it.

We were turned down. My assistant who appeared before the OMB and I then said I was going to appear at the final hearing. I called Bob McIntyre and told him I was going to appear. He said secretaries don't do that. I said this secretary is not going to be here very long and there will be a new secretary coming in and I want the record clear that we are at least leaving a program that my successor can use.

I went over and was turned down again. I asked for a hearing with the President which we were entitled to. I had a very interesting hearing with the President. He said if he had known earlier this could have been given a higher priority but by now the budget was virtually frozen. I said if I had known earlier that this wasn't going to get any consideration, I could have taken it out of my own budget. He said, "I promise you, if we come back you will get this program." I then turned to him and said we ought to leave a legacy of some kind. My own feeling was that when we didn't have an Office of Management and Budget, the managers who approved the work had more freedom than they have now. I was not contending that we ought to eliminate the OMB. I just wanted to tell the President that the people he should be talking to *before* he set the ceiling and not after were the people producing the product, not the people who were talking about it. He said, "I think you're right, but what can I do now?" I said "I don't think you can do anything until the next budget."

We are our own worst enemy when it comes to industrial competition in the world. We had the steel crisis. What did we do? We couldn't cure everything. It had gone too far, but the President, working with industry and labor, established a steel task force. The secretary of labor and the secretary of commerce were the co-chairmen. We did manage to ease the burden a little. We couldn't do as much as we should have done. We started too late.

I can give you other examples. There are ways of improving the present operation of government and its relationship to production. It doesn't mean the government has to interfere in production; it means government helping out when industry can't help itself. We have a mistaken conception that this is still an agrarian economy. The fact of the matter is that the destiny of America depends on how well we get back to a position of industrial competitiveness. It can't be done by praying. It requires a program of complete cooperation and acceptance by industry, in which the whole country is a partner.

Maybe the time has come for what Mr. Jefferson said a long

time ago, that the most effective government is decentralized government. What do I mean by that? I mean that I don't think any president can be an expert in all things but if he has eight, ten, or twelve department heads, and I would consolidate some departments instead of expanding them, and he parts with a fraction of his power to that institution and that institution has the ability like MITI does in Japan in the ministry to go forward with programs within the range of the total commitment, I think you would get more effective government. What you get today is second-guessing before the first guess has to be made. It's a matter of distribution of resources, of manpower, and people.

I had that problem when I was a young fellow and was frightened to run a government agency of 26,000 people. What I did was to get closer to the people. I had my staff meetings very regularly with the experts, then I met with those people who were responsible for really running the government. Just like in a business. In the Department of Commerce, which had over 40,000 employees, I had ten to fifteen people that I had to meet with at least once a week to make sure I knew what was going on. We had forty who were running divisions and operations that we also met with once a week. But every two months the 400 who were really doing the day-to-day work I would report to and they would raise questions with me, so that I was informed and could feel the tremors that were going on through that agency to see where our weak spots were.

Our weak spots were clear almost in the third month. We were in trouble on technology, we were in trouble on productivity; we knew that you couldn't maintain a standard of living in this country unless our productivity improved. We also knew since they had transferred the trade program to us that we couldn't continue to operate with the equipment we had in this modern world unless we improved our exports. It was obvious. I had the authority to go ahead with it, subject to the congressional interferences which takes some time. Someday we're going to have to learn how to keep our division of power without destroying ourselves in the process. Maybe some of our experts can tell us how to do that. The president should be the head of the enterprise. It would be foolhardy to expect him to operate it from his office alone. But some presidents have tried. That's been one of the problems.

I'll give one more example. I served our government in the United Nations in 1957. I happened to be there the day the Russian Sputnik beat us into space. I was given the assignment to bury, if possible, a proposal by the Soviets to establish an international court of criminal justice. We had all the votes we needed until the Sputnik was launched. Then some of our friends began looking at us differently. They didn't say they'd lost faith, but the votes were melting away and we had a difficult time finally winning that struggle.

From 1957 on, we spent $100 billion of government money, using the best sectors of our industry that was available to get ahead of the Soviets in space technology. We didn't hesitate to do that. Why shouldn't we spend the money if it is necessary? Private industry did it working with the government, working on mutually agreed upon programs. We don't want government control. I think the Japanese, who are a different people, nevertheless have practices from which we could learn. Government cooperation is a great deal different than government control.

We have a great government and we want to keep it democratic. We have a free enterprise system in private life and I want to keep it free. But there is a distinction between freedom when you get no cooperation and when you do. We are not going to win this struggle by speeches. We're not going to win it by willing for something to happen. We're going to win it when we take the strength we've got and put energy behind it. The energy has to come from all three sectors. It can't come from the private sector alone.

QUESTION: I served with the Department of Agriculture under Dr. Butz and I'm sure you remember the Nixon embargo on wheat and soybeans. It has been a nightmare for agriculture ever since we did that. We inspired a whole soybean operation in Brazil that never existed before, at least not in open competition. My question is simple. How can you set up an embargo on natural resources and oil? It ends up at a third market in Amsterdam. How do you make one of them stick, other than as a political expression?

MR. KLUTZNICK: Well, I want to be specific because I don't think generally it is a good idea. That embargo would never have been started had it not been clear that the Russians had promised their people an increase in meat. We knew that they were going to have a bad crop and little feed for cattle. Where we failed was not with our enemies, but with our friends. We relied on our friends who, frankly, didn't hold up.

QUESTION: Canada?

MR. KLUTZNICK: Canada and Brazil mainly. That was where the failure was. It wasn't in the idea; it was in our getting the cooperation that was needed. They flunked. That would have worked and worked well if those countries had stayed out of the marketplace.

QUESTION: David Halberstam has written a big book examining why so many million Americans are driving automobiles that come from Japan. He has used all the arguments that you know very well. He faults management in Detroit and praises the Japanese labor force, but he makes one point that is interesting. He pointed out that the industrial energy in Japan has not been diverted since the war because of our restrictions on their military buildup. They don't have much defense spending. From where you were sitting in the Department of Commerce, how much of our lag is due to the fact that the energy of this country has gone into defense spending and that the best brains have gone into the aerospace industry?

MR. KLUTZNICK: I would agree with that but I wouldn't put a percentage on it. You must remember that the first move to increase defense spending didn't come in the Carter administration until December of the last year. Therefore, I would say that it was more negligible than it has been in the last few years where defense spending has built up to a point where undoubtedly it is withdrawing talent and capital. But I think we have enough for both. May I cite an example that is directly related? In the summer of 1980 when it appeared that the automobile industry was in big trouble, the President convened a session of all the top automobile companies for the precise purpose of getting their judgment as to what should be done. I can't forget that session. I won't say too much about it, except that one person spoke up and said, "I don't want any help; all I want you to do is reduce the interest rate below 15 percent." You can guess who that was—Lee Iacocca. He made the shortest speech on record. The others gave extended explanations of why they were in this trouble.

After a long discussion, the President appointed a Cabinet committee consisting of three of us to go to Detroit and continue the dialogue. Since it was in his province, the secretary of transportation was made the chairman. All of the top people were there. Secretary of Transportation Goldschmidt said, "The first thing we ought to discuss is the emissions standard." There had been no preliminary discussion between any of us. It was his job. Phil Caldwell of the Ford Motor Company stood up and said, "Under those circumstances, I'll have to leave because I'm under a consent agreement that the instruments for regulating emissions are an element of competition. I have been restrained by the appropriate court from participating in any discussion of this subject." The meeting adjourned. All of them together were spending about 350 million dollars that the consumer would pay. It is not their money. They were going to sell their automobiles and they would add the costs of complying with emissions standards. They didn't get together and come up with one design for the benefit of the public. That happens time after time in areas where laws are passed that are for the benefit of the public and not for the corporation. Frequently they are restrained from cooperating with each other for the benefit of the consumer.

Here is another example. I went to Cleveland in the midst of all this to look at a change at National Steel. They had spent close to 100 million dollars to produce the purest water to go into the Cuyahoga River. You could drink the water. I went up to the top and drank it. The minute it hit the Cuyahoga River, it wasn't potable. We were requiring them to improve their water so that the river water could be more potable, but nobody had stopped to think that it was upstream where the pollution started. As a consequence, I calculated that the purification requirement raised the cost of steel seventeen dollars a ton. It served absolutely no purpose.

That would not have developed if the steel industry, the government, and labor had worked together. We discovered that there was no way in the world that they could meet this standard in three years and pay it out of their income. We had a special financial committee go through and look at it, and the President gave them an extension. We want enterprise to be free but we don't want it handcuffed. I would acknowledge that there is, in fact, a cost. How do you calculate it? By realizing that a lot of the capital which could be used for productive improvement is wasted for non-productive public good.

There was no sense in improving the Cuyahoga River until it was also cleaned upstream. Here was an investment that increased costs and served no purpose at all. That's the kind of thing you can only develop when you have some understanding of the problem. You can't get that understanding, as the head of a department unless you are working with the people that are intimately involved—the consumer and the producer. There are a lot of people who disagree with that concept because they haven't lived and watched waste that serves no purpose because somebody had an idea that was totally impractical, and there is no way to defeat it.

QUESTION: In the late 1960s and early 1970s, both Japan and Germany were spending almost twice, as much percentage-wise, in research and development as the United States. What causes that?

MR. KLUTZNICK: I think a lack of knowledge more than anything else. Our steel industry is devastated. Why did that happen? In 1958 an American engineer conceived the process of continuous casting. He tried to sell it to American industry, and no one bought it. He went to Japan and sold it. Now American industry, lagging behind the competition, has been putting it in for the last few years at a time when it costs two or three times as much.

Robotics were conceived in this country. Westinghouse was working on them long before Japan used them effectively. But again you get to the gap between creation and implementation. They have an institution called MITI that decides. They go too far in my judgment, but it's effective. Where are they going to put their emphasis? They realized that we were going to be behind them in steel, so they went into steel. That put them into automobiles as well. I don't think we can live in a world free of competition, but I don't think we ought to tie our hands either.

Before I came here I called the head of the National Academy of Science. He made a statement not too many months ago that we are getting more pure science than any country in the world. I asked him if it was still true. He said it's true today as it was before. He said if we don't find a way of using it, others will use it. Anti-trust is one thing. Our inability to develop the instruments for application within our free system is another thing. Our unwillingness to recognize that we have a financial system for corporate operation is a handicap in itself. We have many heads of American corporations who were trained in finance or law and very few that know the production side. The fact of the matter is that we pay a price for that. On top of it, we publicly finance most of our corporations. With our retirement laws, the average chief executive gets his chance for five or six years and then he is gone. He's not going to finance a major redevelopment which, because of interest costs and capital costs, may erode his earning capacity because it will also erode his ability to get a reasonable bonus in the few years that he has. These are very human considerations but we have never faced the human problem in industry. You can't expect a man to cut his own throat just in order to leave progress for his successor. We have a lot of places where we need continuing conversation. I'm not saying that these are the only answers, or the only questions.

NARRATOR: May I ask if we could focus on the Carter presidency? When you discussed issues of this kind with President Carter, did he know what you were talking about? Was he better able to cope with these issues because he had an engineer's background? Was he at home in this area, and did he grasp what you were saying?

MR. KLUTZNICK: Let's take one specific case which I think is important. The steel problem got to be more burdensome than even the government could handle. Ray Marshall and I were directed to see if we could work out some sort of agreement with the Europeans and the Japanese to withhold some of their production in order to reduce their invasion of our market. We got to the point where we thought we had a very acceptable agreement. We went to the President with it. The theory has been that if you eliminate a certain amount of foreign production, you increase the price of the product. Therefore the consumer is really paying for what you are doing. Well, it's never been proven conclusively, but logically it would appear to be the right conclusion. We argued this matter with Carter, and he said, "I want the Cabinet to listen." He turned the deal down. Two and a half months later, the President called and said, "Can you reawaken that deal? We made a mistake." We had, and everybody was excited. We even had a big dinner at the White House with labor and industry and all of us there. After we left, not too many months later, it was dropped again. They started over again about six months after that and recognized that industry could not cope with the product invasions that were coming in. As a matter of fact, some of them were in violation of GATT agreements. He did understand it, enough so that he was willing to take the first risk on the advice of his Council of Economic Advisers. And then when he saw the result, he reversed himself without hesitancy.

You know, government is like business, and like your home. Some things get to a point where they get log-rolled. I think our system of government, as it is presently constituted, doesn't involve the management people who have to produce early enough in the process of manufacturing. He recognized this and was quick to recognize an error. He was not at all ashamed to reverse himself, which I guess is all you can ask.

QUESTION: I would like to press you on a question of the Carter administration's cooperation with business. Perhaps you would respond to this criticism. It is that the Carter administration was correct in promoting cooperation with business, but they were mistaken in not promoting their cooperation more strategically. The Carter administration spent a lot of time and effort reviving troubled industries, like the shoe industry or the steel industry. Perhaps they could have done more in pushing those industries into what economists call "higher value added" sectors of a particular industry, like pushing steel producers into specialty steels where they might be the best in the world and the most profitable in the world. Instead, the administration tried to revive basic steel, where Third World producers like Korea would continue to undercut American producers on the basis of lower costs. Do you think that is a valid criticism, and what does it say about the future?

MR. KLUTZNICK: Well, have you ever tried to push business into something that they didn't want to go into? They are tougher than the government. I could go up and talk to a Senate committee on steel, and they would push, and we had many meetings. For example, we had monthly meetings with the Chamber of Commerce about any issue you can think of. For every industry group that was in trouble, the Department of Commerce would set up a meeting and continue a series of meetings to see what we could do to help. But, you have to make it profitable for a businessman to act and leave the place that he believes is comfortable, even if he is being choked at the moment. I've been on the other side of the fence, and I know what it means to change your mode of operation completely.

I don't think there has ever been a more cordial group cooperating than the group that was set up to study steel. We met regularly; we had experts to advise us all the way through, but they still couldn't take that licking, which I don't think they should have had to take. I think we should have facilitated it. We help the farmer when he's in trouble.

The President properly saw that they needed more time. I think if we had a couple more years, we might have gotten the message across, but we're all stubborn in the areas that we think we know and that we are comfortable with. We tried specialty steel. As a matter of fact, there was a shift. We had meetings, and it was obvious that specialty steel was better. But some of the producers weren't that good. U. S. Steel (now USX) is a competent organization. Even today, while it is down to where it is, we've had to negotiate with them in Chicago, and I tell you, they are not easy to negotiate with when they've got something that they think is right. We don't have the atmosphere that permits a fast change of that kind. If you invite business in to cooperate, you've got first to convince them that you are not trying to take them over. That's what business fears. I don't think we've made the grade yet, though Japan and Germany have.

NARRATOR: Two words that you haven't mentioned that we hear every day in every newspaper article are "trade deficits." Was there much talk of that?

MR. KLUTZNICK: First of all, it was nominal. Yes we were terribly worried when we had a $27 billion trade deficit. There was talk about it. The only way you can stop trade deficits is by offsetting them with sales. I think we've been too long waiting for a new GATT. For example, they are supposed to meet this summer to set up a new round of GATT talks. There were all sorts of violations of the General Agreement on Tariffs and Trade. Now they are going to set up a meeting where they are going to try and include at long last a lot of areas GATT doesn't cover now. I remember my last GATT meeting. I participated in an OECD meeting in which I argued for the inclusion of services. They're not protected under GATT, and America has become a great supplier of services that could offset a lot of this deficit that we have. But they are not protected. Foreign countries don't use our lawyers, accountants, and service capacities. We don't get a fair break on it. Finally, after all these years they agreed to call a special session of GATT. My guess would be that it would be very difficult to get through.

There are a lot of other things we should be trying. The most important thing that we need is elimination of the notion that the government is our enemy. That's a harsh statement, but there are too many businesses that believe it. They are afraid to get near the government because historically they fear that has meant a takeover. We are not going to make it without cooperating. That's where we started, and that's where I end. If we aren't going to accept government as something that is benign and wants to be helpful, and if government doesn't assume its part of the load, I don't think we can beat the Germanies, the Japans and the Koreas. It's a difficult process. But I looked at some recent figures of U.S. Steel. They've managed to reduce their employment and improve their production to a point where their per ton of steel delivered is competitive with our biggest competitors. Read U.S. Steel's latest report. We can do it, if there is a will to do it, and we are not handicapped in doing it. If U.S. Steel could do it, some of the smaller companies could have been doing it. It's doable if you get help. Even better they could do it if we had given them some help earlier in eliminating some of the costs that were incurred that are not evident in the production. That's the core idea I want to leave with you.

NARRATOR: That's a good positive point on which to end. That is usually the way with Phil Klutznick, and twenty years from now he will come back and give us another boost at a time when doom and gloom pervades most discussions. Thank you a lot.

CHAPTER 7

POLITICS AND AGRICULTURE: LESSONS OF THE CARTER PRESIDENCY

SECRETARY OF AGRICULTURE BOB S. BERGLAND

NARRATOR: Nearly everyone wants to talk about nuclear weapons, arms control, or Iran, but it is no less relevant to talk about agricultural matters. We have seen a considerable reduction in the agricultural reserves in the country. Forces and problems in parts of the midwest remind us that agriculture is a very vital element in the challenges we face in the future. So for at least two reasons we are delighted that Secretary Bergland is with us: one, because of the importance of his subject and the work that he did in the Carter administration, and two, because he is one of the politically active Cabinet members who has kindly consented to discuss his President and presidency, the Carter presidency.

President Carter said proudly when he announced Mr. Bergland's appointment that he had pledged himself during the campaign to appoint a farmer as secretary of agriculture and he was proud that he was able to announce Bob Bergland's appointment. Bergland was midwest chairman of the regional agricultural stabilization and conservation service and, before that, of the state conservation service. He was an adviser to Walter Mondale during the first Carter campaign. He was elected a member of Congress in 1970 and served on the agricultural committee and the small business committee. We're very happy that Bob Bergland could be with us today.

SECRETARY BERGLAND: I think it would be useful for me to talk about the Carter presidency and some of the politics of the administration because that is what drives the government. Whether it's this university or any other association, every group has a government of some kind. The science of the process by which these governments function is called "politics." My life has been spent in the partisan political world, a world that is undergoing tremendous change because the role of political parties is being reduced. The techniques used in campaigns have changed dramatically in the last fifteen years with the rise and influence of television. We've seen the campaigns for public office change from what was largely a retailing operation in which candidates would discuss local issues of importance and political parties had an important role to play in shielding candidates from various economic and political subgroups. All that's going by the boards. Now campaigning is wholesaling. Hire an advertising agency. Hire a polling agency. Collect the political profiles. Determine the demographics. Survey the attitudes of demographic subgroups. Put it all in the computer and run daily tracking changes and keep this posted in the computer. Politics has become a very sophisticated business.

When a tracking group shows that a subgroup is starting to veer you change the advertising tempo slightly. Drop something. Add something. This is how politics is run these days. It is no longer an art; it is a science, and it is incredibly expensive. Unfortunately, issues don't really count for much. It is image and impressions. People have allowed themselves to be seduced by the television. To make matters worse we've reduced the role of political parties and we have elevated the role of political action committees. There are now thirty-eight hundred of these committees that raise money and contribute to the persons that they believe best represent their narrow interests. There is no real process by which these narrow interests can be reconciled. Candidates are bought or rented a piece at a time by these political action committees. It's a devastating process. I am very critical of them and yet my organization runs a PAC. I manage a trade association which raises a million dollars every two years, and we contribute money, not on the basis of some altruistic test, but on the basis of our private interest. So does everybody else.

I was not a Jimmy Carter supporter but rather I was a member of Congress and a student of the late Hubert Humphrey. I grew up under his leadership and direction in the populist regions of rural western Minnesota. My parents were Republican populists. There were no Democrats of any real consequence in Minnesota until the late 1920s or early 1930s. As was true in the whole region, from the beginning of time until the Roosevelt realignment in the thirties, everybody there was a Republican. My parent's and my family's politics were what they called the "populist Republican brand." They were big supporters of Robert La Follette and of others who ran groups within the grand old party. The contests were always within the Republican primary ranks.

In the 1930s and 1940s all this changed. The Democrats and the Farmer Labor party, which was the political offshoot of the old populist party, controlled legislatures. Populism was a very powerful political force, not always well led but always well followed. I grew up in a home in which my dad said that politics was important. He thought that all decisions were made in Washington and that these big eastern trusts, big banks and big railroads, were all crooked. Anybody who had made a lot of money, it was reasoned, had probably stolen it and they would have to prove their innocence. That was dad's basic law.

That is the essence of populism and I grew up in that kind of a home, in that kind of environment. Later I became active in politics and especially in local Democratic party affairs in various ways. In the John Kennedy campaign in 1960, until he was nominated, I was a partisan supporter of the late Hubert Humphrey who was trying to gain the Democratic nomination. I campaigned in Wisconsin and other places for him but of course we failed. It was in August or September of that year when Kennedy had been nominated, and most of us were mad. We weren't going to take part in the campaign. Humphrey got the bunch together in the St. Paul Hotel and he laid down the law. He said, "I don't want to hear anything about this business. The choice is between Kennedy or Nixon and that's no choice. We're going to put aside the old wounds." And we did; we went to work.

My job in the campaign was to deal with Lutheran preachers. We knew that religion was going to be an important issue. So, whenever we'd find a Lutheran preacher who got on the high horse about Catholicism and Kennedy, I would find a Democratic parishioner and we'd go see the minister. You'd be surprised how well it worked! We took the sting out of that issue and we did it one on one. It was not done by some grand and glorious debate. It was done with a parishioner who gave money and me.

Those were often difficult assignments but they were effective. That is how elections are often won or lost. Kennedy barely carried Minnesota, was barely elected, and you know the rest of the story. Humphrey was the architect of all this. I grew up in that kind of rough and tumble political environment. We knew how to win, and we knew we'd lose if we did not work.

I was elected to Congress in 1970. I had ran in 1968 and had lost, possibly because the year 1968 was not one of the better ones for the Democrats. Humphrey was nominated as a democratic candidate for the presidency and the Minnesota Democratic party was a disaster. The Democrats had divided on the war in Vietnam and there was no way that they were going to win. Of course, it blew up. I got trapped and lost my way to

Congress, but I kept running and I was elected two years later. I became a member of the Committee on Agriculture. We dealt with problems of agricultural credit, and conservation, and I worked at the job by specializing. That's how Congress is run, by persons who become known for their skill in something; if you don't have skill in something you are of little use to the leadership.

I first met Jimmy Carter in the fall of 1975. Carter was getting organized to enter the campaign in Iowa and in other primary states during the year 1976. He came to Washington to get acquainted with members of Congress. It was organized by the Democratic delegation to the Congress from the state of Georgia. I went there and was not impressed. I thought to myself, "This fellow is not very strong." He didn't have what I thought were the necessary dynamic credentials. I thought he was lacking in many respects.

Carter went into Iowa and took the peanut brigade with him. I was impressed by that. I had done enough retail politicking to know that this was a very effective way to campaign. He brought persons in to Iowa who were all properly dressed, well mannered and methodical. They just went from door to door and from town to town in targeted regions of Iowa. They went only where there were Democrats and they were effective in getting a core of people out to the precinct caucus on that particular day in February of that year. The Carter campaign was, "we need to turn the scoundrels out." It didn't really matter who they were, but we had to rid the country of this bad influence. We had just gone through the Watergate episode. Vietnam had been a devastating political event and the tendency was to look upon Washington as a major problem. Carter ran, literally, as an outsider. That was an appealing strategy because people said, "we've had enough of these professional politicians. It's time we find just plain folks."

I thought that campaign pitch was nuts, but it did work. I thought it was nuts because people should realize that the government has to be run by professionals. It's no place for amateurs and I thought Carter was organizing a campaign of amateurs.

However, he succeeded in piling up pluralities in Iowa and New Hampshire in the primary races. Later he went on to become the Democratic nominee along with Walter Mondale from my state. Mondale was Carter's choice though I'm not quite sure why. I really don't know what the chemistry was, because they had not been good friends. They had no particular problems with each other, but it was an unlikely arrangement.

After the nominating process at the Democratic convention, Mondale called me and asked if I would help organize committees of congressional support for the Carter-Mondale ticket and I said that of course I would. We formed campaign committees and we did the best we could through members of Congress. We used their political organizations back in their districts. Members of Congress have some things in common; they all have good organizations. If they don't, then they don't win. It's as simple as that.

Carter won. I had only met him once during the campaign, however. It was at an agricultural function out in Minnesota and he made a fairly decent presentation. He was not strong voiced, but he was very bright and he had his position thought out. He knew what he was talking about, and so I was very much impressed by the content of his speech. There had been some speculation in the Minneapolis newspapers that I might be appointed cabinet secretary for agriculture. This was during the campaign and I, of course, denied it. As a matter of fact, no one had talked with me at that point. I thought that whole thing was rumor. I was running for re-election and was intent on not getting into that kind of Cabinet politicking.

I won my own election by a good majority. Carter was elected, and four or five days later I was called by a reporter in Minneapolis. He asked me, "How about this Cabinet business?" I said, "Absolutely not. I like what I'm doing." I did indeed like my work in the House of Representatives. He wrote the story just as I told it and Humphrey called me up and asked, "What's this all about?" I told him that I indeed enjoyed my responsibilities in the House. He said, "Well, let me tell you, Carter is not going to be a very good president. He's going to need all the help he can get." He said, "If he calls you, you have no right to turn him down. You have an obligation." I took the whole thing with a grain of salt, and I thought, "It will be a cold day when I'm chosen for the job."

About ten days later, one cold morning, I had a call from Jimmy Carter asking me to come to Atlanta, to the governor's mansion, to meet and to talk to him. I said, "Sure." I hadn't the foggiest idea what the request was about because I was not campaigning for the Cabinet job and I knew a lot of people who were. They had their committees out. There were farm organization leaders and agriculture bankers. People who were looking for appointments were running for this job but I really didn't think about it. However, I went to Atlanta and met the President, and we got along well. We talked about agriculture, international economic development, poverty, hunger and the importance of hunger in world politics, the importance of hunger in the United States, the importance of knowing more about the linkage between diet and health, and the like. The sad irony is that we know everything about the nutritional requirements of a cow and almost nothing about the human body. We were going to change all that. Production agriculture would take care of itself. A land grant to a university would always see to that. What we had to deal with was the other side of the marketplace, the demand side, the human side. I had long thought that this was really important and Carter thought so too, and so we got along fine.

Carter, Charles Kirbo and one of Carter's staff people were all at that interview. They sat there and pounded questions at me for a couple of hours. When I left President Carter asked if I would sign an FBI document releasing my access to the findings so they could do a field check. I said, "Sure." A couple of days later an FBI man called on my mother and said "I'm with the FBI. I'm here to talk about your son." She was sure that I had robbed a bank! They ran the checks and I passed the test.

The day after Christmas the President called me and asked if I would accept the job. I said, "Yes, under one condition." It had to do with the departmental appointments. The appointment of persons to the departments was an important part of the process and I insisted on control of these appointments. He said that was fine, but did say that he had some people he'd like to suggest. I said that was fine. So, we agreed that I wouldn't recommend anybody that he wouldn't agree to and he wouldn't appoint anybody that I didn't want. We each had a veto. The process worked well.

I went to Plains, Georgia. He made the announcement of my acceptance of the post, and we were off and running. I went back to Plains the third of January in 1977. He had assembled all the persons that were about to go into his administration and we talked about macro-economic strategy. There was confusion. There was talk at the time about the need for a fifty dollar rebate. We had to get the economy stimulated and it was suggested that the way to do it was to appropriate fifty dollars for everybody in the country. I thought the whole concept was dumb, but I didn't know anything about it and I didn't take any part in that discussion. I left that to the economists, the lawyers and the scholars.

We were there for about a week and the game plan changed every other day. He really did have a hard time getting his administration organized, but it did finally take off. We all came into office and the President kept his word as far as appointments were concerned. They sent over a long list of people that had been involved in the campaign and I interviewed several that looked like they had some skills we could use. Four of them were absolutely super people—well-qualified and well-trained with good instincts. I wouldn't have anything to do with people that were regarded as a bit shady. They had to be straight arrows or I wouldn't touch them and I didn't have any problem with Carter in that regard. He seemed to attract people like that. They were amateurs in a lot of ways but they were honest about it. His government was really loaded with honest amateurs.

It got off to a terrible start. Some of the President's people regarded Congress as the big legislature and thought that if you gave it time it would go away. The President brought in people to run the Congressional Relations Office who didn't know the speaker of the House, Tip O'Neill. They knew his name because they read it, but they had never met the gentleman. They didn't know the structure of the committees, and didn't know the politics and the subpolitics of the committees. It was an unmitigated disaster.

There were five persons in the Carter Cabinet that had had congressional experience. Walter Mondale was vice president. Brock Adams from Washington State was secretary of transportation. Bob Strauss was the President's trade adviser. Andy Young was the President's ambassador to the United Nations. I was the fifth. We were experienced political people in the Congress and knew the culture up there.

The relationships with the Congress got off to a very bad start. The President struggled with it. He had really not developed any kind of a cohesive national strategy, and he never did develop one. I think this was his weakness. He was an engineer and he delighted in seeing pieces and parts. He wanted to see everything move, but he wanted to inspect all the pieces. For example, in March of that year we were obligated to present a major agricultural initiative to the Congress. Because the current law was expiring, we had to come up with a new approach. We thought this through carefully and decided how we wanted to approach the matter. We had developed a proposal which was a rather lengthy document prepared with the counseling of the Department of State, the Office of Management and Budget, the Treasury Department and the other agencies involved, because agricultural policy is an international event and it crosses all departments and agencies. Agricultural policy is not the kind of thing that's created in a vacuum.

The President liked to have decision memoranda. He didn't really like to mix it up in a meeting. He didn't like to debate or listen to arguments; he was very uncomfortable in that area. There were a few instances in which I would argue with someone in the Cabinet on the substance of an issue and the President would let the argument go on for awhile, and then he would cut it off. What he wanted us to do was to reduce our arguments to writing and to gather dissenting views or additional views and compile these views in a memorandum. His staff would then produce a letter. It would state who's for and who's against. At the bottom of the letter would be a provision to check yes or no with room for comments.

The agricultural initiative went over to the President with about a twelve-page executive summary, a hundred-page detailed documentation and about 600 pages of charts. President Carter called me up on a Saturday afternoon and asked about chart 3 on page 412. I was embarrassed because I hadn't read it. To be honest with you, I had no intention of reading it. But he had. I said, "Mr. President, I don't know." He said, "You don't know?" I said, "No, I don't know. I'm at home, I don't have the report here." "Well, OK, get to me early Monday." So I called up the experts Monday morning at seven o'clock and told them the President had a question about page 412, Chart 3. A technical expert in the Foreign Agricultural Service said, "Well, we thought that might confuse him. It wasn't very clear." We straightened it out and got it over to him. He really wanted to get involved and see all parts to be sure, in his judgment as an engineer, that the thing would finally run when the pieces were all put together.

He didn't like the social life of Washington. He did not develop social friends in his Cabinet. I don't believe there were any. It wasn't until the third year in his administration that he and Mrs. Carter invited my wife and me to a private White House function. We'd been invited to state dinners before. That sort of thing went with the job, but he never did fraternize or get to know his Cabinet or his key appointees in various agencies on a personal basis. He was very much the loner.

Mrs. Carter was important to him in lots of ways. She would sit in on Cabinet meetings. She formed judgments about people and I discovered later that her instincts were very good. She was able to size up a person and tell whether or not he or she was competent, or whether they were incompetent and made up for it by being loud. She would size up a person and would tell the President, "I don't think that fellow is telling you the truth; I think there is something more going on here." She didn't have any evidence, it was instinct. The President depended on her for that purpose.

The relations with the Congress continued to go downhill partly because the President didn't really have an economic game plan. He didn't have a plan, as President Reagan had with the Reagan revolution. President Reagan came into office with a slogan, with a platform, with ideas and with a sense of purpose and a missionary zeal. President Carter didn't want that. He thought those were trappings.

I remember late in 1977 we had been doing a lot of work in development programs in Central and South America. Our theory was that if people go hungry they are going to take up arms. It's just a natural phenomenon. If their kids go hungry, they're going to start shooting something or they are going to steal. The way to avoid having the communists or other radicals in the region gain control is to deal with this problem of poverty. We looked at what Jack Kennedy started down there in the 1960s with the Alliance for Progress and thought it had a great deal of merit. Cyrus Vance and I, and some of our key people, thought we ought to develop a theme. We wanted to repackage the Alliance for Progress. Our basis was to be social and economic development and reform. We presented the President with this idea and it didn't get to first base. He didn't want any part of it. He said, "You deal with the problems piecemeal and as they arise." He didn't want to have any kind of thematic approach to the region's political and economic problems, so we dealt as well as we could with those things one piece at a time.

He enjoyed that kind of an administration. The upside to it was that he never got tangled up on any treaty down there or any major initiative that couldn't be supported or was not well thought out. The downside was that we did a lot of good things in Latin America and elsewhere for which we received no political credit whatsoever. He didn't really want political credit. He thought that he'd be judged on merit and that the country would know he was a good president. He did things that protected the public's interest and he didn't care if the public knew. He hated television; he was no good on TV. By contrast Ronald Reagan is the best I have ever seen. He's been at it for fifty years and knows how to do it because he's a professional television performer. I don't mean that as a criticism; I state it as a fact. And, in this political world that is an absolute requisite. Well, President Carter didn't have television presence, and he wouldn't train for it. He avoided that part which would have allowed him to gain certain credits for certain small wins. Every administration has small wins and big losses, and you just hope the small wins will overcome the big losses when they hit. We muddled along.

The President took a keen interest in the Middle East, perhaps because he is a biblical scholar. He called me one day on the hot line to the Department of Agriculture and asked me if I had read the forty-first chapter of Genesis. I said not lately. (We Lutherans didn't spend a whole lot of time on the Old Testament.) He told me to read it and see if it would work. I didn't have the foggiest idea what he was talking about. It turns out that the first secretary of agriculture was a fellow named Joseph about three thousand years before the time of Christ. His administration was down in an area west of Luxor, Egypt. They had set up an irrigation scheme and the first ever normal granary. You will recall that there were droughts during this time. To combat the droughts, the region set up a grain reserve scheme and when the rest of the world went hungry they had grain. In this way, they became a political powerhouse.

After I had read it, I called the President back. He asked if I thought it would work today. I said, "Yes, it will work." He said, "Let's do it." So we did. I called the economists and I said, "You won't believe this!" I was right, they didn't believe me! I explained what the President wanted to do and they turned all shades of color. I said, "We're not here to pass judgment on the President's opinions in these matters. The question is, will it work?" The economists said it would work, and we went ahead with plans. I prepared an order for the President, and he signed it. With that mandate, we established a grain reserve scheme in which we took surplus grain and, instead of dumping it on the markets, giving the Russians big subsidies or panicking over the surpluses, we put it in reserve. We built granaries and we held the surplus grain. It was a very successful program. It was, of course, intervention. Some of the grain companies didn't like it because they would have much preferred to have the United States remain a grain colony for them. We installed the grain reserve plan and we did it without fanfare. The President didn't want credit for it. He thought the people would find out that it would work and they eventually did. It was done, however, without the usual bells and whistles and fanfare for which Mr. Reagan is so noted.

Carter had always been a biblical scholar and had a keen interest in the continuing disputes surrounding the state of Israel. I don't know what brought things together, but he decided to become a catalyst and to try to bring the Israelis and their Arab neighbors together and to try to figure out some key to the Middle East antipathy.

He became heavily involved in what became known as the Camp David negotiations. He took a very keen, deep personal interest in it. He literally brought that issue into the Rose Garden. He brought it into the Oval Office of the White House where for nearly 18 months, it was a total preoccupation with him. He didn't have time for much else including mundane issues like price support levels and a new highway program. He didn't want to be bothered with those issues because he was so fascinated by his role in bringing together these traditional enemies in the Middle East. Every Cabinet member was involved in the accord process. I was involved. We had a meeting in Cairo with a team of experts taking soil samples, testing water and doing engineering studies on the feasibility of diverting Nile river water to irrigate the Negev and the Sinai Deserts. If the accords had ever come to a conclusion, those regions would have been irrigated and used as a new heartland for transplanted people on the West Bank of the Jordan River. Old Palestine would have become the Palestinian homeland. The Israeli irrigators would have moved to the Negev Desert and we would have made the Negev into the new Bakersfield, California, because it had all the necessary ingredients. Some day that is going to happen.

The President, however, never finished his job. The Iranian hostage crisis brought everything to a screeching halt. It destroyed him politically. It didn't destroy his health but it certainly hurt him deeply. The Iranian hostages were taken on the fourth of November in 1979 and from that day on he retreated into the White House, allowing himself to be taken prisoner. He devoted all of his time to trying to work out the hostages' release. He brought the crisis into the White House and, as a result, wouldn't campaign. He didn't feel that he was free to leave the White House. He felt compelled to be there for all of the delicate negotiations with the Iranians and others who were trying to arrange the release of the hostages. He really was afraid that if he left the White House he would lose an opportunity for their release. Mr. Reagan was the complete opposite. There couldn't be more of a stark contrast between two people or between two administrations.

Some time in the summer of 1979, the Iranians had blown up two big gaslines leading into the Soviet Union and shut down much of Soviet industry in the Caucasus, the region adjacent to Iran. We knew the Soviets were on the warpath about the Iranians blowing up their gaslines, and they started moving arms. I saw the photography taken from satellites and airplanes, and you could read the license tag on the Russian trucks. It was that good. Once in a while I hear people say, "Well, we don't know what the Russians are doing." That's pure nonsense; we know.

The President knew the Soviets were moving arms, trucks, tanks, soldiers and needed supplies and were headed south. The question was, what was this activity about? The President was getting advice from Mr. Brzezinski who said that they were headed for the oil fields of Saudi Arabia. Some theorized that they wanted a warm water port. There were others who argued that they were headed for Iran to take those gas fields. Secretary Vance thought the problem was the fundamentalists' dispute in Afghanistan. I never knew who was right, I didn't get into it. What I did know was that the Soviets were on the march.

It was in December of 1979 that the President called the Cabinet together and presented the evidence. There wasn't any question about Soviet movements, but the question remained about their intentions. We couldn't find out, and that bothered me a lot. I thought that with the world's best intelligence gathering capacities we ought to be able to know, but the President honestly didn't know what they were doing and apparently had no way of finding out what their intentions were. Meanwhile, the Soviets kept moving and kept converging. The President's advisers said he had three choices. He could join the issue militarily by moving the fleet with the Marines and the armies into that region to protect our vital interests. The second choice was to do nothing. The third choice was to be ready with economic sanctions. The first and third options were the only ones that had any teeth to them because anything else would simply be to issue pronouncements and dire statements from the White House.

It was hoped that the Russians wouldn't invade anybody. It was reasoned that they might have been on an exercise. I think it was December 26 or so that the Soviets invaded Afghanistan, and the fat was in the fire. What could we do? We had the same three choices: join the issue with them militarily, do nothing and let them have Afghanistan, or impose economic sanctions. President Carter ruled out the first two and told me and the others in the Cabinet to start preparing a list of things that we could do to stop shipments to the Soviet Union. The big thing was grain. Outstanding was four and a half billion dollars in grain that the Russians had bought but which hadn't been delivered. I told the President, "Mr. President, if you embargo this grain there's going to be political pandemonium in Iowa." This was the end of December and the Iowa Democratic precinct caucuses were on the 26th of February. The President rejected our counsel flat out. He said he was not interested in the political implications of his actions. He said it was a very serious matter with the security of the United States at stake and that if it caused him to lose the election, so be it. He approached the situation very philosophically. He didn't allow me or anybody in his Cabinet to bring up the politics of the issues at stake.

We prepared our assessments of what could and couldn't be done and gave him the list. On the fourth of January he announced the embargo, but he instructed me to take the precautions and actions necessary to mitigate the consequences of the embargo, which we did. We went into the market and bought out the grain company's contracts they had with the Soviet Union and sold the grain to Mexico and China. It's true that there was pandemonium for awhile. We closed the markets for three days and when they opened they dropped the daily limits. I went out to Iowa as one of the President's spear carriers in the Democratic caucus fight. People were scared to death in Iowa. The markets were open and dropping daily limits with billions of dollars at stake. My advice was not to sell. That was not the time to sell anything. That was the time to wait. Interestingly, the market bottomed out and started back up, and by April the markets were strong and by the fall they were very strong. We had the biggest export year in history. The President had three choices in that situation, and the people said we made the right choice. Carter beat Kennedy in Iowa rather handily and went on to gain the nomination.

It was April of 1979 that we attempted the helicopter recovery of the hostages in Iran. It was a disastrous affair conducted by the National Security Council group. I was not aware of it, and I didn't expect to be informed. That wasn't my area, so it was no surprise to me that I had been kept outside of it. There were, however, many others in the government that didn't know about it either. That was bad. I received a call at 4:00 a.m. explaining that there had been a terrible accident in the deserts or Iran and that we had lost soldiers. A Cabinet meeting was called for 7:00 a.m. I didn't know what had happened because nothing had been released to the press yet. We were told what had taken place and why it had gone wrong. We were all asked to engage in damage control with our respective constituencies, to inform them what was attempted and what had gone wrong and why.

It devastated the President. I could tell that he hadn't slept and he looked awful. I have never seen a person destroyed, but I have imagined what they must look like and President Carter looked like I imagined they must. He was drained emotionally and he was drained physically. He was a beaten man. It was really from that day hence that he withdrew to the Rose Garden. He wouldn't come out to campaign. He had Mrs. Carter, myself and a couple of others in the Cabinet campaign, but he wouldn't make an appearance. He said, "I can't afford to leave the White House when we've got these terrible problems to deal with." Mrs. Carter and the small group of Cabinet members served as surrogates in the electioneering process and we came out OK as far as the nomination was concerned. Later Mr. Reagan took up the grain embargo issue as a campaign issue. He argued that the embargo hurt our farmers. It was a phony argument. The notion that the embargo was the cause of all our difficulties was just not true.

Mr. Reagan, however, didn't know that. Somebody told him it was true and he liked the idea. Toward the end of the Reagan administration the department issued a new report on the embargo that said the President was wrong. The embargo did not have any impact on the Russians, or anybody else for that matter. Embargoes are very interesting political devices with little or no lasting economic consequences. What happened was that we denied the Russians eleven million tons of grain and they bought it from the Argentines, the Thais and a few other nations. The Argentinians had to cancel the contracts they had made to deliver grain to the Italian, Spanish and Japanese mills, and we received all that business. We supplied the Japanese, Italians and Spanish and the Argentinians supplied the Russians. That's what happened. President Reagan, however, had the grain growers believing that they could have made more money if there had been no embargo. He appealed to their greedy instincts. They liked what he said, and they voted for him in large numbers.

Carter went on to lose for many reasons. It wasn't just the grain embargo issue and it wasn't just the foreign issues. He lost, chiefly, because he was unwilling to play hard-nosed politics. He was unwilling to package things together. He had been advised by his counsellors to leave the hostage crisis alone, but it weighed him down to the point that he was not effective politically and he lost.

QUESTION: Mr. Secretary, would you comment on the Carter transition team? Did you have a role in selecting any members of the transition team? What is your appraisal of their qualifications, particularly in foreign affairs?

SECRETARY BERGLAND: I can't speak to the foreign affairs side because I didn't know those people. I knew about those that were assigned to agriculture. The head person was Stuart Eizenstat and the main person we dealt with was an economist, Lyn Daft, who had been involved in the campaign as an adviser. He was a competent person who was not particularly skilled in politics. He didn't really know a lot of people, but he knew economic theory. He was very good at that and he and I got along fine. After my nomination was imminent I was given a small office at the Department of Agriculture. As soon as my nomination was announced, the first thing I did was call all my living predecessors. I called Orville Freeman and Earl Butz. I couldn't reach Secretary Benson. He was gone, but I called the others and it was a marvelous experience. I remember when I called Orville Freeman, who was the last Democratic secretary, I told him what was about to happen and he thought it was wonderful. I asked, "What's the first thing I should do?" He told me to find Audrey Warren. He said, "She was my secretary and she knows more about running this place than anybody around." I found her and brought her back. It was the best move I ever made. The transition team itself was helpful in that they gave me the names of people that had been involved in the campaign and, in accordance with my understanding with Mr. Carter, I agreed to look them over and interview them and take as many as made sense. They knew about the understanding that the President and I had and they never tried to override it.

We had to find and install people in positions of authority, to develop the budget and to develop new agriculture programs that had to be sent up to the Hill before the first of April. All of this had to be done in a period of ninety days. Impossible. Absolutely impossible. There is no precedent; no one under those circumstances can do an adequate job in that short time frame. But I don't know any way to avoid it unless we hold elections one year ahead of time.

QUESTION: Mr. Secretary, I'd like to come back to your political action committee statement. Senator Robert Byrd talked to me in his leadership office and was bemoaning the fact that he could no longer exercise his authority as majority leader because every Senator was an independent entity. There is no longer any party discipline. Am I correct in observing that the Democratic leadership is going to try to do something about political action committees?

SECRETARY BERGLAND: They are. They are going to try to curb their influence and the abuse that arises from them. It's a corrupting process.

COMMENT: As a quick observation, I believe they have caused a deterioration in our right to representation in a democracy. I'll be delighted if you can change it.

SECRETARY BERGLAND: I don't know if it can be changed because there are so many people like me around that don't want it changed. There are thirty-seven hundred PAC administrators around the country that are gathering and distributing money. It's big business. It's millions and millions of dollars annually. I run it hard, I run it clean and we raise a lot of money. We are as good as they come. But it's an awful thing we're doing with PACs. It will change, however. I think there will be limits imposed on PAC activities.

QUESTION: I wonder if, in your conversations with the President before you took office or soon afterwards, there was any discussion about your access to him, and about what he expected you to do, or what his charter was for you, if there was such a thing?

SECRETARY BERGLAND: Well, there were a couple of general conversations. He stated early in the formation of his new administration that he was going to use Cabinet government, and he kept his word. We had Cabinet meetings every Monday at 9:00 a.m. Anybody who came three minutes late was not allowed in the room without notice. The meetings would run until 11:00 or so. Some of them were tedious, but most of them were interesting. Some were tedious in that sometimes there were people who would just prattle on, and they didn't have any sense of propriety, proportion or balance. They would take up the Cabinet's time with nonsense. Most of the time, however, it was worthwhile because it allowed a person like me to sit in and listen to a serious discussion between the secretary of defense and the secretary of state, for example, so that I could figure out what was happening. Thus I knew how I could help the President. In that setting, the Cabinet process was very useful. There were many times when I had a problem that required coordination, and I would be able to raise it with the President, and in front of my colleagues. He made this system work, and he used the Cabinet as a discipline. Any time I needed to talk to him I could. He made that clear and he kept his word.

QUESTION: You never felt you were blocked by staff?

SECRETARY BERGLAND: Never. The staff would put their impressions on top of mine if I'd send in papers on a policy issue that was in dispute or under consideration, but I was never censored or blocked. I had direct telephone access to the President in his Oval Office. I didn't come through the White House switchboard. I came through the secretary who sat just outside the Oval Office. If the President was busy, he would always call me back. He was always good about that sort of thing.

QUESTION: You described the President as unwilling to hear an argument in the Cabinet or elsewhere and that he wanted things in writing. Would you describe further his decision-making process after he got the data in writing and had conflicting views? How did he go about making a decision or did he not make decisions?

SECRETARY BERGLAND: He did make decisions. He did not procrastinate, but he wanted to see all the evidence. My colleagues over in the Defense Department, where things are incredibly complicated and with problems much more intense, were absolutely flabbergasted. Harold Brown, the secretary of defense, was telling me one time that there was some national defense issue with documentation that went into hundreds of pages and the President read it all and wanted more. He had gone through the documents and he understood the issue. He was a scholar and a student. He'd make the decision and he'd do it on the basis of what he thought was required as a consequence of presented facts. He didn't care about people's opinions. He wanted to know what the facts were and he wanted to see the hard data. He'd make a choice and, of course, like any president he expected compliance.

He was tougher on compliance than Mr. Reagan. Mr. Reagan allowed an awful lot of internal disorder to go on. I can't quite understand how it can run that way, because Mr. Carter would never allow that. He terminated the services of Joe Califano, for example, for that very reason. Joe kept trying to pull end runs on him after a decision was made. Joe would say, "Well, I'm going to try to politic him on the Hill." Finally, circumstances caught up with Mr. Califano and Carter sacked him. That was it. There was no second chance. You either go along or get out. He made that clear early on. There would be no room for disagreement once a choice was made. He demanded complete and total loyalty to that principle.

QUESTION: I'm curious to know what the reaction was to Mrs. Carter sitting in on the Cabinet meetings.

SECRETARY BERGLAND: It was generally frowned upon. Generally, people thought that they were sort of being snooped on. I think that was the general impression. I was a little uncomfortable and I can't tell you why. I knew that she was sizing me up and there was just something about it that was a little bit difficult. I never had any trouble with Mrs. Carter or the President, as a matter of fact. He and I always got along. We reconciled our differences and I respected his authority. He and I never had any bad words of any consequence because I was very careful about public money and tried to be a straight arrow. In contrast to the Reagan people who are amateurs of the worst sort, he was tough on spending. They haven't the foggiest notion about what money's worth. Jimmy Carter grew up in a home in which money was scarce. All his life he lived in an environment in which money was scarce and, therefore, valuable. He brought that ethos with him to the White House. His budgets were tightly drawn. I grew up in the same kind of house, so I knew where he was coming from when he talked about no waste. I never had any specific reason to be uncomfortable when Mrs. Carter was in the room and we were in the midst of some very heavy discussion, but some of my colleagues rather resented it.

NARRATOR: This is a Center devoted to the study of governance and politics. We were told we would learn a good deal from the secretary of agriculture about both of those dimensions. I don't believe we thought we would learn quite as much as we have. This certainly has been one of the most instructive discussions, Mr. Secretary, we have had and we thank you very much.

SECRETARY BERGLAND: Thank you very much.

PART FOUR:

THE CARTER FOREIGN POLICY

CHAPTER 8

CARTER'S FOREIGN POLICY:
THE SOURCE OF THE PROBLEM

SECRETARY OF STATE CYRUS VANCE

NARRATOR: We are very grateful, Secretary Vance, that you would talk to us about the Carter presidency. Cyrus Vance served as secretary of state in the Carter administration, but earlier had been secretary of the army in the Kennedy administration and deputy secretary of defense in the Johnson administration. He had undertaken a succession of crucial diplomatic assignments including that of special representative of the President in Cyprus and Korea, and U.S. negotiator at the Paris Peace Conference on Vietnam. He became secretary of state in the Carter administration in 1977 and resigned in 1980. Vance is a highly respected international lawyer. In his oral history he responds to questions concerning Mr. Carter and the Carter administration. With everybody who has participated, we have begun our discussion by asking when and how the association with President Carter began. What were your first impressions of him? Did your impressions change, and if they did, how and why did they change?

SECRETARY VANCE: My recollection is that I first met President Carter two or three years before the election and that we met at a conference which was being held in Atlanta by the American Red Cross. At that point I was vice chairman of the American Red Cross. We were introduced at that time and had a chance to chat very briefly. I believe I saw him on one other occasion, again, before he threw his hat into the presidential race, and that also was a very short visit. It wasn't until the presidential race began that I really began to know him.

At the beginning of that race, Sargent Shriver had asked me if I would help him in running his campaign. Sarge, in the early days of the presidential race, had aspirations himself, and as an old friend I said that I would be happy to try to help him, that I had no real experience but I'd try to help him. And so I did, and Sarge jumped in. It was hard going for Sarge, and it did not go well. During those first few months—and this was a year or so before the election was to be held—I received a call from either Richard Holbrooke or Richard Gardner asking whether or not I would be willing to help President Carter. I told him at that time, as I think I indicated in *Hard Choices*, that I was committed to Sarge and that as long as Sarge stayed in the race, I was for Sarge and would do everything I could for him but that if something should change in the future, I'd certainly be willing to reconsider the matter. I think the rest of it I did set out in *Hard Choices*, that Sarge did drop out of the race, and at that point when somebody came back to me from the Carter campaign, I said that I would be happy to help in any way I could. From then on I did help as one of many advisers during the campaign season.

QUESTION: Didn't you prepare a foreign policy statement even before he asked you to be secretary of state?

SECRETARY VANCE: I did in October of election year. I think it was about four weeks before Election Day. The President asked three or four of us if we would prepare a white paper which would lay out what we saw the foreign policy issues of the next four years to be, and to give our recommendations as to what a Carter foreign policy would look like. It would cover not only the substantive aspects of that foreign policy, but the organization of the State Department, the kinds of people that should be included, including, as I recall it, some names; and also a discussion of the budget and how the budget should be constructed. I did put together such a paper, as did George Ball and Zbig Brzezinski—there may have been one other, but if there was I don't remember—and we sent those on down to Carter towards the end of October. I subsequently used that as a sort of basic outline for what I thought the Carter foreign policy should be, and did use it in the State Department as a sort of yardstick against which I measured progress or lack thereof.

QUESTION: The relationship actually must have been fairly close between this document and the priorities that you worked out, where you established priorities for the first year and priorities for the second year?

SECRETARY VANCE: Yes, I did that. One of the things I recommended was that each year we ought to update our priorities and see whether they still stood, and if not to change those priorities and to have the assistant secretaries who had responsibility in those functional and regional areas to do this at the beginning of each year. I would then try to sit down quarterly to see how we were measuring up and dealing with these issues and priorities. I felt it was a very good way to proceed, to force myself and the assistant secretaries into the discipline of staying on top of the issues on a regular basis, yet not losing touch with what the end objectives were. I found it was so easy to get consumed by the present and the day-to-day issues that were coming across one's desk, and to lose sight of what the objectives were down at the end of the road. This was a sort of device for trying to make sure you did both.

QUESTION: Such documents certainly combine the immediate and the broader objectives, such as strengthening NATO, moving toward a second SALT agreement, restoring momentum to the Middle East and Panama negotiations, and so on, for the first year. I wonder, when you were called to Plains, and you and President Carter and Amy had the happy evening together before you put her to bed, did the question of priorities ever come up? Was that something that interested the President?

SECRETARY VANCE: Yes, we did talk about that. I remember that one of the priorities that perhaps would have been questioned by some people was putting Panama right up there at the head of the list. Both the President and I felt that this was a long-festering problem, some thirteen years of discussions which had affected the Panama Canal. It was a very important facility for us and for the world's trade. In addition, if we were able to pull it off, it would indicate the importance which we attached to Third World issues which both of us felt had been badly ignored by the Nixon and Ford administrations. Therefore, we could do two things at the same time: one, hopefully deal with the negotiation of a treaty which would solidify our position with respect to the Canal and to stability in Panama, and, at the same time, convey to the developing world the fact that we placed very high on our agenda dealing with Third World issues which we felt had been ignored in the past. So Panama was raised to the level of one of the top three or four issues, along with SALT negotiations, relations with NATO, and the Middle East, for example, as priority issues which had to be dealt with right away.

We were discussing that kind of thing as early as that first night when I was in Plains for, I guess, my "test" as to whether I would or would not be offered the position of secretary of state.

QUESTION: You found nothing in the President's mentality that made thinking in terms of priorities a problem? James Fallows put forth the notion that one of the President's weaknesses was that he thought in terms of laundry lists on a great many issues and checked them off as he went along, but that he didn't have a clear sense of priorities. You're saying that tendency didn't manifest itself in those early conversations.

SECRETARY VANCE: No, it did not. This question of whether there were too many issues on the list of priorities and, therefore, that it wasn't really a list of priorities, was an issue that was raised by many of the correspondents from time to time. There was something to that argument, but I think it was blown out of all proportion.

It is true that the President saw many, many pressing problems, and sometimes, perhaps, he got too involved in the detail of the individual problems, with the result that not enough attention was directed to the forest rather than to the trees. But by and large I would say that he had a good sense of what the key issues were and where the principal attention ought to be lodged.

QUESTION: The problems which seemed to come up later, of which one finds evidence in your book, Brzezinski's book, and other books, namely, the relation to SALT II to other foreign policy problems like human rights and China, wasn't anything that you were apprehensive about at this early point?

SECRETARY VANCE: Not in the early context, no. As time went on, I did get concerned about it because I saw potential conflicts arising between the timing of China negotiations and the SALT negotiations.

QUESTION: In general, then, what were your first impressions of Carter?

SECRETARY VANCE: My first impression was that here is a man that I liked, a man that I could do business with, and a man whom I would like to work for. I felt all the way through that my assessment was basically sound, a view which in hindsight I still hold.

QUESTION: Regardless of anything that happened?

SECRETARY VANCE: Yes.

QUESTION: Another issue that we talked about is the question of Carter's style of leadership. Some people talk about him as primarily an issue-oriented President. Some critics say that Carter separated the requirements of politics from the requirements of governing. Other people emphasized his obsession with details. But if one had to describe in the simplest terms what distinguished Carter's style of leadership, what would you say?

SECRETARY VANCE: His style of leadership was one in which he had decided that he was going to try and know as much about each one of the problems as any of those who were charged with the principal responsibility for managing the various issues. That was a Herculean task, and I think that as a result of setting that kind of a standard for himself, he made it very difficult at times to manage the variety of problems that were pressing in upon him. That, I think, is the criticism that Fallows and some of the others have talked about.

He was a prodigious worker, would work late into the night, get up at five o'clock in the morning, and would be back at work again. You never had to worry about the fact that your President wasn't going to be on top of all of the facts with respect to particular issues with which you were involved. But from time to time the fact that he was dealing with so many problems—both domestic and foreign—did make it difficult to get him to focus on some of the broader aspects of the problem in a way that a Cabinet officer who was charged with responsibility in that area would like them to have been dealt with. On the whole, he was a very good leader to work for and certainly a very bright and thoughtful individual. I think of all the presidents I've worked with—and I've worked with many—in terms of sheer intellect, he had more brain power than any of them.

QUESTION: If you had to mention a single weakness, whether it flows from a strength or is independent of a strength, what would it be?

SECRETARY VANCE: I would cite two. First, he had a tendency of becoming too involved with details, and therefore, losing sight from time to time of the forest for the trees. That wasn't always true, but it happened from time to time.

Secondly, he was hindered, not only by a lack of knowledge of the Washington scene and the Congress, but by almost a contempt for the Congress which the members of Congress felt and which made it difficult to carry through difficult political issues where you needed the Congress's help if you were ever going to get your programs put into effect. I think those were probably the two biggest problems that he had.

QUESTION: Did he get as much help from the White House staff as other presidents have received in dealing with Congress?

SECRETARY VANCE: No, I don't think he did. I don't think his staff really recognized the importance of that in the way that the Larry O'Briens and the like did for Jack Kennedy. On the other hand, Jack Kennedy was a creature of the Congress, and he knew the importance of having the Congress with you if you were going to carry through your programs. He picked people around him who had that kind of know-how.

My own view is that if you had the Lloyd Cutlers and the Hedley Donovans there in the earlier stages, many of these things would not have taken place, because those right at his elbow in the White House would have been guiding him and protecting him against some of the pitfalls; as people who had lived and worked in Washington, they knew it from top to bottom and knew the importance of dealing with and cultivating the leaders of the Congress, and sharing concerns with them and seeking their advice. There is an awful lot of good advice that one can get from the Hill, that unless you have been a part of it yourself, you don't know and you therefore not only make it more difficult to keep your objectives but you may lose some good, wise advice that you could otherwise get.

QUESTION: Did President Carter's attitude toward Congress make your own foreign policy dealings with Congress more difficult?

SECRETARY VANCE: Yes.

QUESTION: More generally speaking, did he use his White House staff in the way that you think a president should?

SECRETARY VANCE: No, I think he should have involved himself much more with the Congress than he did, and he should have used his White House staff more effectively in dealing with the Congress. The master at this, in my judgment, was Lyndon Johnson; he was superb.

I can remember night after night when President Johnson would have the key people on a particular issue over at the White House. He would sit them down, eat with them, drink with them, talk with them—from time to time he'd make sure their wives were there as well—and thus a relationship was developed that was invaluable to him. Therefore, his intelligence about what was going on in the world, and how to move them in the direction which he wanted them to go, was like day and night when compared with what President Carter was able to achieve.

QUESTION: How would you describe your own relations with Carter?

SECRETARY VANCE: My relationship with him, I thought, was very good. I believe that I was as close to him as anybody in the Cabinet, and perhaps more so than almost anyone. I liked him as a person; I liked working with him; and therefore I have no complaints whatsoever with that relationship.

I do have complaints about the way in which the White House system was designed and how the role of the National Security Adviser was defined, both of which were less than satisfactory. I do not feel that the President adequately enforced what I think is essential in dealing with foreign affairs and national security issues—namely, to tell the principal players in the White House and in the departments that he expected them to work together in a collegial fashion to advance the best interests of the country and those of the President. He did not tell them that he did not want them going out and building empires for themselves, because if they were going to do that, they had better get themselves a job elsewhere. He did not say that if he caught any of the people doing that, he was going to fire either one or both of them as, for example, if there was such an incident involving the secretary of state and national security adviser. He did not enforce sufficiently that kind of a tough policy with respect to the principal players who were his senior advisers.

COMMENT: In a sense, there is a third weakness, making statements in public. He didn't demand of his staff what Franklin Roosevelt did. Jim Rowe told story after story about Roosevelt knocking somebody down after they had talked in public without explicit authorization and in seeming derogation of policy on which a consensus existed.

SECRETARY VANCE: I think that's true. You have to do that, in my judgment, if you are going to be an effective president and have a staff doing the president's business in the most practical way.

QUESTION: Did he know Stu Eizenstat personally before he chose him as domestic policy head?

SECRETARY VANCE: I believe he did. How well I don't know.

COMMENT: He wasn't quite in the category that the Georgians were.

SECRETARY VANCE: No, I think his closest advisers clearly were between Jody Powell and Ham Jordan.

QUESTION: It seemed to work with Stu Eizenstat—and the books that have come out emphasize this—and he played the role of brokering and coordinating differing viewpoints. It didn't work in the foreign policy area. I wonder if Carter didn't know what a lot of us knew about some of you who became the key players in foreign policy? Was there a gap there? Maybe that's something you don't want to get into.

SECRETARY VANCE: Well, I really didn't want to go into it. I think that probably ought to come from others. It was an unsatisfactory relationship between myself and the national security adviser on a number of things—not all of them—but particularly on U.S.-Soviet matters. I think it hurt the President.

COMMENT: It has come up in every one of the sessions we've had, and one of the things that has puzzled so many people is that those who knew the persons involved predicted it from the beginning. We've been puzzled why those of you who were there didn't expect problems from the beginning.

SECRETARY VANCE: I really did not know Zbig that well. He would not have been and was not my first choice, but he was clearly the President's first choice. I felt that I did not know Zbig sufficiently well to be able to say to him, "This obviously cannot work." The President obviously has a right to choose whomever he would like to have around him. Not having that depth of knowledge, I did not feel that I ought to say that this was not agreeable or satisfactory. That was a mistake.

QUESTION: Well, you never know how a given person in a particular situation will react. Some of us remember Zbig pulling out letters at the Council on Foreign Relations and saying, "Look what I've managed to get from Henry Kissinger, an admission that he hasn't done this right; I would have done it this way." Knowing the sense of rivalry he exhibited toward others, we weren't surprised by what followed.

How did he use the Cabinet and how did President Carter deal with Cabinet members? Brzezinski is pretty scornful about the Cabinet meetings.

Carter's Foreign Policy: The Source of the Problem 143

SECRETARY VANCE: Well, the Cabinet as an institution was really not effective, because discussions often took the form of a rather routine kind of exercise when one went to a Cabinet meeting. I don't think that the best was gotten out of this body of very intelligent individuals. The President worked much better in dealing one on one with individuals than in using the Cabinet as an institution. I think that's often true, not just of President Carter. The Cabinet can be a marvelous sounding board, because you have people from different parts of the country with different backgrounds and different experiences. A lot of the problems you are dealing with are basically domestic problems at heart, and you have wisdom and experience represented in Cabinet members, whether you consider foreign affairs issues, national security issues, or straight domestic issues. This is something that a president ought to know how to do and ought to use or learn how to use. He didn't have that.

QUESTION: Would he make presentations to the Cabinet?

SECRETARY VANCE: From time to time, yes.

COMMENT: But not consistently.

SECRETARY VANCE: I don't think the Cabinet meetings were sufficiently well organized.

QUESTION: Did you feel that the White House worked well, by and large, in its relationships with the Cabinet secretaries, the departments, and the agencies? Was there good coordination between people such as Hamilton Jordan and the Cabinet heads?

SECRETARY VANCE: I really had very little to do with Ham in the government, until we got involved into things like Iran, and then we worked very closely with Ham and I found it very satisfactory working with him. He was very helpful in our attempts to free the hostages and those kinds of things in the latter part of the administration. But although Ham sat in on the weekly breakfasts, I really did not have much day-to-day contact with Ham Jordan.

COMMENT: The complaint that one or two of your colleagues in the Cabinet has made is that too many responsibilities were assumed by the White House and that if you had 40,000 people covering an area like commerce or foreign policy in a large department, they thought that the department could have done that job better than the White House.

SECRETARY VANCE: I agree, and what's more you have an institutional memory in an organization like the State Department that you don't have in the White House, and you lose a lot by not using that to the utmost. I understand the argument that presidents make that it gets too cumbersome and that you don't get your answers quick enough. I don't think that's necessarily true, nor do I think it is something that if true you can't get around.

COMMENT: Even John F. Kennedy held that view.

SECRETARY VANCE: He did, very much so, and I think Bush is apparently developing that view now in saying, "I can't get the quick answers I need," at least at the Kennebunkport meeting at which he made the breakthrough and came up with what seemed a sensible approach.

NARRATOR: Thank you for a most informative discussion.

CHAPTER 9

CARTER'S FOREIGN POLICY:
SUCCESS ABROAD, FAILURE AT HOME

DIRECTOR OF THE POLICY PLANNING STAFF
ANTHONY LAKE

NARRATOR: Tony Lake is representative of a small group of extraordinarily able younger men and women whom Secretary Vance brought into the State Department. He had worked in Senator Muskie's campaign for the presidency in 1968. He had previous government experience and was known for the clarity of his writing and thinking. Following his service in the Carter administration, he became a professor of international relations at Mount Holyoke College.

QUESTION: One question we've asked everyone is how and when did your association with President Carter begin? What were your first impressions of him, both as a man and as a political leader? Did your impressions change over time or not?

MR. LAKE: I first met him when I was invited down to Plains during the shuttles that they were running for various people to go and discuss various issues with him at the Pond House. I was one of a group of ten discussing general foreign policy. I was very impressed. On the way to Plains, I really hadn't known what to expect. He was, of course, running a campaign that was almost as popular in what it *wasn't* doing as much as in what it *was*—which is to say he was not running on charisma so much as catching an anti-government wave in public opinion. So people didn't really know him terribly well, especially in the early stages of the campaign. On meeting him, I was extremely impressed with his intelligence, and with his undoctrinaire approach. He asked very probing questions about the various issues we discussed. What especially impressed me was that after the three-hour session was over, when he went out to talk about the session with the press, he had mastered the issues in an extraordinary way. His comments not only showed that he knew facts, but understood the nuances of the issues. And of course that stood him in very good stead later, in the debates with President Ford, especially on Eastern Europe. I was very impressed.

NARRATOR: Did that impression that you had at the first meeting persist over time?

MR. LAKE: It did. But that same strength that I noted at that meeting, of course, later became in other contexts a weakness. The same grasp of details led him, sometimes, away from keeping track of a general strategy.

NARRATOR: How would you describe Carter's style of leadership in terms of its being a mixture of strengths and weaknesses?

MR. LAKE: I'm sure a lot of people you have talked with have related this to leadership of the nation as a whole. Let me address something else. One thing that has always struck me about the bureaucracy in which I worked under various presidents is that they can't lead it by ordering it around or even through fear, so much as by treating it like any other political constituency—by capturing its loyalty and imagination. I think he was very good at that in the beginning, largely again because he was very interested in the issues and had very clear, attractive moral values. But I don't think he was successful, as time went by, in gaining personal loyalty in the bureaucracy; he never really reached out to it, less than he reached out to the Congress. That was a shame, because I think he could have, and he might have had a more successful presidency, one his personal qualities or high intelligence and moral purpose could have produced.

NARRATOR: Would you think that was due to his lack of experience in Washington, or was it inherent in his style and his attitude toward the bureaucracy?

MR. LAKE: I think there were probably three reasons. First, he did come to Washington running against Washington, as an "anti-president" in a sense. I admired all of his symbolic gestures of being a "republican" president, trying to correct the perception of the presidency as having become "imperial." But sadly, he did lose something symbolically when he set out to diminish the trappings of the office. It diminished his own personal standing with some of the bureaucracy as well as the public. I still admire the way he saw the role, but it had real costs.

The second part of it was what he had experienced in Georgia. The style of governing that had worked there was unsuccessful in Washington.

And third, Washington hates it when presidents don't treat it with the respect it *believes* it deserves.

NARRATOR: Do you think it hurt him more than it hurt Reagan, because Reagan didn't show Washington a lot of respect, did he?

MR. LAKE: But Reagan built up the office in a way that Carter didn't, and he seemed to love being President in a way that Carter didn't. Reagan attacked Washington when he was out in the country, but within Washington he made sure he talked to all the right people and stroked the right folks in a way that Carter absolutely refused to do. So while giving the impression to the rest of the country that he was antigovernment, Reagan made Washington purr in the way he acted there, and the way he treated the presidency.

And there was a question of personality. Carter was and is highly admirable, but he was a very private, public man. He did not convey his personal qualities with the kind of warmth that can inspire a bureaucracy or the Congress.

NARRATOR: Several people have said that they would work with him and he would be reasonably outgoing, but the next time they saw him he not only did not remember their names but didn't seem to remember their faces in a fairly recent relationship with him. Did that happen to any of you in the foreign policy sector?

MR. LAKE: No. What did happen, and it was very unfortunate—it happened in other administrations also—was a growing sense of mistrust of the State Department by the President, a mistrust possibly even encouraged by some of those closest to him.

NARRATOR: Kennedy of course had that, but would you say it was worse for Carter and was accentuated by people close to him in the White House?

MR. LAKE: Yes, I think so. There is always that rivalry. It was the worst I've ever seen under Nixon, but it got to be bad under Carter. There was a famous meeting he held with all the assistant secretaries of the State Department.

148   *Director of the Policy Planning Staff Anthony Lake*

There had been a leak on Iran early in 1979, and he was furious and called in all of the assistant secretaries in the State Department. He had us all sit around the Cabinet table, and then stalked in and berated us for a lack of loyalty, for a catalogue of sins, and then walked out. He obviously was furious. But he was attacking exactly those people who were his natural constituency in the State Department.

NARRATOR: Do you think the fact that the NSC, and particularly Sam Huntington and Brzezinski, were said to be leaking to figures like Senator Moynihan as well as leaking to the press, led to the opposing criticism that the State Department was doing its own leaking? Carter must have heard this numerous times during the day. Brzezinski says in his memoirs that he never once complained to the President about what the State Department was doing, as I remember it, but he charged that Vance frequently complained to the President. Vance engaged in defense of the State Department and sought to protect it.

It sounds as though this is a little different than some previous administrations, where Kennedy and others came in distrustful of the State Department and it remained that way. With Carter, the relationship appeared early and then intensified.

MR. LAKE: I think there are a number of reasons for that.

NARRATOR: It would be interesting to hear you talk about them.

MR. LAKE: The press itself was one factor. I don't want to start with the press, because everyone always blames them for everything, and that's wrong. Nothing in the Constitution says that officials have to wash dirty linen in view of reporters.

I think part of the problem was the NSC system itself, which was unusual in the Carter administration. What they designed was in essence two central committees below the NSC itself. One was the policy review group or PRG, which was supposed to manage policy decisions and planning on general foreign policy issues. The other was the security group, the SCC, which was to deal with crises, and security or intelligence issues. The policy review group was to be chaired by a Cabinet officer. *Which* Cabinet officer chaired it, and therefore which department would prepare the basic paper to be discussed at the meeting, depended on the issue. That was a natural invitation to constant struggle among the various departments as to who would chair which issue. More important was the question of whether something was a crisis—in which case it would go into the SCC, chaired by Brzezinski—or a general policy question, which meant it went to a group that would be chaired usually by Vance and the State Department. This also became a constant source of struggle, because it matters who chairs discussion of an issue and it matters who writes the paper.

Thus one of the sources of conflict was a flexible system that depended on collegiality, if it was to work smoothly. It had the effect of undercutting collegiality, as people competed in the weekly struggles to decide which agency would take the lead of which meeting. I think in retrospect it would have been better to have had a clear structure in which issues always went to one committee or the other and the system decided it rather than the people.

A second reason why relations between State and the NSC worsened were simply historical. The competition had been getting worse over the last ten or twenty years; people assumed, based on previous experience, that those conflicts were going to take place. Almost from the start, everyone started looking for evidence that "they"—whether "they" were the State Department or "they" were the NSC staff—were launching some sort of bureaucratic offensive.

I remember that on the first day, when we on the transition team in the State Department came back to our offices from the Inaugural, we received a description of the new NSC system from the White House. A number of us were irritated that there hadn't been more consultation as to what that system would be at the start, and we were worried about these competitive aspects. We all met with Vance and said that we thought this was a bad start, that there should have been more consultation, and that we should pursue the issue. Vance got very angry. It was perhaps the angriest I saw him in the four years. He said he was not going to have this kind of behavior, that it had shattered other administrations, and that we should absolutely not pursue the issue.

That raises the next reason, the press. I can remember that in the first few months of the administration a number of reporters came into my office saying—and this was before the competition had really gotten very intense or very nasty—that their editors had told them to write stories about the "Vance-Brzezinski rivalry." This was at a point in time when Vance felt no rivalry, and most of us didn't either.

NARRATOR: This happened very early in the process.

MR. LAKE: Very early. What I found happening fairly often thereafter was reporters coming to us in the State Department, saying, "Did you know that over at the NSC staff they are saying that this successful policy was really the child of the NSC staff and that the State Department opposed it [or that a failure was the child of the State Department and the NSC staff had opposed it]? Would you comment?" You either had to sit there saying, "I'm not going to get into that kind of stuff," or you had to defend your own institution.

David Aaron at the NSC and I used to get together from time to time to try to track these things down, and sometimes we would call in reporters to meet with both of us. We would put our arms around each other, grin at the reporter, and say, "Look, we both work for this administration, we agree on the issue you are writing about." But more often than not there were a few on the NSC staff and a few in the State Department who could not resist doing what they thought was defending themselves against what the reporters said were the allegations from the other side. I don't think the reporters were absolutely making it up, but it becomes a chicken and an egg thing, and once it all starts there is no end to it.

NARRATOR: Is there a fourth factor? Is there something in the relationship between the two principals that in hindsight people should have seen? In the interviews we've had, Vance says that he recommended Brzezinski but he didn't really know him all that well, and that he didn't anticipate some of the things that came up. Brzezinski says that Vance probably was a good administrator and he recommended him, but he was not much of a conceptualizer and moreover he underestimated the struggle between the Soviet Union and the United States and overestimated the role of the United Nations and the importance of the Third World.

MR. LAKE: Certainly, Vance's very clear concepts were simply different from Brzezinski's. The latter was more concerned with the Soviet Union as a global threat, Vance more with resolving regional issues and negotiating SALT II. That certainly would be a fourth factor: there were substantive differences. On the other hand—and of this I absolutely am sure—for at least two years, if not more, Vance simply refused to take such arguments into the realm of bureaucratic backstabbing.

NARRATOR: Even though he was as much or more experienced than Brzezinski was with the workings of the bureaucracy?

MR. LAKE: Yes. In one way I admired Vance for it, because he was right; the growing public perception of divisions did hurt everyone in the administration more than they helped any individual official. Vance knew this and was very gentlemanly about it all. A number of his subordinates became very frustrated that he wasn't fighting back more. In the third and fourth years, he did fight back, mostly by way of the President. But Vance always refused absolutely to be critical of Brzezinski, either with reporters or with his own colleagues. I still admire the way he behaved.

NARRATOR: There is a fifth element that we've all puzzled about. Carter seems to say that these interpretations of the institutional or particularly the personal rivalries are a tempest in a teapot and that he self-consciously used the two men and the two organizations for the extension and projection of his own policies. Vance was not very interested in being a public spokesman on policy, whereas Brzezinski was always willing to do that, and Brzezinski never undertook this role without consultation with Carter. Despite all the criticism, Carter felt this was a good thing for his administration. How do you assess that?

MR. LAKE: Well, I disagree. Having two rather conflicting *public* spokesmen on these issues hurt us. Certainly it was true that Vance was uncomfortable with public relations exercises because it might look like personal self-promotion, and that was absolutely abhorrent to him. In Washington as it is, this did limit his strength as a secretary of state. So some missed how strong he was in promoting his views within the government and as a negotiator.

NARRATOR: Camp David.

MR. LAKE: Yes, on the Middle East and other issues, he was very good at making decisions, had wonderful judgment, was very pragmatic as well as principled. But he was limited in his willingness to push things publicly. That's true. I don't think, however, that the system can work when the national security adviser then becomes too public himself. Brzezinski certainly liked doing that, and he was quite good at it. I think Carter perceived rightly that he needed a spokesman out there. The problem was that the more Brzezinski did it, the more an impression was created of more than one voice speaking for the administration. That hurt the administration more than it helped it.

The answer would have been a much clearer definition as to what the respective roles of the secretary of state and the national security adviser were. In a nutshell, the national security adviser is the coordinator of policy. Only the NSC can do that. The secretary of state has to be the negotiator and public spokesman. I think Carter should have gotten Vance to do more public relations.

NARRATOR: He admits that he should have done more.

MR. LAKE: That would have been the answer, rather than letting the two voices start contending.

I also think there was a problem politically, in that the White House sometimes hyped the Soviet threat more than claiming the credit we all deserved for meeting it—for example, instead of emphasizing our role in helping meet the Shaba crisis in Zaire, we got bogged down by our claims that the Cubans were behind it all when we couldn't prove it. Later, in 1979, promoting a sense of crisis that helped produce a *Time* magazine cover of a huge bear about to devour the Middle East did nothing to encourage the belief among the American public that the administration was dealing successfully with American foreign policy challenges.

NARRATOR: Is this the key to the difficulty?

MR. LAKE: Another example: in 1978, when the Ethiopians were driving the Somaliis back out of the Ogaden, we went to the Russians and gained their assurances that the Ethiopians would not cross over into Somalia. And they did not do that. Instead of claiming credit for a success, the NSC continued to emphasize the role of the Cubans and the Soviets in the region and the threat this posed to U.S.-Soviet programs on arms control. Certainly, we wanted to continue to work for a reduced Soviet and Cuban presence. But why focus the public more on the threat than on our actions to counteract it?

NARRATOR: Is this the key to the difference between the Carter administration and, for instance, the Bush administration? Nobody seems very excited that Brent Scowcroft is a public spokesman and often speaks on these issues. But he never seems to be advancing an independent view, does he?

MR. LAKE: Or implicitly attacking anybody else. I think that during the Ford administration, he played the role of national security assistant better than any we've had in the last twenty years.

NARRATOR: Could you say a little bit more in terms of policy about Carter's role in one or two specific foreign policy areas? The Carter administration, despite all its woes, has quite an agenda of achievements in the Panama Canal, China, Camp David, the environment, human rights, etc.

MR. LAKE: I hope that what the historians will say is that his foreign policy was a tremendous, substantive success even while it failed politically at home. Maybe we should talk about that.

I can't think of another administration since Truman's, and perhaps 1972 with Nixon-Kissinger, that produced so much diplomatically (often building on things that Nixon and Ford had accomplished) in negotiating the Salt II Treaty, in the normalization of relations with China; at Camp David, in the Panama Canal Treaty; and in Zimbabwe, where we helped keep the process alive until the British with our help finally solved it. We also had successes on the environment and in the human rights policy, which constituted a number of specific successes that we didn't want to talk about because they would have discouraged other successes. We also succeeded in encouraging people in the Third World, both leaders and the people, to have a new kind of confidence in the United States. This was important to our interests as well as our ideals. For example, I have no doubt that our position on human rights in South Africa encouraged African leaders to cooperate with us in specific diplomacy regarding Zimbabwe.

NARRATOR: What was Carter's role in all of this? Was it primarily Vance and the State Department that moved these things ahead and that had a vision, or was it Carter's vision? And was it Carter's negotiating skill and his diplomacy generally?

MR. LAKE: I think both. On those issues, Carter and Vance were very close and worked very closely together. Vance had Carter's confidence, and on some of them it was very much Vance. For example, the Panama Canal Treaties involved Vance or a number of his lieutenants, always working of course with the NSC staff and the President, who took a close interest. On Camp David it was very much Carter, although Vance was very much involved. China was more Zbig.

NARRATOR: Partly because Vance was busy with other things?

MR. LAKE: Yes, because during that period Vance was very busy with the SALT II negotiations, on which Vance did most of the negotiating. Zimbabwe was Vance mostly, but again working very closely with Carter, who took a very useful interest.

Carter took as detailed an interest in all these things as any President has. Vance was a very good negotiator. Correct me if

I'm wrong, but I can't think of another diplomatic creative burst like that since the late 1940s.

NARRATOR: No, I can't either.

MR. LAKE: They all served American national interests.

NARRATOR: Do you think these achievements are achievements which at the time they occurred had an enormous importance for peace and world order? Or do you think they were achievements whose full impact will be seen ten or twenty years from now when we look back and say, that Carter's vision of the future turned out to be prophetic?

MR. LAKE: I think both, depending on the issues. Some of them are achievements because of what we *don't* read about. God only knows that would have happened with Noriega, for example, in Panama had there not been the treaties. Without the treaties, Noriega would have had a nationalistic issue to seize on with his public, to create even more chaos. It would be very damaging to our interests.

In Zimbabwe it is hardly a perfect situation, but there is no conflict making headlines. Perhaps most importantly, the security of Israel, because of the disengagement with the Egyptians, was enormously enhanced. A part of the achievement of Camp David was in defusing a conflict in the Sinai that might have happened. In all these cases, it is fair to say that there are people alive today who wouldn't be, even if we don't know who they are.

On the longer term implications, there was a vision of peace and human rights that President Carter held which was diminished for some years, but may be coming back now. I wish we had created more of a popular base for it through a stronger public appeal during the Carter years.

NARRATOR: In your book, you, Mac Destler and Les Gelb talk about substance, but you also talk about procedures and methods. To what extent did the procedures and methods make possible these successes? To what extent were the successes achieved in spite of the methods and procedures?

MR. LAKE: As we discussed before, the NSC procedures and the committee structures were not a success. They relied on a collegiality that was eroding, and they should have been more clear from the start. I think the successes, as we get back to why Carter's foreign policies could succeed abroad and fail at home, came in large part because of a pragmatic approach to issues.

There was an effort to take each issue as it came and try to resolve it. This approach fit both Carter's and Vance's outlook on the world, which meant that they concentrated on one negotiation and the next negotiation as it unfolded. All that led to practical success. The problem was that such an approach did not translate into clear, coherent, ideological pronouncements that easily translated into public support. This is generally a dilemma in American foreign policy: the simpler the formulation, the better it is politically at home, and probably the more difficult and possibly even dangerous to apply abroad.

For example, I would mention the human rights policy. I used to do a fair amount of speaking on human rights and the question I always got was: Why was the administration inconsistent in its human rights policy? Why are you beating up on this nation while not beating up on that nation? Why are you using carrots here and sticks there? My answer was always that a perfectly consistent human rights policy, in its *tactics*, would be fraudulent. Our goal was consistent, but our methods, in the real world, had to vary. Different governments respond best to different kinds of inducements, and there are different kinds of violations of human rights to be addressed. That was the right answer in explaining the complexity of reality, but it was not one that was going to encourage confidence in our consistency or an easy understanding of what it was that we were trying to do.

NARRATOR: Tony, could you say just a word about the ways in which and the extent to which Vance and Carter used the policy planning staff?

MR. LAKE: Let me first complete some thoughts on politics. There is one other point here that I cannot prove, but I would like to mention. I don't think it was Iran that lost Carter the election. I don't think that foreign policy generally wins or loses elections in any case. Foreign policy issues are politically important in two indirect ways: First, they provide a test of the character of candidates. People seem less interested in the details or what candidates say they will do than in whether the candidates seem capable of taking care of business in a dangerous world. And secondly, a foreign policy problem can become symbolic of other things that are bothering Americans. I think that to some degree a public sense of helplessness over Iran reflected a sense of helplessness about the economy.

NARRATOR: One last point on that subject. Do you think this pragmatism you mentioned began to dissipate after Afghanistan?

MR. LAKE: Yes, in large part because it was an election year.

156 *Director of the Policy Planning Staff Anthony Lake*

NARRATOR: Two final questions if we could. One, would you say a word about the policy planning staff and its role in the administration. Two, how will historians judge this presidency ten or twenty years from now?

MR. LAKE: On the second question, we went over his great diplomatic successes. And also, I hope that Carter's performance as a *former* president will be remembered as very inspiring. He seems to be doing things on their merits, whether his housing projects or his forays into diplomacy, rather in than an effort to recapture headlines.

NARRATOR: Yes, it tells one something about the man. You know that the era of General George Catlett Marshall and George Kennan and Paul Nitze is the era that people have written about pro and con, and one hears about the policy planning staff in that period. Did Carter and Vance seek to use the work of the policy planning staff, and did they do it in a way that you thought was effective and appropriate?

MR. LAKE: I think the most appropriate role for the planning staff is whatever the secretary of state wants or whatever will be most useful to the secretary of state.

Toward the end of the administration, the President told me that he wished the planning staff had sent him more ideas directly, and my answer was, as tactfully as I could put it, that that would have been difficult while I was providing those ideas to Vance. Obviously if I had sent ideas to the White House that Vance didn't like, then I would have been undercutting my immediate superior. So my focus was very much on the secretary.

What I did as director of policy planning was very similar to what Winston Lord had done before me. It gained both of us some criticism from academic analysts of policy planning. Both of us got very involved in current issues. This reflected very much what Kissinger wanted Lord to do and what Vance wanted me to do. Neither of our staffs concentrated on lengthy analyses of possible future events. In my experience at least, when policy planning staffs do that, no senior official has time to read them, and they become essentially academic exercises. Successful planning staffs try to be involved in current issues that have important policy implications, to bring a longer term perspective to them, and to help relate one issue to another.

So we got very involved. Secretary Vance established a system—it wasn't my suggestion, it was his—in which all of State's papers for the interagency policy review group meetings were prepared jointly by Policy Planning and the relevant assistant secretaries. We were also involved in all of the secretary's speeches and public statements and helped coordinate the department's position on AID budgets. I encouraged staff members also to write longer think-pieces, but mostly we tried to interject a planning perspective through continuous involvement.

NARRATOR: That's a good point on which to end. Tony, is there anything we've not touched on that you think is more important than what we have touched on or about which you'd care to comment?

MR. LAKE: Not really. I just hope that for historians, the President's substantive accomplishments are not dimmed by the bureaucratic conflicts. What matters in the end is what he actually accomplished.

NARRATOR: That's the real legacy. Thank you for your reflections.

CHAPTER 10

THE CARTER PRESIDENCY AND THE UNITED NATIONS

AMBASSADOR DONALD McHENRY

NARRATOR: Donald McHenry is a triple-threat figure on the American scene. He has been a diplomat, a public relations company executive, and an educator. Currently he is professor of diplomacy and international relations at Georgetown University, a position he has held since 1981. Don received his undergraduate degree from Illinois State University and his graduate degree from Southern Illinois University. He taught at Howard University and then served in the State Department from 1963 to 1973. He joined the staff of the Brookings Institution in 1971 and became project director at the Carnegie Endowment for International Peace from 1973 to 1977. He was U.S. deputy representative at the United Nations from 1977 to 1979 and ambassador to the United Nations from 1979 to 1981. He has also served as a director of the International Paper Corporation, Coca Cola, the First National Bank of Boston, Smith Kline Beckman Corporation, and the First National Boston Corporation. He has been a member of the Board of Governors of the American Stock Exchange and a trustee of Mount Holyoke College, the Brookings Institution, the Ford Foundation, and the Phelps Stokes Fund. He is a member of the board of directors of the Ditchley Foundation. He has been the recipient of the Superior Service Award of the Department of State and the Family of Man Award of the New York Council of Churches. He is also a member of the editorial board of *Foreign Policy* magazine.

In all these respects—public, private, and educational—Don has made major contributions. He certainly served with great distinction in the U.N. Though his style was quite different from that of his predecessor, Andrew Young, he established good working relations with the Third World countries. In the U.N., he worked quietly and most effectively on a number of very sensitive issues.

AMBASSADOR McHENRY: Thank you very much. I should begin by saying how very important I think the Miller Center study on the Carter White House is. In fact, one of the real contributions to the study of contemporary politics is found in the recording of memories of those who participated in the process before those memories completely fade. There is something about time which plays tricks on you. First, one forgets much more quickly than one realizes. Second, there is a tendency to romanticize the further one gets from the situation. One tends to omit important details.

My own participation in the Carter administration was, in one sense, somewhat accidental. It is generally believed by some that I have been active in politics; the fact is that I have never been active in politics. That belief comes from my appointment as the ambassador to the United Nations. Because that position has traditionally been held by political appointee, it has been assumed that the same is true in my case. It isn't.

An article in a *New York Times* "Man in the News" clip—an article which serves to constantly remind me of how lazy newspaper writers around the world are—reported that Don McHenry was a long-time associate of Andy Young and a participant in the civil rights movement in the South. I still see that article over and over again in my bios in various places around the country and around the world. Nothing could be further from the truth. I met Andy Young after he was appointed ambassador to the U.N. I was on the Carter transition team assigned to brief various new appointees. We were called from Plains and told that this guy Young was going to be appointed ambassador. Who was going to brief him? Two people with the requisite background were available: Bill Maynes and Don McHenry. It was late on a Saturday afternoon, and because we both had been working extraordinarily long hours, neither of us wanted to brief Andy. We flipped a coin and I went home, so I still hadn't met Andy Young at that point.

Nor was I active in the South. I had not been active in politics in general. I was in the State Department throughout the 1960s, having gone there in 1963 to serve in the foreign service.

How, then, was my association with the Carter administration established? Quite simply, it was because I had been active in foreign affairs. I had been in the State Department for about ten years, and at the Brookings Institution and the Carnegie Endowment as well. I also had done a little writing. That is why I was asked by Cyrus Vance to serve on the

Carter transition team. During the campaign while at Carnegie, I'd been approached by a number of the candidates for advice on one subject or another. As a charitable institution, we were under instruction from the Board of Trustees to speak with all candidates, and we did. Contact with the Carter campaign landed me on the transition team.

It was during the transition team period that I first met Jimmy Carter. One of my assignments during that time was to organize a rather innovative approach to introducing the President-elect to Washington. Mr. Carter wished to have an all-day briefing session on foreign policy with various figures in Washington. The decision was made to have that briefing at the old Smithsonian Castle; there in that very large room gathered a bipartisan group of congressional foreign policy experts. The president-elect sat there for the day and engaged in very lively discussion on foreign affairs with those individuals. It was the assignment to prepare that conference—and to make all the arrangements, from the grubby details of food to microphones—which gave me my first occasion to actually meet Jimmy Carter.

After the inauguration I went to the United Nations as part of the United States mission, serving as the third ranking ambassador there. It is generally not known that we have five ambassadors to the United Nations, and I was the third-in-line for responsibility for the U.N. Security Council. Mine was a rather curious job. If the ambassador is in town, he or she will be the Security Council representative, and if that representative is absent, the number two ambassador takes over. Only when seemingly everyone is traveling around the country or on vacation do you finally get down to number three. More than anything else, this means that number three is responsible for the issues that arise, for sitting in on the interminable meetings when number one and number two don't want to be there, and for occasionally moving up to the front chair when they are gone. It also means that number three has responsibility for the political sections of the United States mission and, therefore, the overall coordination of the political issues which arise or are likely to arise. That was my responsibility. It was as a result of that responsibility that I had my first direct association with President Carter.

Working at the mission with Andy Young and Jim Leonard, who was number two, meant that we enjoyed a very close association with Cyrus Vance. Vance was a very strong believer in the United Nations; he continues to be so. He is very active in U.N. affairs to this day. Because the three of us had been close to Cyrus Vance over a period of time, it wasn't difficult for us to begin work quickly joining with him in developing policy initiatives. One of our first initiatives concerned Namibian negotiations. These negotiations led to the creation of the so called "contact group." It was through my leadership of that contact group, composed of the U.K., Germany, Canada, France, and the United States, that I had my first immediate association with the President.

We set off trying to settle the Namibia question and inevitably became entwined in the question of Southern Rhodesia. These negotiations got off to a pretty good start. The one thing that one should know about Jimmy Carter is that he follows everything and, if anything, he follows everything too closely. He was very much involved in the day-to-day developments of all our major initiatives. He followed in great detail what we were doing on the Zimbabwe, Rhodesia, and Namibia negotiations. Not only would he follow these in great detail, but he would offer a piece or two of advice here and there. I frankly was surprised, not because the President was interested, because these were relatively important initiatives, but because he knew as much as he did about them.

As we were developing policy for these particular areas, the President became directly involved as a result of visits to the United States by various heads of state. Nyerere came to Washington, as did foreign ministers and prime ministers of the U.K. and West Germany. Inevitably, there was a discussion of Namibia, and because of that I was called in on a number of occasions to brief the President. I also had occasion to brief the President on my negotiations with the South Africans. I suspect that it was through these briefings that the President drew whatever impression he had of my participation in government. It was certainly through these briefings and discussions that I had my closest view of Jimmy Carter in his early stage.

Later on, there were other issues which brought me into the White House in a position to observe closely the President and his staff. These included, obviously, the numerous questions concerning the Middle East, starting out with our effort in early 1977 to develop the so-called Geneva Conference with the Soviets. I was involved in the President's visits to the United Nations. Indeed the President visited the U.N. devoutly every fall. In fact, Mr. Carter came to the U.N. long before a president would normally do so. A president normally visits in the fall, and Mr. Carter was there within two or three months of his inauguration. That was an indication of his interest in the U.N., an interest which was on the one hand very well focused, yet on the other hand somewhat naive. I say the latter because, as you know, the President was pulled, I think, in various directions because of his Southern background, which was relatively conservative despite his reputation for being very liberal. He was both liberal and conservative. He was conservative on military affairs and liberal on issues such as civil rights. He was conservative in his view of the great powers' prerogatives and liberal about the United Nations. He probably expected more from the U.N. than it could in any way accomplish.

I would suggest that the working relationship which developed between New York, the State Department, and the White House was fairly typical of the working relationships generally between these three institutions. On the one hand, it was cooperative on many issues; on the other hand—in part because people see issues from the vantage points of different institutions and have different responsibilities—there were at times great difficulties. There were difficulties particularly on issues concerning the Middle East. New York and the State Department would be lined up in my view—and I'm still prejudiced on this point—on the same substantive side of an issue, while the White House, having to be much more concerned with domestic politics, would oppose us.

From personal experience, I can give you examples of Jimmy Carter's manner of working closely on issues. I've mentioned the Namibian and Rhodesian negotiations, where the President was very closely involved. In fact, he was probably too closely involved. There were times when he knew more about the subject, I dare say, than I did. This was quite different from my own approach. My own approach was to make sure that my staff knew more about the subject than I did. But there were times when Mr. Carter knew things, which in my judgment, he probably should not have known.

The ballerina incident has probably faded from your memory, but it was indicative of the way the President operated. It also led to an even closer relationship between the President and myself. You will recall that a Soviet Bolshoi ballet dancer defected and left his wife in the hands of the Soviets. The Soviets sought to take her out of this country, and we ended up with a seventy-two hour standoff at Kennedy Airport. That incident, which brought out the worst in various sections of the United States government—that is, the inability of Immigration, Customs, and the FBI, and any number of other agencies to cooperate smoothly in such an emergency—was an example of the manner in which the President could be decisive. He quickly established a line of authority in New York so that we weren't speaking with several voices. I think that for the first time in a long while, at least for such foreign policy incidents, we had lines of responsibility quickly established.

It was this incident, occurring just before Andy Young's resignation, that led to my appointment by the President as representative to the U.N. Here too, Mr. Carter operated in a very decisive—maybe too decisive—manner. While I had worked with him on a number of occasions, I had had no long, close association with the President. A few days later, Andy Young resigned and I was called to Washington by, I think, Hamilton Jordan. I saw the President in the evening in the upstairs White House quarters. We talked about the problems which Andy Young had run into and I gave him some of my own views, which weren't actually too different from Andy's. Where we differed, I guess, was in the way I would handle things. Anyway, without going much further, the President said that he'd been considering me for this job, but that he would have to talk it over with Cy Vance. He told me that Cy wanted me to have it and he thought he agreed with Cy. So the President and I went outside to wait for a car to pick me up. The car came and he went back into the White House. But before we had gone ten feet, he came back out the door and said that he had already decided. And that was that. He never talked with Vance.

We had a further brief conversation in which the President indicated that he accepted my view about how the job should be handled. I had told him that there had to be a close working relationship between the ambassador to the U.N. and the secretary of state. I also felt that the ambassador had to have a close working relationship with the president. If I was to be ambassador, I wanted the ability to see the President whenever I wanted— and to see him "unfiltered." I told him that I would never do this without clearing it with Cyrus Vance, because that was part of my working relationship with Vance, but that I felt I had to have an opportunity for direct presidential contact. It was then that I established weekly meetings with Vance and they were held when I came for Cabinet meetings. On occasion, I also saw the President.

Now actually seeing the President, despite his agreement with my condition, was not the easiest thing in the world. Staffs inevitably wish to shield the president, and that was quite true in this case. So very early I had to establish two things with, I regret to say, Zbigniew Brzezinski. One was that when I saw the President neither Brzezinski nor any of his staff would be present unless I invited them. That was my agreement with the President. But apparently Mr. Brzezinski either didn't get that message or didn't believe in it. Therefore, at my first meeting with the President, I had to disinvite one of Brzezinski's people from the President's outer office. I never again had a problem with that.

Secondly, I had to counter an effort to cut me out from information channels. I did that by telling the President that I had an information problem that I would not specifically discuss with him, but that if I didn't get it cleared up by our next meeting, I would tell him and request his assistance. He told me to work on it, whatever it was, and if I felt that I needed some help to come back to him. I then had a meeting with Brzezinski and told him of my agreement with the President. I said that I had not told the President the substance of the problem, but that I could assure him that the President was going to stand with me if I had to take it back to him. I never took it back to the President because it was resolved. I hadn't wanted to involve the President at a stage that I thought was premature. On the other hand, I wished to be assured that if there was a need for some kind of assistance that it was there.

The hostage crisis was another instance in which the President was consumed with details. In a sense, the hostage crisis consumed the Carter presidency. The President approached it in the same manner that he approached other problems, and involved himself in the slightest of details. He followed up on every avenue, whether or not it had much likelihood of success. And, of course, he followed in great detail what was going on in the U.N. with regard to the hostages. There were times when he wished, in a sense, to not follow the very slow political process necessary in a parliamentary institution like the United Nations or Congress for that matter (the processes are very similar). For example, he strongly wished early on to go for sanctions, but both Cy Vance and I resisted that. We felt that it was necessary for us to bring the international community along, to bring them to an agreement about the fact that we had exhausted all reasonable efforts before we went the sanctions route. We felt that if we tried to implement sanctions too early, we would run into a Soviet or a Chinese veto, or that we would give some of the nonaligned countries an excuse for not going along with us.

On one occasion, it was necessary for me to jump on an airplane and come down to tell the President not that he was wrong, but that there was a better way of proceeding in the U.N. At that time I did suggest to him that we go into the Security Council with a phased approach so that we could bring the other countries along; that would make it more difficult for the Soviets to exercise their veto. He agreed and we did go through with this. It was necessary on a number of occasions to get the President to pick up the telephone and call Prime Minister Manley in Jamaica. This he was willing to do. There were times late at night—twelve, one, two o'clock in the morning—when I would pick up the telephone and get Jimmy Carter. Unfortunately, there were also times when Jimmy Carter and Cyrus Vance, with their early bird habits, would pick up the telephone at six in the morning and call me. But it worked both ways, and the President was very closely involved.

I think it was at Thanksgiving of the year the hostages were taken (1979) that Kurt Waldheim and I came down to see the President to discuss a trip that Waldheim would be taking. There were very few times when Jimmy Carter wasn't available to discuss an issue. In fact, there were probably too many times when he involved himself in a discussion that might have been better left to subordinates or left for his involvement later on.

Mr. Carter never resolved the differences between the State Department and his own National Security Council. He seems to have tried to follow both paths. Let me be specific. His Annapolis speech, (that curious speech) read as if one person wrote the first part and a second person wrote the second part. It was written almost exactly that way. We in New York, and Vance at the White House, did intervene through Andy Young at the last minute to make some changes in that speech. Unfortunately, it should have been redrafted and what happened was that it ended as a whole series of compromises.

Angola was an example of Carter's inability to resolve the conflict between the State Department and his White House. In a sense, this dilemma was an illustration of the two tendencies in Carter: Carter, the southern conservative, and Carter, the very liberal individual. On any number of occasions, Mr. Vance suggested to the President that the United States should recognize Angola. We had a very close working relationship with the Angolan government. Yet, almost every time that this recommendation was made, Mr. Brzezinski put a little note on the paper that was illustrative of Morton Halperin's book, *Games Bureaucrats Play.* The note never stated that the President shouldn't recognize Angola. Rather, it was that the President had gotten one iron in the fire in the Congress already, and that he had made them mad. Further, the President probably didn't want to send the Angola case up at the same time, and perhaps he should wait until it cooled down a little. Brzezinski's other suggestion was that he ought to engage in extensive consultations but he'd list about six people whom he knew would oppose the recognition of Angola. I am sure that the President recognized what was going on; he definitely recognized that there was a sharp difference over this issue. In the end, he decided by not deciding, which means that he never really took hold of the issue and resolved it.

A third instance of the division, the hostage crisis, led to Cyrus Vance's resignation. Vance would tell me over and over again on the telephone that we had to keep following every peaceful avenue because (these were his words) "the crazies down here want to start something military." It was as much to ward that off as anything else that we undertook some things that we knew weren't going to get anywhere, but we also knew that they were necessary in order to hold off military operations. As you know, we did not succeed, and the rescue attempt occurred with disastrous results.

Finally, I tend to believe that in the long term people will look back at the presidency of Jimmy Carter and, at least concerning foreign policy, assess it quite positively. I had worked, though not as closely, with Kennedy, Johnson, and Nixon. I was surely more impressed with Carter's foreign policy knowledge than that of these others. I didn't find the cynicism in Carter that I found, for example, in Mr. Nixon. One evening Nixon told me that he knew I was right about the fact that we shouldn't have a new Bureau of Latin American Affairs and Canada, and that we shouldn't have raised the new undersecretary to the undersecretary level, while leaving all the other geographic bureaus at assistant secretary level. Nixon argued, however, that it would make the Latins feel good, even though he knew we shouldn't do it. Well, I never heard that kind of cynicism from Jimmy Carter in any instance. Even on the most difficult issues, I never heard the cynicism that was in Nixon, or sometimes in Lyndon Johnson. It wasn't there in Jimmy Carter.

I think people will recognize that, in close person to person contact, he was an impressive figure. Indeed, he was one of the most impressive figures that I have known. That is, Jimmy Carter in this room would be a great communicator. Double the size of this room and he would be a disaster. But in a room with a small group of people he was a very impressive, communicative figure. It was the ability to handle mass communications and to have his sincerity ring true, as opposed to naive or phony, that Jimmy Carter never mastered and probably never will. It's just not in him. In a sense, Carter and Mondale have something of the same problem. They are both very impressive, well-informed figures, particularly in a small group. But the larger the group, the weaker they become in their ability to communicate their ideas and in their perceived sincerity.

Yet, on foreign policy, I think Jimmy Carter will stand out in history. This is true particularly because of the Middle East, Southern Africa, his appreciation of the United Nations and his dogged pursuit of SALT II. He will, in my view, be criticized for domestic policy and for his, as well as his staff's, total—and I mean total—inability to communicate with Congress. But on foreign policy, the Carter presidency will be rated highly.

NARRATOR: We probably should allow Jim Young, who is directing the Carter oral history, to ask the first question.

QUESTION: I am fascinated by your impressions of Carter, especially since we've heard most of his staff describe their impressions and their working relationships. The point that you've noted about Carter's speaking to anonymous mass audiences as opposed to his speaking in a room among intimates, is one that a number of us here have personally experienced, as Carter has visited the Miller Center. I wonder if you could describe your first impressions of his performance at the initial foreign policy meeting with members of Congress. There he seemed to have no such communication problem. It was your first, and probably his first, major substantive meeting with congressional leaders, at least on foreign policy. Would you say that things got off to a bad start there, was he impressive, or was he mostly listening? How did it go?

AMBASSADOR McHENRY: Things didn't get off to a bad start there; actually they got off to a very good start. The idea for the meeting was Carter's, and it was innovative. It was a closed meeting so that there was no need for posturing for anyone. Already by that meeting, with what seemed to me a highly inquisitive mind, he was picking up an impressive knowledge of foreign affairs, despite starting off with very little knowledge of them. And he is one of the first to admit that. But I think he got along very well in that first meeting. In fact, many of those present hoped that it was a sign of what would continue, this kind of immediate effort to enlist the views of the Congress.

You have to keep in mind that Carter ran as an outsider, as a non-Washington person. His staffers had made some devastating comments even before he had arrived in the capitol. Had the kind of relationship that began at the Smithsonian continued, I think Carter could have slowly offset some of this impression; but he couldn't do it. He started with a chief congressional adviser who was already in dutch with the Congress. He never changed his people; he was intensely loyal to those around him. Though he generally recognized their faults, he rationalized the problems with the hope that they would learn or that people would eventually see the good and valuable side of them. That never occurred and he never made the changes that were necessary. At one point he did bring in Lloyd Cutler and Hedley Donovan of *Time* magazine. Both of these appointments were efforts by Carter to get a better feel of Washington, but he still never made it. By then it was too late, and in any event, the hostage crisis came along and killed his presidency.

QUESTION: Would you care to comment on the future of UNESCO and the U.S. role in it?

AMBASSADOR McHENRY: We are now in a presidency (Reagan's) that up until a year and three months ago was anti-multilateral in its approach. I think it still is. However, about a year and three months ago, they suddenly looked up and realized that they were going to get blamed in history for having destroyed the U.N. system. So they told themselves that although they wanted to wound it, they didn't want to get blamed for destroying it. Even if it is a terminal case, they want to make sure it expired after they left, so somebody else would get the blame. Having decided this (about a year and three months ago), they started turning things around by being a little less unilateral in their approach. But they still have a problem. The resignation of Alan Keyes, despite the headlines in the paper to the contrary, was not racial. It wasn't at all racial. It was because Mr. Keys and the right wing never got the message a year and a half ago that Mr. Shultz and Mr. Whitehead wanted to turn things around.

UNESCO is a perfect example of where a wrecking crew has an opportunity to be very effective if the institution is already structurally weak. UNESCO has had very serious problems. It has had poor leadership. It has a mandate which is not all that clear, certainly not as clear as the mandate for civil aviation or health or weather or something of that nature. UNESCO has a very fluffy mandate that allows it to cover all kinds of things. It is the perfect institution on which one can start a wrecking operation. Then we pulled out. Some changes have taken place, but apparently not enough. Most of the changes that we had asked for, though, had been made by the time we pulled out. Yet the Reagan administration was dead set for pulling out and they did. UNESCO needs new leadership, and until it gets new leadership, I don't have much hope of its turning around.

QUESTION: Would you comment on the allegation that the Carter administration's efforts to free the hostages were sabotaged when a Reagan cabal made a secret agreement with the Iranians to delay the release of the hostages until after the elections, and that the *quid pro quo* supposedly was some arms received through Portugal and Israel, to be delivered within a year?

AMBASSADOR McHENRY: Well, I'm no fan of Mr. Reagan, but I don't believe that. I just don't think that the Iranians would have cooperated. They were so confused at that stage in their history that they wouldn't have cooperated with anybody. I think two things occurred with regard to the hostage situation. The first was that for most of the year in which the hostages were held, there was no Iranian government. If there is no government and no one with authority, there is no one with whom to negotiate. It took all of that year for a government to develop, for the mullahs to finally win over the various factions to form the so-called government. Until that occurred, we were spinning our wheels. That is a lesson, by the way, which Mr. Reagan did not learn, because his arms-initiative was designed to negotiate with the so-called moderates in the Iranian government. He should have learned that any time you are trying to carry on a negotiation, it can only be with those who have power to deliver. Reagan didn't have that in mind during this situation.

The second thing was that Iraq decided it was time to initiate the latest twist in their fifteen-hundred-year-old land battle with Iran. The Iraqis, who had been humiliated by the Shah only a few years before and had been forced to accept a settlement that they didn't want, figured that the Iranian government was weak, that chaos prevailed, and that, therefore, they could move in and very quickly restore their honor. So the Iranians now found themselves with a reason for ending the hostage situation in order to open up a pipeline for arms with which to defend themselves.

I think those issues were the two most significant factors impacting on the hostage situation. The establishment of authority within Iran and the Iraqi threat led to the change. The timing of the hostages' release was just one final act of spite. But even if Mr. Carter had been re-elected, the Iranians would have released the hostages because, at that point, there was a government that had a problem on their own hands.

NARRATOR: What do you think of the evaluation of someone close to both of us, Hans Morgenthau, that he never knew a president with whose objectives he agreed more, but who at the same time was more inept in pursuing those objectives? How does one evaluate a statement like that, and, in particular, Carter's role in relation to the statement?

AMBASSADOR McHENRY: As you know, I had the greatest respect for Hans. I think that Morgenthau, while sharing Carter's concerns, would have pursued a very different human rights policy and probably wouldn't have placed it so high on the list of priorities. For him there was a "fluffiness" about the way in which Carter pursued foreign policy. Hans was of the old school. Though not as unfeeling as many young students interpret him, Morgenthau was, nonetheless, concerned with foreign policy factors more tangible than human rights.

QUESTION: Several times you mentioned a common criticism of the Carter administration: that Carter followed details too closely. You mentioned that at times he knew more about the Namibian negotiations than you did, and that he involved himself in ongoing discussions too many times. I wonder if you could give us several illustrations of when this type of attention was actually counterproductive.

AMBASSADOR McHENRY: I didn't mean to say that Carter's involvement was counterproductive in terms of the Namibian negotiations. The President's participation actually was quite valuable. When I made that comment, I was talking about his overall presidency. What I am concerned with is the amount of time that one spends projecting leadership. This overall projection is what Mr. Reagan seems to excel at, and at which Mr. Carter never succeeded. In the few instances that he tried, such as the "malaise speech" or the Notre Dame speech, where he talked about our long national obsession with communism, one didn't get the impression of this man as leader.

Moreover, his attention to detail tended to carry over to the way in which he discussed policy matters with the public. The public doesn't want, in my view, to hear a recitation of the detailed complications of foreign policy. It doesn't want a pro and con presentation. The public tends to want to know how you, as president, are going to act. Then, of course, the public beats you over the head if you do the wrong thing. Nevertheless, the people want to believe that, with all the expertise available in Washington, the president has arrived at a decision and is taking charge. If you do a pro and con, if you appear at a press conference and say "on the one hand . . ., and on the other hand, it demonstrates your knowledge and the process by which you have decided. The question is what kind of message does it give the public regarding leadership? It is this kind of approach which Carter pursued with all his considerable detailed knowledge, and I'm afraid that carried over in the perception of Carter by the public. This perception of being a specialist rather than a generalist was what I'm talking about when I expressed concern about his knowledge of details. It is not that his knowledge ever interfered with specific negotiations.

NARRATOR: In this room President Carter said that the reason he retained both of his warring chieftains, Brzezinski and Vance, was that each of them could do different things, and that he badly needed someone who was at work in both traditional and public diplomacy. He said Vance was a skilled diplomat and an outstanding technician, but that no matter how hard he tried, he could not get Vance to articulate American foreign policy. He said that Brzezinski was good at articulation, and that he did it because Vance wouldn't do it. He said that Brzezinski never made a "Meet the Press" statement without his (Carter's) knowledge and, most of the time, his full approval.

AMBASSADOR McHENRY: I've heard the President make that statement a number of times. I disagree with him. Even if one were going to take that approach, he would want to make sure that the person articulating the policy, in this instance Brzezinski, did so in a way which was consistent with the policy. What you had was Mr. Vance pragmatically pursuing policy and Mr. Brzezinski viewing everything through his hardline Soviet lens. I may be a little harsh on Brzezinski, but this is about the way it was. Mr. Vance, on something like the Horn of Africa, was trying to work with the intricate details of the situation, which for the most part had absolutely nothing to do with the Middle East nor any particular Soviet strategy. Mr. Brzezinski, on the other hand, talking expansively about the "arc of crisis," would put an East-West spin on every situation. From my point of view, this didn't make any sense.

Concerning foreign policy statements, Brzezinski relished all these things. I'm sure he never appeared on "Meet the Press" without the President's approval, but I'm also sure that 99 percent of the time, the idea of an appearance came from Zbig. He loved it.

I must tell you that I have some reservations about this way of operating the presidency. I happened to be on the Nixon transition team. (How I made that team is difficult to understand, but I did. Actually I was in the State Department and was simply assigned to it.) I remember at that time mentioning to Secretary Rogers that some of the papers coming down from the Hotel Pierre were an indication of real trouble, that he was being cut out, and that a structure was being established which would either directly take the State Department out of the decision-making process or do so indirectly by overwhelming it with minutiae. And he said to me, "Don't worry about it. I'm a friend of the President and when any decision is made, I can take it right to the President." And I responded, "Mr. Secretary, by then it will be too late." I think experience proved me right.

Then along came the Carter administration. I remember Vance calling together the transition group one Saturday to express concern about the structure being established. Vance told us that he was going to insist upon some changes. He later did so, and they were made. He also said that he wouldn't tolerate any backbiting between State and the NSC, that we were going to work with the NSC instead of fighting with them, and that he would have the head of the first one of us he heard was participating in one of these squabbles. That was his approach.

I don't agree with the President on his view of Brzezinski's participation. I think Brzezinski's own memoirs tend to undercut the President's analysis.

NARRATOR: Did the changes Vance insisted upon concern committee chairmanships? Wasn't the NSC adviser chairman of at least three out of the seven committees?

AMBASSADOR McHENRY: That's right.

QUESTION: How should we deal with the propensity of incoming administrations to regard everything done previously as utterly incorrect? From your State Department perspective, what can we do to retain some degree of continuity in our foreign policy?

AMBASSADOR McHENRY: It is very difficult. We have little institutional memory and what little memory we did have is practically gone now that the Reagan administration has put political appointees at the desk level in the State Department. We have known all along that political appointees would be given deputy assistant and assistant secretary level posts, but now they fill positions at the desk level. And the next administration is going to want to "clean out" these appointees. Quite frankly, if I were with a new administration, I would clean house too because I think that they've brought in a pretty lousy bunch of people. The thorough politicization of the State Department is a real problem when trying to establish policy continuity.

I learned a valuable lesson from Cyrus Vance during the Ford to Carter transition. We both felt very strongly that Mr. Kissinger was following a bad policy in southern Africa. We felt that if his initiative succeeded, the United States would be terribly embarrassed, so we wanted to state right off that the United States was changing its policy. But Vance thought such a maneuver was unwise, saying, "No, we're not going to do that. We can't send the world a signal that we will simply change our policy because a day has passed. We shall follow through on Kissinger's initiative and try to change it as best as we can, but we are not going to renounce it." He sent us out to follow through on this hideous policy.

Fortunately for us, the South Africans, in this instance, didn't recognize a good thing. Since they are always playing for time, they like to teach every new crowd a new trick by starting them over from the beginning. They didn't recognize that starting over from the beginning was exactly what we wanted. So they took the initiative of denouncing Mr. Kissinger's proposals, which was the answer to our prayers. Thus despite our approach of preserving continuity, we arrived at where we wanted to be.

I can't fully solve the problem of greater continuity. We currently have a Council on Foreign Relations group, co-chaired by Henry Kissinger and Cyrus Vance, which is trying to discover if there is a basis for the re-establishment of a bipartisan foreign policy. About fifteen or sixteen of us have been meeting for the last year. I don't know what the conclusions will be because the two of them, Vance and Kissinger, dismissed the rest of us after a year and they have been off writing themselves. So it will be very interesting to see what their conclusions are. I think it is very difficult to establish a bipartisan foreign policy in an environment in which there is so little consensus. Consider the divisions over Vietnam, Central America, "Star Wars," etc.

QUESTION: I would like to address two of your very interesting points: the President's concern for detail and the difference between Brzezinski and Vance. Is it possible that the President's emphasis on detail prevented him from seeing what you might call the "strategic contradiction" between Brzezinski and Vance?

AMBASSADOR McHENRY: It could be. On the other hand, it also could be that Brzezinski's conservative view was more consistent with that of a traditional, Southern conservative who had not been active in foreign affairs. I believe that, while on the one hand Jimmy Carter was attracted to Brzezinski's overview, on the other, when dealing with specific problems such as human rights and Namibia, the more humane, practical side of Carter came out. I think to this day he has never solved this contradiction.

COMMENT: Two Faustian souls dwelt in Carter's chest.

QUESTION: Don, during your very informative presentation, you noted the organizational shortcomings of the Carter foreign policy apparatus. At the same time you emphasized in great detail the personal characteristics, which in this case were marked by bad chemistry, responsible for the administration's foreign policy. Is the fault with the structure as it exists or with the personality differences, to which we shall always be subject?

AMBASSADOR McHENRY: I was mainly trying to outline the perspective from which the President viewed foreign policy issues. No, I don't think that you can do much in terms of changing the structure. I have one suggestion which I have somewhat facetiously made, which is that I would probably change the title of the assistant to the president for national security affairs to the assistant to the president for paper shuffling or something of that nature. That would emphasize what I think is the responsibility of that individual: coordinating paper. The national security adviser should be responsible for assuring that various views come to the president, not for being an adviser to him on substantive matters. Somehow this change must be made. A president can still have a close adviser, whether in or out of government, who has great influence on him. But I'd rather have that individual enjoy a personal relationship, as opposed to a professional relationship, whereby other governmental agencies and individuals are affected.

We are stuck with this structure; there has to be an official to insure that the president has received the views of all the parties, agencies, and offices which must have a say on foreign policy decisions. The number of interested agencies will increase; it will never decrease. We are going to see more and more previously domestically oriented agencies with a say in foreign policy matters. That is the nature of the world in which we live.

I guess this brings me to the point that these personal relationships are extraordinarily important. You did not have a battle between the ambassador to the U.N. and the secretary of state during my tenure. But how many battles have there been? I think that a battle has occurred in almost every other administration.

NARRATOR: You had no battle with Muskie?

AMBASSADOR McHENRY: No. My relationship with Muskie was excellent; we enjoyed a very close working relationship. We realized that we were both working for the United States government. I did not necessarily always agree with him, or with Vance, but I never tried to upstage him or do something without consulting him. I expected the same thing from the secretary, and in both instances I wasn't disappointed. The personal relationship is very, very important. Regardless of what structure you establish, if you have people in the final analysis who are trying to stab one another in the back, or who don't recognize that they are working on the same team, it won't work.

COMMENT: As you well know, it is the same in the corporate world.

NARRATOR: Don McHenry has been a marvelous colleague in every group with which any of us have been associated, and the kind of presentation he gave today is illustrative of his human qualities that we've all come to respect. Thank you very much.

CHAPTER 11

THE CARTER PRESIDENCY
AND FOREIGN POLICY

SECRETARY OF STATE EDMUND MUSKIE

NARRATOR: It's a special privilege for the Miller Center to welcome Edmund Muskie, former secretary of state, United States senator, and Democratic candidate for vice president in 1968. That he has not been at the Miller Center before is merely a result of his own heavy obligations. Since the founding of the Center we have wanted him to visit, because so much of his thinking represents a parallel effort to what has gone on at this place seeking to understand some of the great issues of the presidency.

Senator Muskie was born in Rumford, Maine; he received his B.A. from Bates College and his law degree from Cornell University. He is the recipient of approximately thirty honorary degrees from institutions such as William and Mary, Bowdoin College, Boston University, the University of Notre Dame and others. He practiced law in Maine and was elected to the Maine House of Representatives, serving from 1947 to 1951 and as Democratic floor leader for two of those years. He was governor of Maine from 1955 to 1959, and United States senator from Maine from 1959 to 1980.

In the latter position he was recognized and respected as a trusted leader in the Senate. He was deputy majority whip at one time and also an acknowledged authority in certain basic and well-defined areas such as energy, the environment and arms control. He was a member of the Senate Foreign Relations Committee but gave it up temporarily to become chairman of the Senate Budget Committee. He served as sub-committee chairman of the Senate Governmental Operations Committee, and left the Senate to take the position of secretary of state at a very crucial stage of the Carter administration. He's received numerous awards: the Presidential Medal of Freedom, Former Members of Congress Distinguished Service Award and others. It's a great privilege for those of us who have known Edmund Muskie, even in a limited way, to welcome him to the Miller Center.

SENATOR MUSKIE: Thank you, Ken. One of the reasons I've not been here before is the intimidating reputation of this group. In any case, I understand that the productive part of such a meeting is the questions, but I also understand the importance of saying a few words at the outset to stimulate questions and to enable us to adjust to each other so that we can have a free exchange. I discussed this with Ken in advance and thought perhaps the most useful way to serve our purpose would be for me to give you a little anecdotal material on my experience in the State Department and how it happened to come about.

I suppose it begins with my application to law school. I have forgotten what I said on that application, but I was offered a scholarship to Cornell Law School. I had never thought about being a lawyer, so I asked to have the summer to think about it. To postpone the decision on something of that kind in the middle of the depression was a rather foolish thing to do, but I did. I finally agreed to take the scholarship, and I applied to law school. However, in my application I made it clear that I wasn't sure I wanted to be a lawyer; I thought that law school might be a good way to get into the Foreign Service. Well, that took me fifty years, and I'm not sure that my law school education had a thing to do with it!

In any case, I have always found executive responsibility more stimulating and interesting than legislative. I enjoyed being governor, enjoyed being secretary of state, but merely tolerated being United States senator.

At the time that Cy Vance resigned from the State Department, which of course was the occasion for my nomination to the State Department, I was traveling. I was in the West. I traveled to Arizona to campaign for Mo Udall, who was running for re-election, and on that occasion I met Bruce Babbitt for the first time. Then I went to Colorado to campaign for Gary Hart, who was running for a second term in the Senate. On my way back to Nashville to make a speech to a group interested in water pollution legislation, we landed in St. Louis where there was a message for me to call the White House switchboard. I had no idea what that was about, and I hadn't heard about Cy Vance's resignation at all. So I called the White House switchboard from St. Louis, but the operator didn't know who was calling me. So I got back on the plane, got off at Nashville, and there was another message at the airport. I tried again to reach the White

House switchboard, and again I struck out. I went on to my hotel and prepared to deliver my speech that evening.

In the meantime the White House had been in contact with my wife, and she had heard the news about Vance's resignation. She immediately concluded that they were looking for me to replace Vance, but I didn't have access to her either. I made the speech and got back to the room about 11:00 p.m., where the President finally reached me. He didn't indicate what he was calling me about and I couldn't guess why he was calling me. In any case we chatted for a while, and then I thought, "Well, maybe he wants to go fishing." I had invited him to go fishing in Maine several times. He loves fly fishing. Finally, though, he said, "I suppose you're wondering why I'm calling?" I said, "Well, yes." He then said he'd like me to be his secretary of state. That was the first indication I had that there was a vacancy, and it left me speechless, which is a condition I'm not accustomed to. The President then asked me for my response and I told him that the position had "some appeal." (I think those were my exact words.) Then he asked me if I saw any problems with accepting the job and I replied that I needed to talk to my wife, to my accountant, to my political advisers, and to the governor of Maine. The President asked me how long that would take, and I told him I was going back to Washington in the morning and that I would try to get all that done sometime tomorrow.

He hung up after that, but he was on the phone again at 6:00 a.m. the next morning. He said he was on his way to Texas and could drop down to Nashville and pick me up and we could talk. I told him that I didn't need to talk to him; I needed to talk to my wife, my accountant, my political adviser, and the governor! So he asked me when we could talk, and I agreed to meet him at 5:00.

I went back to Washington and had those conversations, except for the governor, but the one problem that I wasn't able to resolve that day was how I could protect my staff. After all, they had come with me and expected to be with me during my term, which still had two years left. I wanted to be sure that their futures weren't jeopardized by my taking this sudden turn. So I met with the President, and the first thing I wanted to know was whether I would be his foreign policy spokesman or whether I would be sharing that responsibility with somebody else. He made it quite clear that I would be his foreign policy spokesman. I told him about the problem of my staff and that I really had to talk to the governor about whom he would appoint as my successor. I had to ask the governor to what extent I could get a commitment from him to urge my successor to protect my staff. The President told me to take a White House plane up to Maine and see if I could resolve the problem, and I did so.

I called the governor, and he happened to be having supper—we only have supper in Maine, we don't have dinner—with four or five noted journalists on the Maine political scene. I couldn't tell him why I was calling, but he guessed. So I met him at the Brunswick [Me.] Naval Air Station the next morning, and we discussed the problem. He already had a list of potential candidates to succeed me in the Senate. I told him what I wanted and acknowledged that it was his responsibility to pick my successor. I also said that I wouldn't try to suggest who it ought to be, but that I would be glad to discuss the candidates if he wished. I told him that primarily I wanted to protect my staff, and he said he would take care of that. I called the President and said that the light was green and that we could go forward. He told me to come back to Washington, and we had a press conference that evening at 5:00.

The thing I remember about the press conference was that after the President announced my appointment, the press began to throw questions. Particularly I remember Sam Donaldson who was trying to press me on the Vance resignation as to whether I thought it was justified and if I would do the same thing, and so on. I did my best to answer the questions. Finally, as I began to walk off the stage Sam said, "Senator, you've left us a little ambivalent." I said, "Well, then it's been a successful press conference!"

From that moment on it was an interesting eight months and twenty days. The immediate problem, of course, was what to do in the aftermath of the failed rescue attempt of the hostages and what our policy was going to be regarding Iran. Among the immediate chores that I faced, though, was a meeting in Brussels of the NATO defense secretaries. It seemed an appropriate place for me to launch my career with the NATO allies. Following this was the Austrian State Treaty ceremonies, the Twenty-fifth Anniversary in Vienna, where all the wartime allies would be gathered, including, of course, Mr. Gromyko. That offered a challenge because following the invasion of Afghanistan, I don't think there had been a meeting at the foreign secretary level with Gromyko. So, there was the question of how to deal with that. In response to the Afghanistan situation, we had imposed embargoes, the Olympic boycott, and other policies with which I had to grapple. That was almost an immediate challenge for me after taking office. After that was the economic summit in June, and following that I made a commitment to visit with the ASEAN [Association of Southeast Asian Nations] foreign ministers in Southeast Asia. In the first month and a half I had a very busy schedule.

Of course, I also had the problem of adjusting to the State Department and establishing my position there. It was a very different kind of situation than normally occurs when a new secretary takes office with a president. I ruled out immediately any notion of forming my own team. I felt that in the interest of continuity and coming to grips immediately that I would take the team that Vance had assembled, deal with it, and offer them my confidence and credibility. This first step that I took proved well advised, and I had no reason for the next eight months to have second thoughts. I received all of the cooperation I could expect from the staff. They were very forthcoming and apparently welcomed my willingness to dispose of that problem immediately.

I did have some problem persuading Warren Christopher to stay on. He, of course, had hoped that he might be appointed secretary, and I could understand that. He was eminently qualified to be secretary, but I gathered that the President, in an election year, found it useful to appoint a member of the Senate. The Senate was a problem through the hostage crisis and other pending issues. Also, politically speaking, he needed someone who had a national constituency of sorts. I thought that was his reasoning, and so I was able to persuade Warren Christopher to stay on. Our relationship was perfect, as far as I was concerned, for the rest of that year, and he was invaluable in the course of the Iran hostage negotiations. So with the team in place I made it clear there was to be continuity.

After the NATO meeting in Brussels, I went on to the Austrian State Treaty ceremonies, and that was interesting because of the confrontation with Mr. Gromyko. Each of us made speeches on that occasion. I followed him, and in the course of that speech commemorating the Twenty-fifth Anniversary of the Austrian State Treaty, which technically ended World War II so far as that country was concerned, I made clear and unambiguous reference to the invasion of Afghanistan. The press regarded that as a confrontation with Mr. Gromyko. At lunch that day, he and I were seated side by side, and we had an interesting exchange. I remember him saying to me, "We in Moscow are facing this question. Who is Muskie? We understand that on the one hand he has a terrible temper and is very hard to get along with, but on the other hand, he can compromise." I said, "Mr. Minister, I hope that you are always in doubt on that score." At that point I waved my finger under his nose, and it was a picture of that gesture that appeared on the front page of the European edition of *Newsweek* magazine.

Yet we had civil discussions; on that occasion we met privately for a couple of hours. Our second meeting was at the opening of the United Nations Assembly in the fall of 1980. I had the feeling that if I had continued in office, there was a basis for a constructive relationship, if not one based on friendship. We found that we could talk to each other civilly even in disagreement, and also that it was possible to explore possibilities. I found that encouraging.

Coming back to the United States, there was a lot of work to be done preparing for the summer ahead. The June summit in Venice was the next big challenge, and problems with our allies were serious. There was the usual complaint that there was inadequate consultation on our part with our NATO allies before taking important foreign policy initiatives. The personal relationship between President Carter and Chancellor Schmidt, particularly, was far from favorable. They simply didn't hit it off well with each other. Fortunately, I got along well with the West German Foreign Minister, Mr. Genscher, who is still in office, incidentally. He's the longest sitting foreign minister in the free world—and now that Gromyko is gone, on both sides of the Iron Curtain. Genscher is a very able man who, I gather, has regained his position of influence which he lost temporarily when his party almost lost a necessary percentage of the vote to qualify for representation in the Bundestag. So he's back, and I think he is back in full force. It's good to see some of these people continue. The other ministers who were there when I was there are all gone. The Venice summit, as I think back, was most notable for the personal confrontation and explosion between Schmidt and Carter, which was very private except that Brzezinski and I were present. It was a very unpleasant situation. Otherwise, that summit wasn't notable for anything else.

We went on from there to a foreign ministers' meeting in Ankara, which was the first such meeting, I think, ever held in Ankara. The issues there were the current internal instability of the Turkish regime and the violence which resulted in an escalating number of deaths attributable to political instability. Shortly after that, the military took over. At that point there was even serious concern about the safety of the visiting foreign ministers. It was an interesting personal experience for me. It was my first NATO foreign ministers' meeting, and it happened to be our country's turn to be the public spokesman at that point. So it was my first opportunity to make an impression publicly and on my associates at the State Department level. The Greek-Turkish dispute has been a problem for a long time and it was a problem then; the situation in Cyprus is an ongoing problem. I had separate meetings with the Greek foreign minister about Greek bases—a problematic issue that still persists in our relations. So there were a lot of old problems of that kind.

I went on from there to Southeast Asia, stopping in India on the way, and had what I think was a very constructive experience with the ASEAN foreign ministers. I was the only outsider present. We got along very well. The principal issue of concern, which is still a concern, was the refugee camps on the Thai border. The Thai government wanted some military assistance to help control the border to protect the refugees. I was able to arrange for that. The other issue was Kampuchea and whether or not the current representatives to the United Nations should be seated or whether representatives of the new government in Kampuchea should be seated. That issue is a continuing one, but we succeeded, with the help of some others in the United Nations, in keeping representatives of the government there rather than those of the new Vietnamese satellite government in Kampuchea.

I came back to this country, and the Iranian hostage matter was on the front burner. The presidential election continued with its ups and downs, mostly downs for the President. Our Iranian policy, as it emerged, was a very simple one. Number one, we decided to use patience as an important instrument. We would wait until the Iranians had their government in place. I think it was in August that the Majlis [Assembly] was finally in place, and they elected a prime minister. I wrote him a letter which we hoped might begin the slow process of negotiation. You may remember that they wanted us to apologize for having put the Shah of Iran on the throne. In my letter I did not offer an apology, but I indicated that we had mutual grievances against each other and that we ought to find a way of discussing these, either directly or through third parties.

The Speaker of the House read that letter to the press without comment, and it was toward the latter part of August or the early part of September that I got a message from Genscher, the German foreign minister, indicating that the Iranians were interested in beginning a dialogue indirectly, under German auspices. It was then that we began the negotiating process. We sent Warren Christopher to West Germany, and Schmidt acted as host. We had to find a way to exchange messages indicating that we were in touch with each other. We wanted to be sure that these talks were going on with Khomeini's knowledge and approval, and they, of course, wanted to be sure that they were in touch with us and that we were positive and interested in going forward. Our signal was made in my speech to the United Nations General Assembly that fall, and Khomeini himself used his code in a public statement that he made. So we were in contact. Those contacts continued slowly, because there were a lot of things to grind out.

The Iraq war broke out in late September, about the time that we were meeting with the United Nations General Assembly. It's traditional for the United States secretary of state to use the opening of the United Nations General Assembly to hold bilateral talks with as many foreign ministers as possible. That's quite an exercise. I think in a period of a week or ten days, I met with twenty-five or thirty foreign ministers on a bilateral basis. This involved extensive briefings from the State Department people on the state of each of these relationships, which, of course, I had not been exposed to as a United States senator. That was a real education for me.

So far as the Iran-Iraq war is concerned, the Iranian minister came to the General Assembly looking for support, and I think that was an important event. He was told in no uncertain terms, not only by those he consulted in Europe but by those in the nonaligned world, that if he really wanted to get a sympathetic response from the United Nations with respect to the Iran-Iraq war, he ought to straighten out the hostage situation. The United Nations voted overwhelmingly in support of us on that issue, as did the World Court. He got that message, loud and clear. In the meantime, we had persuaded many of our friends among the European nations and elsewhere to make interventions in Iran on behalf of a solution to the hostage crisis, people who regarded themselves as friendly to the Iranian people. Those interventions continued on almost a daily basis. This exposure to the United Nations' attitude, I think, undoubtedly was helpful in persuading the Iranians to begin the talks that ultimately resulted in success.

The election was the next event, politically at least. To this day I'm not sure why the Iranians at that point opened up the hostage issue to the media once again. I'll never forget that weekend before election day when Americans, via television, relived all over again the agonizing days of the original hostage taking. It was repeated on television, and the Iranians also relived the event. They laid down terms at that point, which were unacceptable to us, but I think they may have thought they were doing President Carter a favor. Of course, to the contrary, they completely destroyed his prospects for reelection in that weekend. At the beginning of that weekend, the polls showed Carter and Reagan almost equal, I think, and by the evening before election day, he was hopelessly behind. It happened that quickly.

The secretary of state traditionally does not get involved in the politics of the election campaign itself. I did make speeches around the country on foreign policy in order to lay out the President's foreign policy and what we were doing, but he lost. After that, we filled the interregnum with continuing negotiations.

The Iranians wanted to shift from the West Germans as the intermediary to the Algerians. The Algerians came in and were superb. Farsi is a very difficult language to penetrate, not just in terms of speaking it but in terms of the substance of discussion. The Algerians were good at Farsi and so they were helpful. They did not act as mediators; they simply carried these messages back and forth and undertook in each case to explain the circumstances in which the new position was taken. All three persons in the Algerian group were experienced in the negotiations that separated Algeria from France, so they had excellent background and were truly expert.

I met with them, but Warren Christopher had the primary responsibility for traveling back and forth, as he had to do from time to time. We also had a team. There's an excellent book on this published under the auspices of the New York Bar Association, and all of the people on our team contributed to that account, which is accurate and comprehensive. If you want the details of the negotiations, you can get them there. Warren Christopher was part of that group as were people from Treasury. The transfer of funds involved was enormously complicated, and if it weren't for the development of electronic transfers, it probably could not have been done because we had to arrange for the exchange of the hostages and the transfer of the money at the same moment through the national banks in London, Algeria, and ultimately the central bank in Iran. That all had to be done before the hostages would be allowed to move to the Algerian aircraft to fly out of Iran. So it was a touch and go situation, and it wasn't finally completed until a half-hour into the new Reagan administration.

Those negotiations were frustrating because we had to constantly reassure the Congress that movement was taking place. Just about every weekend I was asked to appear on "Meet the Press" or "Issues and Answers," in which the media undertook to get as much detail about what was going on as possible. We had to be very careful about not disclosing those details lest we interrupt an initiative that had some promise of success.

Of course, all this time the incoming administration was undertaking to "pooh-pooh" these arrangements. They really didn't have a plan themselves, as they disclosed later. We had to keep a cool and steady hand on things as they were proceeding. We had to tell the American people enough to show them that things were progressing without telling them more than we could risk publicly exposing. So it was an interesting game from week to week.

I remember the toughest time was when a demand made by the Iranians surfaced, which looked like a $24 billion ransom demand. It wasn't that, but it would look that way unless you understood what was going on and what they were really saying. I think what we finally transferred to them was only $2 or $3 billion more than that needed to meet the claims of Iranian creditors, who had attached holdings in the United States and elsewhere. But in any case, it worked out, and we worked on the principle that if they would undo what they had done with the hostages—in other words, release them—we would undertake to undo what we did in blocking their assets. The difficulty was that courts were involved to the extent that creditors had brought suit and put attachments on these assets. So an arbitral tribunal was established for the purpose of presiding over a resolution of all those issues, and that was the principal legal issue which ultimately had to be decided by the Supreme Court after our administration had ended.

The court held that the President had authority to transfer jurisdiction over these claims from our courts to the arbitration tribunal. That work continues; it's not yet finished. I think it's nearing completion now, eight or nine years after the fact. Our last act, made possible by President Reagan, was to fly to Wiesbaden, West Germany, to meet the hostages. That was our reward for all this effort, a reward we thoroughly appreciated.

QUESTION: During the negotiations, to what extent did you keep the incoming administration advised about the details, between the election and the inauguration? And secondly, is it true that your successor, Alexander Haig, wrote that immediately after negotiations, they had a long discussion as to whether to honor your agreement with Iran?

SENATOR MUSKIE: We did not advise them on an ongoing basis, but we did keep them involved to the extent that they sought information. The first meeting was between Mr. Reagan and President Carter in his office. From President Carter's description of that meeting, Mr. Reagan didn't appear to want a thorough briefing. There were a number of issues to cover, of course, including the hostage negotiations, but to the extent that Reagan wanted a briefing, it was available.

Now with respect to the State Department, it took quite awhile before President Reagan selected a secretary of state. I think it was in December when Haig was finally selected, and Haig's first act was to meet with me. I undertook the briefing to the extent that he desired it. We did not go very far; I think it would have been very difficult to go beyond that on an ongoing basis. It was difficult enough to keep the negotiation going, and we couldn't be sure from day to day or from week to week whether or not the track we were currently on would be productive.

One of the very low visibility issues was whether or not, in restoring the assets to the Iranians, we would also restore to them military equipment that the Shah had bought and paid for. The new administration, through those people who ventured to speak on the subject, including Mr. Kissinger, assumed that we were preparing to do that. Well, we were not, but we didn't want the issue raised publicly. For their own reasons, the Iranians were not considering it, and we simply didn't want to discuss those reasons or to raise the issue in any way that might make it an obstacle. It would have been a very serious obstacle. If we had been truly committed to the principle of "you restore us and we'll restore you," they could have used that logic against us. The fact is that it was not raised. I don't know what has happened to those supplies since then. Possibly, much of it is now obsolete. Whether or not they should be reimbursed is an issue that might be raised at some point. Whether they should be reimbursed is an interesting question.

With respect to the time that the administration gave to deliberating on whether or not to accept the agreement, I am really in no position to answer that question. I don't know. I do know that shortly after the new administration took office, we were asked to testify on Capitol Hill on these agreements. At that point they seemed to have made up their mind that there was no question about it. A representative of their administration, whose name I do not remember, said specifically that he was glad the problem had been dealt with because the new administration had no plans for dealing with it. I think they were really appreciative of the fact that the matter was closed. President Reagan was in the position to take credit for welcoming the hostages back home and enjoying those glorious ceremonies at the White House without having to worry about how to get it done. Of course, since that time, he's had other educational experiences on the problems of dealing with hostages.

QUESTION: There was a well-publicized dispute between Vance and Brzezinski. Let me ask you a question about your relationship with Brzezinski. In his book he suggests that you were not well-informed on foreign affairs, very heavily dependent upon Warren Christopher, and more discursive than Vance, but you were less contentious. He found it easier to reach decisions with you at State.

SENATOR MUSKIE: I find that amazing.

QUESTION: Were there substantial policy disputes between Brzezinski and you, and were there any problems created by the institutional structure of the National Security Council (NSC)?

SENATOR MUSKIE: There were annoyances. With respect to your description of what he said in the book, of course I was not as informed in foreign policy matters as someone who had spent his life in that area. As a senator, I had been involved to the extent that the Senate, as one of the institutions of government, shares foreign policy responsibility. I had been a member of the foreign policy committee. I had taken trips abroad at the request of the President. In the year before, I had spent two weeks in Brussels, West Germany, Poland, Portugal, and Spain at the request of the President. I had led a congressional delegation to mainland China a week before normalization.

I gathered from what I learned later, after I had been secretary of state, that a report of my performance on those assignments had in part led to Carter's asking me to be secretary of state. So I had been exposed to foreign policy, but I will not pretend that I was an expert. I certainly wouldn't suggest that I could compete with Brzezinski on his knowledge of foreign policy. He is knowledgeable—there's no question about it—sometimes overly knowledgeable! It seemed to me that every time a new problem arose that had not been discussed before, he always had a multipoint answer. It was as though he had deliberated over it for some length of time, and then he produced the findings for us. He has a great facility for that. He's not a man at a loss for words. If he is as persuasive in the Polish language, which I do not speak, as he is in the English language, he would be a formidable man to come to grips with in foreign policy.

I think that whatever problems he had with Vance, and I'll let each of them speak to that himself, they certainly were at odds over the desert rescue operation. That was a Brzezinski initiative, something that Vance opposed. I think that, sometimes in annoying ways, Brzezinski concluded that (1) President Carter couldn't afford to lose a second secretary of state; and (2) this was a presidential election year and as a former national candidate myself, I was of value to the President. He didn't want to rock the boat on that account. On a personal basis our relationship was congenial. How could you expect two Poles not to get into some arguments?

QUESTION: Can you enumerate some of your differences with Brzezinski on the Polish situation? He suggests that you were much softer towards the Russians than he was.

SENATOR MUSKIE: We certainly had differences. We went through several exercises in the National Security Council meetings. We had frequent meetings, about once a week. We went through exercises that were very much like the one that we did for Ted Koppel's show. It was on the same subject: the Soviets were deploying troops along the Iranian border and also along the Polish border at the same time. We went through exercises to interpret what those moves suggested and to determine what our response would be to the hypothesized developments along those lines. What might they have in mind? If there were a threat, what would we be in a position to do? What forces were in a position to be deployed? Now as I remember those discussions, which were all hypothetical situations to prepare for different contingencies, there were no discussions that separated the hawks from the doves. But I doubt that he found me dovish in the arguments with him.

QUESTION: In regard to the Palestinian autonomy talks, the second part of the Camp David Accords, how much input did you have in the negotiations during your eight months as secretary of state? Was that solely of Sol Linowitz's responsibility?

SENATOR MUSKIE: He, of course, was our on-the-spot negotiator. He did an excellent job and kept us fully informed. There were several developments that had the effect of interrupting the Camp David peace process. At one time, Geula Cohen introduced a motion to establish Jerusalem as the capital of Israel, which did not have the support of the Israeli government. Their description of their reaction to it was that it was a mischievous thing. But once it appeared on the floor of the Knesset, it was very difficult to defeat it, and for any Israeli member of the Knesset to go on record as opposed to it. But I think they were able to defeat that one.

There were other developments in the United Nations that required a response. On one occasion, we abstained from voting on a resolution when the Israelis wanted us to vote against it. Some resolutions in the Security Counsel were very ingeniously put together in order to make it difficult for us to present the motion as one-sided against Israel and as irrational. By and large we tried to give support, but then the Israeli government would take an action that Sadat took issue with. I think at least twice, while I was secretary, he interrupted the peace process. Because of the action taken by Geula Cohen, he interrupted the peace process. I think there was one other. So we at State were involved in this sense: when the negotiations were on, Linowitz was in charge. But when the negotiations were interrupted, we had to get involved to try to resolve the reason for that interruption and resume the negotiations. The result was that we didn't make very much progress.

There is always difficulty when you have such issues as partial autonomy for the Palestinians. Another very explosive issue was the Israeli resettlement of the West Bank and the Gaza Strip, which I think we all regarded as stirring the pot unnecessarily. Now, of course, after all these years, those resettlements are part of the enormous difficulty of arranging for any Palestinian autonomy on the West Bank or in Gaza. So the problem has not been eased by the resettlement policy, and the Israeli government should never have instituted those resettlement policies. In the Camp David Accords, that kind of subject was implicitly left to the negotiation process. The resettlement policy was established by unilateral Israeli policy for reasons that are understandable but which make agreement very, very difficult. At least during that process, until President Sadat's death after we left office, the peace process was regarded as valuable, something that needed to be kept alive. It took enormous patience on both sides to do so.

QUESTION: In your illustrious career you've rendered distinguished service in the legislative branch and also in the executive branch. Recently, there has been considerable public discussion having to do with the participation of members of the legislative branch in foreign affairs in one way or another. Without asking you to comment on the personalities involved, unless you care to do so, would you comment on the principles involved in connection with the implementation of the constitutional intent?

SENATOR MUSKIE: I suppose you are talking about Jim Wright. Ken and I both worked on the publication, *The President, Congress and Foreign Policy*, which I think contains an excellent discussion of that subject. I was co-chairman of that project along with Kenneth Rush. We had the assistance of forty to fifty distinguished Americans to discuss the subject. Ken was rapporteur of the project. I thought we came out with a good report, which I still use from time to time to discuss this subject. There's no question that this is an area that the Constitution, in my view, established as a shared responsibility, and there's a cyclical response to that constitutional arrangement. I think we said in the book that the constitutional arrangement was an invitation to struggle between the president and the Congress. The president, of course, not by any explicit requirement of the Constitution but by virtue of being the chief executive officer, is the principal representative of the United States in dealing with foreign governments. There is no other way for that to be done. Because of that advantage, he's able to conduct discussions and negotiations with representatives of foreign governments. Over the 200 years of our country, the president has expanded the perception of his role that probably was dominant at the time of the Constitutional Convention.

There is a resistance on the part of the president—and a proper resistance I think—to that kind of role being played by representatives of the congressional branch. It is interesting that the first negotiator picked by President Washington to negotiate the Jay Treaty was the chief justice of the United States. Notwithstanding the doctrine of separation of powers, Washington reached into the Supreme Court to pick the negotiator of the treaty. That also precipitated an issue between the President and the Congress regarding the Jay Treaty, which undertook to clean up some of the unresolved issues left by the Treaty of Paris following the Revolutionary War. That negotiation hadn't met with President Washington's approval altogether, but the Senate requested the confidential record of those negotiations. The President shared those secret instructions and private negotiations with the Senate, and the Senate acted on the treaty.

Subsequently, the House asked for that secret information, and the President turned them down. He said that they can share in areas where there is a constitutional area for the House to act, such as impeachment. But beyond that, the Senate and the president share the foreign policy powers under the Constitution. Washington fulfilled that provision, and that was sufficient. The President made clear a very sensitive and selective approach to this problem.

Let's take the Jim Wright situation head-on. It is a fact that today, unlike in earlier periods, foreign governments deal directly with the members of the Congress because members of the Congress handle legislation of importance to them. I know the Canadian ambassador has contacts on the Hill that he nurses and nurtures. There is a trade agreement pending for the Senate's consideration, so what do you expect? You see the Central American leaders come up to Washington, and they are sent to the Hill by the president, or they go on their own volition. They are invited, I'm sure, by members of Congress, and particularly of the Senate, to come up to the Hill to discuss their problems. That kind of contact is ongoing.

It's inevitable that a member of Congress like Jim Wright, who is under pressure to establish his leadership position particularly in an area where the President and the Congress are sharply divided (aid to the contras), should undertake to accept leadership responsibility from the congressional point of view to influence policy in a direction that is consistent with congressional wishes. I don't think there is any prohibition against it except one's own views about the proper role of each. The Logan Act doesn't even successfully inhibit private citizens from conducting talks with foreign governments. Jesse Jackson has been doing it all over the map, and nobody has raised the Logan Act as a possible sanction against that sort of thing. Of course members of Congress travel all over the world expressing foreign policy views, which are not necessarily equivalent to negotiations. I think that by this time, foreign governments are sufficiently attuned to the disarray of the American policy-making system that they accept it and understand it and suffer through it. Public opinion can impose restraints, and I suspect that even Jim Wright has felt some public pressure to be a little more private.

COMMENT: I didn't mean to restrict my inquiry to Representative Wright because there are a number of other examples.

SENATOR MUSKIE: I picked one because it's a little easier to comment on one, but it does happen relatively often. In my case, President Carter sent me to Europe to talk to Schmidt about important issues between us, especially the new missiles that Schmidt had been largely responsible for getting us to develop. In Portugal we had military base problems, and we had to meet with the Spanish king to talk about the looming base problems that we had there. We went to Berlin to talk about the West Germans' *Ostpolitik* policy. It's not that we negotiated any agreements, but we discussed these things for the purpose of serving the needs of Congress and serving the needs of the President. So it happens, and I think we've got to be accustomed to that.

What really bothers me about the Congress is its inclination to attach legislative conditions on the State Department or the president that I think are out of place. There were eighty-seven amendments to the State Department Appropriations Bill last year that involved a whole range of annoying examples of congressional intervention. So that happens, but it is attributable to a different cause.

QUESTION: Would you be more concerned about the transition period when Mr. Richard Allen, for instance, traveled throughout Europe and met with foreign leaders prior to inauguration? Is that a troublesome part of this greater involvement of parties other than those with constitutional authority?

SENATOR MUSKIE: Well, I think there is a good answer and a bad answer. Obviously, the new administration needs to position itself with our allies, with the Congress, and with the American public on policy initiatives. The problem that really troubles me about transition periods is that there is a disposition of new presidents—whether they are from the same party as the outgoing administration or from the other party—to disown current policies. They want to establish their own new policies.

One example of that was Saudi Arabia's request to purchase the AWACs planes. In connection with the Iran-Iraq war, we had approved the assignment of these planes, which were, in effect, on loan to the Saudi Arabians as a protection against possible Iranian aggression across the Gulf. Toward the end of our watch, the Saudis asked to purchase them. It's been an ongoing problem for several years now of providing arms, and the F-15 aircraft for example, to the Saudis; the objection comes from Israel that these weapons could be used against Israel. So Congress had established constraints within which we had to operate. Congress had to be informed, and there was a waiting period of about sixty days before any agreements of that kind could be implemented. The Saudis asked us if we would sell them the AWACs planes that they were already using. We concluded that we didn't have time. We indicated our support for the idea and said that we would undertake to discuss the matter with the incoming administration, which we did. The President discussed it with Mr. Reagan as I did with Mr. Haig. We offered to go to the Hill with them while we were still in office to recommend the sale with them if it was their disposition to agree to it. They did not want to do that. They wanted to separate themselves from us on that issue. So they waited eight or ten months before they initiated that proposal themselves and had a very difficult task, but it finally succeeded. They finally got congressional approval that I think they could have gotten without any difficulty at all eight months earlier and without the public controversy that emerged. There was no harm done in all of this, but the point that I'm making is still valid: The inclination of the Reagan administration was simply to separate themselves from our ongoing policy to the extent that they could, and to start fresh.

This has relevance, incidentally, to the Tower Commission studies. In the case of people like Richard Allen traveling around Italy, you've got to grant an incoming president the option of doing that. However, I would hope that someone in that position would not undertake to do so in a way that would frustrate an ongoing policy of the United States because it was being conducted by the outgoing administration. There is always a risk; it involves a very sensitive approach.

The historic example, from my point of view, was the refusal of President-elect Roosevelt to meet with President Hoover on the economy in advance of his taking office in March of 1933. Roosevelt would have nothing to do with it. He simply refused. Whether this would have made a difference is hard to say, but he was obviously willing to take full responsibility for his administration. He also wanted the responsibility of putting his policy in place without relying in part or in whole on the Hoover administration. Presidents have to do what they want to do, and I don't think you can institutionalize a change in that practice. I don't think you can put in place a set of prohibitions or guidelines that incoming presidents will honor. They are going to do it their way. That's what they're elected to do, and there isn't much you can do about it.

QUESTION: Senator Muskie, during the last few days we've been seeing references in the newspapers to Admiral Poindexter's diaries, and I believe the Tower Commission was not given access to those diaries. Do you believe this would have made a difference?

SENATOR MUSKIE: It would have been helpful. We had no subpoena power. Our authority for getting information was the President's directive, which was very clear and was contained in the Tower Commission report. It was honored, as far as we knew, by all relevant agencies of the government. We were very satisfied with it. That did not make available to us the testimony or records of individuals who chose to take the Fifth Amendment. The President was in no position to overcome their constitutional rights in that respect; so we did not take testimony from Oliver North, John Poindexter, Richard Secord, Albert Hakim, or Fawn Hall.

That doesn't mean that written records still in the possession of the government weren't available to us. But the fact is that the most difficult period for us to get the facts was the period of August and September of 1985. It was in that period that the first decisions to approve the Israeli transfer of weapons to Iran were made, and there were no formal records of this that we could discover. The principals had differing recollections of what had happened and when. The secretary of defense and the secretary of state, who were statutory members of the council, did not agree in their recollections of what happened and what decisions were made and who was present in August of 1985. The chief of staff's recollection did not match that of those two gentlemen. The President's recollection was uncertain, at best. He recollected approving, but the time when he approved was of significance, and there his memory was weak. Robert McFarlane's record was the most comprehensive and the most detailed, but it wasn't reinforced by anyone else's recollection. So there we were. It seems obvious that because of their preoccupation with the importance of maintaining the secrecy of the operation, they have as little written record as possible. I find that hard to accept. That, at least, was the way we saw it when we were through.

Now, McFarlane told us that Poindexter was appointed as the note-taker at meetings of the Security Council during that period. This was before McFarlane had resigned in the last part of November. Yet we could find no evidence of any notes that Poindexter took in the thousands of documents that were turned over to us. If there were notes, that confirms, in my judgment, McFarlane's testimony to us that Poindexter was indeed the note-taker and that there should have been notes available. If he had taken notes and they weren't available, then presumably somebody destroyed them. We have some evidence of the destruction of records, so there's a very interesting sidelight to the whole thing. Unless we know what is in the notes that have now been discovered, I can't really judge. If there were notes in addition to whatever notes he took at the Security Council meetings—his personal notes, similar to some notes that Ollie North took keeping a record of his own involvements—then maybe we would have learned earlier that he had not informed the President of the diversion of funds, as he testified. The notes I would like somebody to discover are whatever notes Bill Casey had! There's the big gap in the whole story.

NARRATOR: Maybe the most treasured judgment anybody can have is the judgment of his peers, particularly of peers with whom you work hour after hour on difficult issues. This last question reminds us that when we mentioned that we hoped to have Secretary Muskie visit the Miller Center, one of his colleagues on the Tower Board told us to do all we could to bring that about. "Secretary Muskie is a great man," he said. That kind of a judgment is repeated by others who have worked closely with him. Evidence of that quality is pretty clear in the discussion we've had today. We're pleased that all of you came, but we're especially pleased that perhaps we've merely had the first of several exchanges with Secretary Muskie of the Center. Thank you so much.

PART FIVE:

THE CARTER PRESIDENCY: PUBLIC PHILOSOPHY AND PRESIDENTIAL STYLE

CHAPTER 12

CARTER'S POLITICAL RHETORIC

PROFESSOR GADDIS SMITH

NARRATOR: One of Gaddis Smith's main contributions has been his influence over a stream of people who have gone on to become leaders. One of his students recently won the Porter Prize, which is the distinguished prize for the best Ph.D. dissertation in humanities, arts, and sciences at Yale.

Professor Smith has done extensive and important work in the field of American maritime history, and all of us have benefitted enormously from his contributions in the field of diplomatic history.

On our subject today, he is the author of the book *Morality, Reason and Power*. Its value lies not only in its reporting of what happened, but also in its framing of the issues in terms of a coherent set of ideas against which he undertakes to judge the Carter presidency. He wrote an earlier book on Dean Acheson as secretary of state, as well as a history of wartime diplomatic relations in the tradition of his mentor, Samuel Flagg Bemis, who was one of the earlier great figures in the field of diplomatic history.

Gaddis Smith was born in New Jersey, took both his undergraduate and graduate degrees at Yale, taught for three years at Duke University, returned to Yale, and has been there ever since. He has been chairman of the History Department and master of Pearson College, but fortunately for his students and for all of us who are some distance from Yale, he has greatly illuminated our understanding of the field of diplomatic history through his writings.

PROFESSOR SMITH: When Professor Thompson asked me to discuss Jimmy Carter's rhetoric, I was delighted to accept but rhetoric as such is not a subject on which I have focused in the past. I've seen it as an essential part of government, but I do not pretend to be an authority on rhetoric in a technical sense. I'd like to start by giving you my working description of what it means to study a president's rhetoric, and then describe some standards that we might apply to presidential rhetoric generally before going into Jimmy Carter's rhetoric itself.

Rhetoric in its broadest meaning is the use of words in discourse. That's too broad for our purposes though, and so I propose that Carter's public use of words, those delivered orally in person while he was President, be used to define the texts that we will study. This might be a bit arbitrary since he undoubtedly used a good deal of rhetoric in private dealings with the National Security Council or in secret sessions with foreign ministers, but we don't have the transcripts yet for use of that rhetoric. There is also rhetoric in private written communications but, again, the vast bulk of President Carter's papers are not yet open for historians. We also have second hand reports of what Carter said in situations where his words were not recorded, but these sources are problematic, and I'm going to exclude those. We also have purely written texts, such as annual budget messages which go on sometimes for hundreds of pages. These texts weren't written by the President himself, and so we can exclude them. We will also, for convenience sake, exclude texts prepared before he was President—the campaign speeches of 1976, for example—or things written since he stepped down from the presidency, his memoirs and his several other books.

There is always a problem of authorship, and this is a problem for anyone studying a president. We all know that presidents have large staffs of speech writers and that their public statements are often an amalgam of material presented by different Cabinet agencies and departments, and then worked over by the speech writers.

It is possible when all of the archives are open to trace out exactly which sentence and which paragraph came where and to know exactly how a speech was changed by speech writers and then by the president. But we don't yet have full access to that material for President Carter, and it is an enormous task to reconstruct that kind of literary history for every speech. I haven't done that kind of reconstruction, so I'm going to assume that if Jimmy Carter said it personally, then that's his rhetoric. He chose to say those words even though they may literally have been written, in many cases, by other people. Indeed, if we excluded from a study of presidential rhetoric every word that was produced by somebody else, we would have swiss cheese that was all hole and no cheese.

The source of the material that I'm using for my remarks are the familiar volume called *The Public Papers of the President*. For Jimmy Carter they are the green and blue volumes, a set of which are on the shelf in that room to my left; everyone who has dealt with American presidencies in recent years in the 20th century knows those invaluable volumes.

Now what is it that we want to study about presidential rhetoric? That's a much more complex question than to ask simply what the texts are for the rhetoric. We certainly do not want to engage in a purely literary analysis, like graduate students in literature trying to find something new to say about Shakespeare. We don't want to concentrate on Carter's use of the conjunction in his State of the Union addresses, or gastronomical metaphors in the press conference. We are concerned with rhetoric as part of political persuasion.

The best modern book on rhetoric is *Modern Rhetoric*, by Brooks and Warren, and they say that there are four elements to the art of rhetoric: *Argument*, which attempts to persuade people; *exposition*, which attempts to explain and inform; *description*, which attempts to make the listener or the reader see and feel a situation; and *narration*, which tries to show what happened and why. For our purposes, the first element, argument, is preeminent because that is what political rhetoric is about. Political rhetoric uses the other elements—exposition, description, and narration—but they are servants to the principal purpose of argument.

The next question is what standards of judgment should we apply to Carter's rhetoric as argument. We cannot divorce ourselves from the larger political context or from the degree to which the President's goals were achieved or not. But we don't want to maintain the position that good rhetoric is that which works, or that rhetoric which doesn't work is bad rhetoric. For that would be rather reductionist since we know that there are so many other factors which will determine whether a bill passes or a treaty is confirmed, or whether the Democratic party wins or loses an election. There are many other factors at work, and we must recognize that rhetoric is only one element.

An additional complexity flows from the many different audiences which a president especially seeks to influence. Let's take a nonpresidential and rather simple example. If Knute Rockne is in the locker room before the big game, and he exhorts the team to "win one for the Gipper," and the team goes out and wins, then we immediately know what the rhetoric was and who the audience was: the team. There wasn't any other audience at the time. We know the purpose and the outcome is easy to assess. We can determine it quantitatively by the final score.

But how many different audiences and purposes are there for a president in a State of the Union address? In Carter's case, consider the State of the Union address in January 1980 which dealt somewhat with the hostage crisis in Iran and even more with the Soviet invasion of Afghanistan. In that address there were layers upon layers of audience, both domestic and international. We as historians are part of the audience, especially in dealing with someone as recent as Jimmy Carter. I think everyone in our audience here at the Miller Center was an adult during the Carter administration. We were part of the original audience just as we are part of the historical audience now. We have our own values and our prejudices. We reacted at the time to what Carter said, and if we are now trying to be historians, the memory of how we reacted will affect our judgment. Our memory, in fact, may not be accurate, but what we think we remember affects our current opinions.

On that point, let me confess my own bias right now, because we all have biases. I respected and admired Jimmy Carter's integrity and his goals when he was President, and I respect and admire the way he has conducted himself since his retirement from the White House, but I cannot call him an effective president. Much of his difficulty can be attributed to bad luck due to circumstances beyond his control, but much of it can also be attributed to his own failings, including his failings of rhetoric. My judgment on his rhetoric is harsh, as you will see in a moment, but it is also sad because I think the rhetoric was being employed in a good cause. My judgment is also quite subjective. It draws on my own taste in rhetorical techniques, my own sense of the context of what Carter was trying to achieve, and my own comparisons of Carter's rhetoric with that of other presidents.

A moment ago I dismissed the usefulness of any purely literary analysis, but literary analysis in the sense of how words are used must be employed to some degree. I must also give you two disclaimers. First, I have not interviewed Mr. Carter or any of his aides about the subject of rhetoric. I cannot say how much of Carter's rhetorical style was deliberate and calculated, and how much of it was inadvertent. The other disclaimer is that being a neophyte in the formal subject of rhetoric, I've not researched the professional journals of speech and communication on this topic. My hunch is that there probably is already a body of literature on Carter's rhetoric by the professional students of rhetoric and the communication arts; there may even be a doctoral dissertation or two. I haven't read that material; perhaps I will at some point, but I haven't done it yet.

Jimmy Carter was a talking President; he spoke on an extraordinary number of occasions. There were news conferences twice a week during the first two years of the presidency. After midterm in 1979, however, as both domestic and international crisis mounted, he reduced the number of news conferences. But before that time, there were actually call-in shows where you could dial an 800 number and have a one in a million chance to put a question over the telephone to Jimmy Carter. There were town meetings throughout the United States and abroad. One of the most interesting ones that I came upon was a session in Shimoda, Japan. There were informal question and answer sessions with all manner of groups. I haven't done a quantitative comparison, but I suspect Jimmy Carter may have had more of his spoken words recorded in the four years that he was President than any other president in our history. And there certainly wasn't any of this shouting over the clatter of the helicopter with Jimmy Carter.

Despite the quantity and variety of his public communication, there is a sameness to his rhetoric. He doesn't seem to alter the way he uses words to meet the audience or the circumstances. He spoke as if the audience for Jimmy Carter was Jimmy Carter, and I'm going to emphasize this theme. There is a very personal quality to his rhetoric, a constant reference back to his own life and his own experience. Whether this is deliberate or self-conscious, I don't know. He was not a widely read or traveled man, and his illustrations, his references, and his comparisons were drawn very largely from his own life.

I have a question that I'm going to put to this audience: who was the first person mentioned by name by President Jimmy Carter within seconds of his taking the oath for President?

QUESTION: Wasn't it his daughter?

PROFESSOR SMITH: No, it was Julia Coleman, who was his high school English teacher. He refers to her in the very beginning of his inaugural address as someone who had a great impact on his life by teaching him spiritual values.

In the conduct of his term of office, a president has to mention thousands of individuals. He presents people, nominates people for office, and frequently has to refer to congressmen, senators, foreign leaders, his staff, and his family. I am struck with how few individuals, except for those that he has to mention in an official way, were quoted or mentioned in the whole body of Jimmy Carter's rhetoric. There were a few biblical figures and biblical quotations, and he did cite Martin Luther King, Reinhold Niebuhr, and Paul Tillich by name; he mentioned other presidents only rarely. Sometimes he used rhetoric which is reminiscent of other presidents, especially Woodrow Wilson, but seldom did he mention Wilson by name. There is indeed a thinness, a poverty of historical and literary references in his discourse.

Perhaps his emphasis on himself was calculated as part of an effort to present himself as a president of the people. He was drawing strength and wisdom from the people, people just like himself, demonstrating that in America any person, from a background no matter how obscure, could become president. (That's a paraphrase of a remark that he made often about himself.)

I sense that this self-reference was more than deliberate calculation, that it reflected a fundamental loneliness in the man, an introversion, an uneasiness in applying to the role of government the experience of others with whom he was not intimately connected. I believe he was speaking truthfully when he told a group in 1979 that his rural childhood near Plains, Georgia had been the happiest time of his life. He said something like this to that group, "When I am now in the White House in Washington, my greatest hunger is to be alone, away from the security officers, away from the press, and to be in the fields and woods again."

As a teacher and adviser to students, I, like any teacher concerned with writing, constantly harp on the importance of the lead paragraph and the lead sentence within each paragraph. Whether it is a newspaper story, a State of the Union address, or an inaugural address, it is that first sentence and that first paragraph that will have the biggest impact.

In that context I find it extraordinary that so many of Carter's leads refer to himself directly or implicitly. There is his reference to Julia Coleman and her impact on Carter at the very beginning of his inaugural. There is the famous spiritual crisis speech of 1979 known as the "malaise speech" (although he did not in fact use the word "malaise" in that speech). That speech begins with these words: "This is a special night for me. Exactly three years ago on July 15, 1976, I accepted the nomination of my party to run for president of the United States." One could be cynical about this; who cared that his nomination was exactly three years before? And why begin the speech with that, which was certainly one of the most important speeches, he thought, in his whole life? In the opening sentence of the 1980 State of the Union address, another very important address, there is an implicit self-reference: "These last few months have not been an easy time for any of us." It refers to himself: the "us" is almost the royal "we," I think, in that circumstance.

The spiritual crisis speech is one of the most interesting of all of Carter's statements. The particular substantive problem in that summer of 1979 was the energy crisis, and Carter tied that crisis to his most oft-repeated idea, that the fundamental issue was the spiritual health of the people. At the beginning of his presidency he continued to use the theme that had been very important in his campaign, which was that the spiritual health of the American people was rock solid. He said that he had enormous confidence in the American spirit, and that he was drawing his own strength from it. He promised a government as good as the people.

There was also a contradictory claim at the same time; Jimmy Carter believed that Watergate and Vietnam indicated that there was a lack of spiritual health and that now somehow there would be a rebirth, which he would lead. So just two years after his inauguration, he spoke grimly of "a crisis that strikes at the very heart and soul of our national will. We can see this crisis in the growing doubt about the meaning of our own lives, and in the loss of a unity of purpose for our nation. The erosion of our confidence in the future is threatening to destroy the social and political fabric of America."

You will recall, I am sure, the immediate circumstances of that speech. He originally had intended to address the nation on the energy problem early in July, but his speech was canceled at the last minute. He retreated to Camp David, and for ten days invited to join him—as he said himself—people from every segment of society: business and labor, teachers and preachers, governors, mayors, and private citizens. They were to tell him what was wrong. He filled a huge notebook in his own handwriting with their comments, and he quoted quite a bit of this in his speech. I'll just give you a sampling of the quotes from these other people: "You don't see the people enough anymore." "Some of your Cabinet members don't seem loyal." "I feel so far from government. I feel like ordinary people are excluded from political power." "Mr. President, we are confronted with a moral, spiritual crisis."

I would be interested to hear how any of you reacted to that speech. I recall that I myself did not feel that this alleged spiritual crisis was within me. I didn't feel a spiritual crisis, nor did I sense it was really widespread throughout the nation. Instead, I interpreted the speech as self-revelation; I sensed that Carter was talking much more about himself than about any objective reality in the nation. I feared that Carter was undergoing a crisis, and it did not enhance my own confidence in him at the time.

This brings me to the question of what quality it is which inspires confidence in a president's audience and constituents. I've been searching for a single word to describe it, and I've come up with "serenity." Although I have some problems with that word, I'm going to use "serenity." "Serenity" is sort of a Pennsylvania Avenue version of "the right stuff."

In his fireside chat on February 2, 1977, his first address of that kind, Carter said: "I have spent a lot of time deciding how I can be a good president." I think that was probably true, but it was bad rhetoric. Someone once said that FDR never had to think about what it meant to be President: he was President. Most importantly, he was serene in his own identity. One sensed that no matter how serious the crisis—the Japanese attack on Pearl Harbor, or the terrible economic crisis of the Great Depression—FDR's own personal stability was not at risk. This calm quality that I have in mind is not the same as passivity by any means, because serenity can be the companion of enormous activity, energy, and commitment. Thinking of twentieth century presidents, I would say that Theodore Roosevelt had it, as well as Franklin Roosevelt. Wilson had it through 1918, and then lost it very emphatically. Eisenhower had it and so did Kennedy. Lyndon Johnson had some of it. Hoover lacked as did Nixon, Ford, Harding, and Coolidge. I would rank Truman as somewhat neutral on this. Whatever you think of Reagan, he had serenity. It's too early to tell about Bush, but Carter was decidedly without it.

I, as well as virtually everyone who has written on the foreign policy of the Carter administration, have commented on its schizophrenic nature, torn between Secretary of State Vance's efforts to solve conflict through negotiation, Zbigniew Brzezinski's passion to change Soviet behavior by threat, intimidation, and the infliction of pain, and Carter's own moral sense. Both Vance and Brzezinski had quite different approaches, and they both appear in Carter's speeches. Carter's failure to recognize the tension in these two approaches at times led to an awkwardness that bordered on incoherence. I'm not saying that he should have opted entirely for one or the other because the tension is there; it is real, but I think it has to be confronted and explained.

The confusion in policy and the confusion in rhetoric were much the same thing. Indeed, I think the problem of the way in which his speeches were put together was that sometimes these conflicts appear within the same speech. This confusion found expression in Carter's shifting invocation of historical meaning, rare though the invocation of history was. It also found expression in his unfortunate penchant for exaggeration, which is characteristic of his rhetoric.

In his Notre Dame speech of May 1977, which came closer than any other early statement to expressing his personal vision of a better world, Carter made the famous declaration that, "Being confident of our own future, we are now free of that inordinate fear of communism which once led us to embrace any dictator who joined us in that fear. For too many years we have been willing to adopt the flawed and erroneous principles of our adversaries, sometimes abandoning our own values for theirs.

This approach failed with Vietnam, the best example of its intellectual and moral poverty." It is a very, very interesting passage.

Two and a half years later the Soviets intervened in Afghanistan, and Carter indulged in great exaggeration. He called that event the greatest threat to world peace since the Second World War, and then he described its relationship in history in a way that was completely different from his reading of history back in the Notre Dame speech. He said, "Since the end of the Second World War, America led other nations in meeting the challenge of Soviet power. In the 1940s we took the lead in creating the Atlantic Alliance in response to the Soviet suppression and consolidation of its East European empire. In the 1950s we helped to contain further the Soviet challenge in Korea and the Middle East. In the 1960s we met the Soviet challenges in Berlin and faced the Cuban missile crisis," and so on. There was no mention of Vietnam, and no mention of moral and intellectual poverty.

I think both of these interpretations of history have some validity, and a president with a greater historical sense could have shown how they were interrelated. But Carter, with his penchant for hyperbole, exaggeration and oversimplification, seemed to throw out one interpretation without any trace whatsoever in order to embrace another.

Let me end on a more sympathetic note. I see Jimmy Carter as someone who tried simultaneously to think and act in several different realms. First, he was most comfortable in the lonesome, somewhat introverted role of the boy growing up near Plains, wandering in the woods and fields. He was also comfortable with a small circle of friends and family from Georgia.

As for the second realm, he was definitely uncomfortable at the level of national politics. He, like Ronald Reagan, campaigned against Washington as something alien to the true American character. But when Ronald Reagan got to Washington, he gloried in it. He triumphed and really loved the place. He may have continued to engage in anti-Washington rhetoric, but he was really in his element. Carter hated Washington, and he hated it even more at the end than at the beginning of his presidency; this shows in his rhetoric.

The third realm was that of the universal world of all mankind and of the human spirit, and Carter tried to be most truly American by seeing himself and the nation in service to all mankind, not just to the narrow interest of one nation. It is in this sense that he was the most Wilsonian of our recent presidents. This vision and the tension between the world view and the national view was eloquently expressed in Jimmy Carter's farewell address, which is my favorite. He simultaneously reaffirmed the necessity of maintaining American armed strength, while eloquently describing the consequences of nuclear war and the threat of environmental disaster. "We see our earth as it really is, a small and fragile and beautiful blue globe, the only home we have." I think that echoes both Plains and the whole world. "We see no barriers of race or religion or country." Of course, the reality was that the barriers were everywhere, but this was his vision. "We see the essential unity of our species and our planet, and with faith and common sense, that bright vision will ultimately prevail." And that, I think, was Jimmy Carter at his best, both in rhetoric and in thought.

QUESTION: Do you think that his failed rhetoric accounts for his incredibly low popularity rating with the American people? Thirty-seven percent against Reagan's sixty-seven percent? He never sold himself to the American people.

PROFESSOR SMITH: That's correct. Especially in the "spiritual crisis speech," he attacked the American people. He was basically saying that the problem here was that we were spiritually sick, that we had this spiritual crisis. That wasn't the problem; the problem was the Middle East, OPEC, and some difficulties we had in the distribution of oil. Jimmy Carter's gloominess certainly contributed to his own unpopularity. He also had a lot of very bad luck and bad timing.

COMMENT: I was interested in the popularity rating. Not only was he very low among the American people, but the American Bar Association ran a popularity rating among the lawyers, and it was just about as bad as for the American people as a whole.

PROFESSOR SMITH: As I said at the beginning, I admire him as a person and I admire his goals, but I have to rate him pretty low in terms of effectiveness.

QUESTION: Do you think his record would have been viewed differently if the hostage crisis and the oil crisis had not occurred?

PROFESSOR SMITH: Yes, I think that these issues are where you have circumstances that were in part beyond his control. I think the Soviets were the most important factor of all. The Soviets were in a period of incredibly bad leadership, which Gorbachev and almost everybody else in the Soviet Union now are recognizing. "Brezhnev" is becoming one of the dirtiest words in the Soviet rhetorical vocabulary today. This was the period when the Soviet Union was led by a succession of zombies and people who were quite literally on the edge of death. It was paralysis, rigidity of the worst sort leading to incredible Soviet blunders, in both domestic and foreign policy. The worst blunder of all was the invasion of Afghanistan, which seemed to undermine what little there was left of the more positive view that Jimmy Carter had held concerning possibilities for international cooperation. We can speculate about what might have been had Gorbachev somehow come to power in Moscow at the same time that Jimmy Carter came to power in Washington. My guess is that Jimmy Carter would have been reelected and things would have been quite different.

The hostage crisis in Iran was the end product of thirty years of American-Iranian relations. It cannot be blamed on Carter himself. There is a lot of speculation as to whether he could have handled it differently. Carter believed, and I think this is part of his moral code, that the most important issue concerning the American hostages in Iran was their lives. He would do everything possible to preserve their lives. Some of his advisers said, "No, Mr. President, there is a national interest that transcends the lives of hostages, and we basically have to affirm our strength and act quickly and immediately." Zbigniew Brzezinski, the national security adviser, wanted the United States to take military action within a few days of the taking of the hostages. It might well have killed the hostages, and Jimmy Carter might have come out with little more damage than Ronald Reagan did from the death of 243 Marines in the barracks in Beirut, but Jimmy Carter refrained from doing that. He did then authorize the rescue attempt, which failed very early on, long before the team got anywhere close to Teheran. In the end we all remember that the hostages were released within minutes of the beginning of the Reagan administration, and no lives were lost. The hostages were certainly a dark cloud that hung over the last year of Carter's presidency, though.

QUESTION: Did he actually legally change his name from James to Jimmy?

PROFESSOR SMITH: I don't know. He signs all his presidential papers Jimmy Carter rather than James Earl Carter.

QUESTION: Didn't the Camp David Accords give him a great deal of satisfaction and also elevate his image in the eyes of the American people?

PROFESSOR SMITH: I think they did. He had substantial achievements in foreign affairs, one of which, the Panama Canal Treaties, in fact hurt him politically despite being quite an achievement. He narrowly got them through the Senate, and public opinion polls pretty consistently showed that the majority of the American people were against them, but I still think it was better to have signed those treaties than not.

Camp David was an achievement. It wasn't a panacea, which we now certainly know. It ended the formal state of war between Egypt and Israel and led to the withdrawal of Israel from the Sinai, but it did not lead to the Palestinian autonomy in the occupied territories, which was envisioned in the Camp David Accords. I think Mr. Carter was suckered by the Israeli government on that one. He had much higher expectations than the reality of Israeli policy warranted. How much the Accords contributed to his popularity ratings in the polls is hard to measure. It certainly wasn't enough to get him reelected. In fact he wasn't all that popular at any point with the organized American Jewish lobby. Some of them were more hard-line than the settlement in the Camp David Accords.

QUESTION: Did he rely at all on Madison Avenue for his presentation?

PROFESSOR SMITH: No.

QUESTION: To what extent do you think that his delivery had an effect upon the message that he was trying to get out?

PROFESSOR SMITH: He consciously tried to avoid the trappings of the imperial presidency. He wanted to speak in ordinary, almost conversational tones, person to person. I see why he wanted to do that and I can respect him for it, but I think it was a mistake for a president. I think in a presidential setting, especially major policy addresses, you have got to be a little bit more ceremonial than was his style. My hunch is that a lot of people said, "Well, this guy really isn't much of a leader. He's just kind of an ordinary guy; we want someone with more "oomph" in his delivery style.

PROFESSOR HARTT: A lot of us thought that when Carter reached the White House, piety would become an "in" thing along the Potomac. And yet it really didn't work out that way. I am interested in the self-referencing character of so much of his discourse, and with how intimately related it is to the quality of his piety. The kind of pietism to which he was exposed and which clearly influenced him comprises a very large component of his self-referencing tendencies.

I wonder if your suggestion is that there is indeed a schizophrenic element in this piety. On the one hand, we get the insistence on the importance of salvation, whatever secular value that might have, while on the other we get a scolding of what the preachers would have called sin: I see his "moral crisis" speech as a kind of scolding. However, you don't see any point at which his rhetoric is significantly loaded with the biblical imagery that some of us would have expected. His vision does not seem to be either that of the Old Testament prophets or the vision of Reinhold Niebuhr. Do you see any point at which his rhetoric was decisively influenced by what he himself took to be his very deep Christian convictions?

PROFESSOR SMITH: You, of course, are a scholar of religious thought, and I'm not, so I'm a little bit out of my depth here. It is interesting that in his inaugural address, after introducing Julia Coleman, he did make an explicit biblical reference. He had in the first draft of the address a passage from Chronicles. The passage that he wanted to use was: "If my people"—my people—"shall humble themselves and pray and seek my face, and turn from their wicked ways, then I will hear from Heaven and will forgive their sin and will heal their land." But at the urging of aides who claimed some listeners might think Carter was equating himself with Solomon and condemning all Americans as wicked, he chose instead Micah, 6:8. The message was similar although muted: "What doth the Lord require of thee but to do justice, love mercy, and walk humbly with thy God." There are relatively few other explicit biblical references thereafter in his public discourse.

COMMENT: I do not think Carter wanted to be a southern Baptist preacher—that doesn't get to the core of his rhetoric nearly as much as he wanted to be an engineer. It was Rickover, not Niebuhr or Tillich, that he sought to emulate. You can go back to older, wider and better definitions of rhetoric than those you get from the English Departments. These older definitions all have speaker, speech, and audience, while the defining element is the sense of audience. We had the best and the worst rhetoricians in the modern sense of rhetoric riding down Pennsylvania Avenue together in January 1980.

Carter, really, was all thumbs rhetorically speaking. In the South, southern Baptist preachers have a sense of their audience.

COMMENT: Jimmy Carter did not have that. He did not have a sense of an audience, either in the old sense of his immediate face-to-face audience in a congregation or a political hall, or in the modern sense that Ronald Reagan has. Reagan knows when there is a camera and a mike present; he knows that there is a great audience out there, and he knows how to play to it. Carter had neither of these skills and I think this is really the core of his failure. There are a number of books about Carter's rhetoric, but the only one I could think of sitting here was one which defined rhetoric in a very spacious, modern way. It said in effect not to just think of speeches and what is in speeches, and what appeals we use, but to think about the whole context of persuasion. I guess that gets bigger as the apparatus gets bigger.

PROFESSOR SMITH: Right, and it includes the nonverbal imagery, such as walking on inauguration day.

COMMENT: Hogan, on the other hand, presents the Panama Canal as an example of a rhetorical victory for Carter. He did accomplish something important, even if most people would call it political in the narrower sense of getting the treaties through.

There has been a problem in rhetoric which goes back to the ancients: Do you merely study technique, or do you also study the goals for which the rhetoric is used? Good technique doesn't always mean good rhetoric to some people, because there is some question about what it is used for. You might say, "Well, Carter wasn't any good at it; he was all thumbs." But here was something he cared about; he did, and he did successfully persuade in a difficult situation. As you said, the treaties even succeeded against the current of popular opinion.

QUESTION: I was struck, of course, by the terrible bad luck that President Carter had, but also I think it is an interesting speculation as to how he would have done had he been in the White House during the time of Franklin Roosevelt's first two terms. Roosevelt had the best luck you could imagine. He had the bad guys to attack, the "pirates of privilege," and he made the most of it. He got people cheering, and he got the votes. I wonder if Carter, with his religious bent or convictions, might have botched that and not done Franklin Roosevelt's job.

PROFESSOR SMITH: I don't think he would have done Franklin Roosevelt's job. Herbert Hoover hadn't been doing very well in confronting the crisis up to the time he left office. Roosevelt was a master politician in so many ways. He worked magnificently with Congress; he knew how to flatter and win the support of the members of Congress. Of course the nation was united in a sense of a crisis with perhaps 90 percent of the people agreed that extraordinary measures would have to be taken as a matter of national life and death in 1933. Jimmy Carter never, ever had that, but his handling of Congress was incredibly inept in spite of the case of winning, by the narrowest of margins, the necessary Senate votes on the Panama Canal.

QUESTION: How much, if any, of the contrast between Mr. Reagan's superior rhetoric and Carter's ineffective rhetoric, do you think came out in the presidential debates in 1980?

PROFESSOR SMITH: I was biased against Reagan personally in those debates, and I must say that my reaction, I'll have to confess, was a rather elitist one. I thought, "Are the American people so dumb that they are going to be fooled by Reagan?" I wasn't for Reagan. I thought Jimmy handled himself pretty well in those debates. He handled himself quite well in the 1976 debates and scored a good point against Jerry Ford on the question of whether Poland was a free nation or not. Not being a professional student of rhetoric, I am still puzzled, frankly, as to the enormous appeal that Ronald Reagan has to so many people. It's almost as if it is a visceral feeling people have—this is somebody I like; this is somebody I'd like to have in my living room or sitting in the car as we drive down the highway together. This feeling seems more important than everything else.

QUESTION: It seems the malaise factor preceded Carter to the White House. I was a career employee in the foreign agriculture service, and we were made to feel guilty about everything from the parking space to the amount of gasoline that our cars used. I never went through such a grilling as those fellows put out. I don't know how Carter managed to get these people around him or whether he attracted that type of person. He himself was not doing it personally.

PROFESSOR SMITH: His close advisers were from a very narrow circle, overwhelmingly from the state of Georgia. I think you are quite right: this guilt trip that they were trying to make a lot of us feel wasn't very effective politics. Jerry Ford was in a unique and difficult, almost impossible situation: having pardoned Richard Nixon, he could not free himself of the taint of the Nixon presidency. This made for a not-to-be-repeated situation which, I think was really extraordinary. Carter had bad luck once in office , but he also had had unbelievable luck in getting elected because of those circumstances.

QUESTION: Can you see any relation between Hoover's and Carter's background, both having been engineers? How might it have affected things?

PROFESSOR SMITH: Any similarities would be superficial. Hoover's world experience, of course, was incredible. He had been operating for two decades before his presidency for two decades at the highest level of affairs: running the Belgian Relief and the European Relief during the First World War, being a major world figure in international mining before 1914, and then being the most important member of the Cabinet in the Harding-Coolidge years. Hoover clearly had enormous experience. Hoover was a much more, I would say, authoritarian person. Although Hoover had never been in the military, and though he was a Quaker, I would say he had characteristics that we often associate with military command. He commanded things to be done. When the circumstances responded to his commands, he was marvelous. When they no longer responded, as with the collapse of the world economy, he was in a pitiful condition because he didn't have political skills; he only had command skills. So I think my basic answer is no: the similarities are too superficial to be pursued too far.

NARRATOR: Whom did Carter like? Whom did Carter feel at home with?

PROFESSOR SMITH: The relationship between Jimmy and Rosalynn Carter is a very important one. Ken reminded me that I say in my book on Carter, and it is something I still hold to, that Rosalynn Carter is the most politically aware, astute, and intelligent First Lady since Eleanor Roosevelt. I still hold to that.

In the realm of foreign leaders he had good relations with some Third World leaders. The closest relationship he had was with Sadat of Egypt, and he had a surprisingly good relationship with Torrejos of Panama, who was of questionable character, but Carter liked him. He had very poor relations with and did not like major European figures, Helmut Schmidt being the most notable example. Schmidt did not make it easier by publicly calling Carter incompetent. I would say he had difficulty dealing with people who considered themselves his equal. Maybe a lot of us have that trouble.

NARRATOR: I'm sure we all now realize why Professor Gaddis Smith has such a tremendous reputation as a scholar of diplomatic history and of the Carter presidency. We thank him very much for being with us today.

PART SIX:

THE FIRST LADY AND THE VICE PRESIDENT

CHAPTER 13

THE PERSPECTIVE

OF THE FIRST LADY

FIRST LADY ROSALYNN CARTER

NARRATOR: James Sterling Young, who won the Bancroft prize for his great book *The Washington Community*, and who has been the director of our presidency research program and of the Carter Oral History project, will introduce Mrs. Carter.

MR. YOUNG: Looking back on our time, historians of the next century will notice something few of us immersed in these times have been aware of. Future writers will comment upon the transformation of the presidential spouse from a familial role into a role of very considerable public and political responsibility. Historians will no doubt look back to the time of Franklin and Eleanor Roosevelt to see the beginning of this transformation. Many will want to ascribe the further development of the first lady as a public figure to the time of Jacqueline and John Kennedy. But there is no doubt whatever that historians of the next century looking back will regard the first ladyship of the 39th presidency, Jimmy Carter's presidency, as an extremely important chapter in that development and will study it accordingly. Not just because of who Rosalynn Carter is, but because of where she was in history. We are very honored to have you here, Mrs. Carter.

MRS. CARTER: Thank you. I didn't prepare any formal remarks for this morning. When looking at the directory of my computer, I did find something that said "First Lady," so I looked it up. What I found were the answers to some questions that I had received from a student about being the first lady. I thought I would go over these answers with you and then answer your questions.

I played many roles as first lady of the United States: that of wife and confidante of my husband, mother, hostess, and almost full-time volunteer. I'm not sure my influence on the President ever made a difference in his decisions. I always told him what I thought, and he always listened to me. He didn't always react the way I wanted him to react.

However, the first lady can influence the decisions of her husband and of other high ranking government officials on certain issues. If, for instance, she selects a project to work on, it gives the issue visibility and creates interest in government circles. She also has more contact with people. It's easier for a first lady to get out and talk with people and find out how they feel than it is for a president. The first lady has an advantage in that way. For the president there is no possible way for people to really express their views to him. In fact, sometimes people are simply awed just by meeting a president, no matter which president it is.

I only had that happen to me once. When Deng Xiaoping was coming, we did some research on him and China and found out that the camellia plant in our country came from China. So I called an old friend in Moultrie, Georgia, where every year they have a Camellia Festival. I asked him to save camellias so that we could decorate the White House with them, and he did.

When this long-time friend came to the White House, I met him in the diplomatic room and said, "Hello, Mr. Mayor." He couldn't say one word. He really tried. I felt so sorry for him. I started talking to him, and he just handed me some of the camellias. When he came back in the afternoon to decorate, he was fine, and we had a nice conversation. But this happens often with the president.

As first lady I had projects that were important to me, and my position was one of influence in working on these projects. My major objectives as first lady were to promote acceptance of and better care for the mentally ill and to pass the Equal Rights Amendment. I hope I had some impact on the first; I failed on the second. We did what we could on the Equal Rights Amendment at the federal level and got an extension for it passed. Promoting volunteerism and dealing with problems of the elderly were two other issues I was concerned with.

I was not granted a specific sum of money for these projects. I had a staff at the White House to assist me with all White House entertaining, events and correspondence. I had a press secretary and a project secretary who had one assistant. I often had to depend on volunteers because I had so many things going on.

If I had a chance to change anything about the role of the first lady, I think it would be to provide her with a staff large enough to pursue her projects. Contrary to popular belief, I had a very small staff. They were competent, dedicated, and much overworked. The lights burned late in my offices every night.

I was provided transportation by the government for all of my activities. The so-called chores were not unpleasant ones. Social events filled the calendar. There were groups to greet daily, meetings with staff to plan events, meals, entertainment, activities for visiting dignitaries, and events associated with the projects I was working on. Correspondence was voluminous and time-consuming, particularly autographing photographs, postcards, programs, newspaper clippings, quilt squares, and whatever else was sent to me to autograph.

If a president and first lady have a close relationship, criticism and advice will be accepted in good nature. As in all close relationships between husband and wife, criticism and advice are sometimes taken and sometimes not.

When we were in the White House, Jimmy had been in politics for a long time. I had had the experience of being the first lady of Georgia, and this was very helpful to me by the time I got to the White House. I had learned when Jimmy was in the state Senate that you're going to be criticized no matter what you do. If you stay in the White House and pour tea, you'll be criticized because you don't get out. If you get out a lot, you'll be criticized because you are trying to do too much. I had learned even before I got to the White House to do what I thought was important, because the criticism is going to come. I think to be able to do that, you have to be very secure in your beliefs and know what you want to do, what you stand for, what you want to accomplish, and to believe that you are doing the right thing. If you believe these things, the criticisms just roll off; you get used to them.

I actually found local politics the hardest, because you know everybody, those who support you and those who say bad things about you. You feel as though everybody at home ought to be for you. When you get to the state and national levels, it is much easier because you know that everybody is not going to support you.

Eleanor Roosevelt was my favorite first lady because of her activism and genuine concern for the less fortunate. Lady Bird Johnson was a special friend of mine. She had come to Georgia when Jimmy was governor and helped me start a roadside beautification program. I had been to the ranch and visited her. She is still very special to me.

In February 1988 we had a conference on Women and the Constitution at the Carter Center as part of the bicentennial. Lady Bird Johnson, Betty Ford, and Pat Nixon all agreed to co-convene that with me. Betty Ford and I went to the LBJ ranch and spent a couple of days with Mrs. Johnson in the planning. It was wonderful to be with them, because if we ever see each other it's in receiving lines when we all go some place for a special event. It was the first time we had ever had just to sit and talk about the things we are doing now and the things that we had done in the past. We sat on the front porch at the LBJ ranch for much of the two days and talked about common concerns. What do you do, for instance, about accepting the honorary chairpersonship of an organization that you might be interested in but which you are not going to be able to work with? How do you just lend your name? How did you handle various other kinds of situations? How do you handle your mail and so forth? We all agreed that the position of first lady was one that we liked and enjoyed. We also all agreed that the position of former first lady is exciting.

I'm glad that I had the chance to be first lady. I enjoyed the experience, particularly the access to people and leaders in our country and from all over the world. But the thing I enjoyed most of all was the ability that comes with the position to focus attention on problems that were of importance to me.

I want to make one additional comment. Since we left the White House Jimmy and I have found that we still have the resources to work on any project or undertake any interest that we have. Because Jimmy was President we can call on experts in almost any field and they will help. It puts a big responsibility on us, and we are still facing the question that has been part of our lives for a long time: are we using the influence we have to make life better for people, for all our people?

Now I will be happy to answer your questions.

QUESTION: Do you have an opinion, Mrs. Carter, on whether there should be a salary for first ladies or for women whose spouses are in the diplomatic corp, positions in which the wife is often called on to play a heavy role?

MRS. CARTER: I have never thought about other diplomatic wives particularly, but I've had that question a lot. As much of a feminist as I am, I've always said I was glad I didn't have a salary. If you have a salary, then the position will become institutionalized and there will be duties that you have to perform. I was glad that I could do what I wanted to do.

The White House will run without a spouse. The cooks have been in the kitchen for years. The major chef who was there during our term had been hired by Lady Bird Johnson. The presidents come and go, but the staff stays on. Those who are indiscreet are not kept very long.

You have a social secretary who can plan all of the events. You have enough staff in that capacity in the mansion (we call the middle part of the White House the mansion). The kitchen staff—the maids, the cooks, and so forth—has done state dinners forever. There was not much I could teach them about state dinners. I had to do that at the governor's office because we only had prisoners for help, and the first lady preceding me had not done any entertaining. When I went to see my predecessor after Jimmy was elected governor, I asked her who helped her with entertaining and she said, "I do it myself." I said, "Well, who does the cooking?" She said, "I do." "Who does the waiting on the tables?" She said, "I do." I went home and asked Jimmy, "What have we done?"

So my secretary and I had to train the prisoners who were the help, and it was really frustrating. I remember one day we had the press in the basement, and we had submarine sandwiches. I went down just before the press came, and the staff had trimmed the crust off of all the bread.

When I got to the White House all of that was done for me, and I felt free. I didn't have to worry about it. It's good that you do have that staff, because there are so many duties that I don't know what you would do if you had to worry like I did at the governor's mansion.

I finally got the governor's mansion running, but it was all so new to me. I have told people often that it was a bigger job to go from Plains, Georgia, to the governor's mansion than it was from the governor's mansion to the White House. Nobody has believed it, but it is absolutely true. Whereas in the White House you have state dinners and entertain heads of state and so forth, in the governor's mansion you entertain ambassadors. In the White House you entertain the Congress, and in the governor's mansion you entertain the legislature. So you have a lot of the same responsibilities. Being in the governor's mansion was a great help to me when I got to the White House.

QUESTION: Would you like to speak about the effect on children of growing up in the White House?

MRS. CARTER: We are a very close family, and we had always worked together on everything. When Jimmy had gotten out of the Navy, we had come home to Plains. Our oldest son was in the first grade; we had three little boys—our boys were 20, 17, and 15 when Amy was born, so she is almost another generation. After we had been home in Plains for about a year, I started going down to the office to help Jimmy. We had an agricultural supply business. I went down at first just to answer the telephone for him so he could get out and meet the farmers. (His father had died, and Jimmy had gotten out of the Navy to go home; so this had been his father's business. It was a small business.)

Soon I started cleaning up while I answered the telephone, and then I started entering the tickets for the farmers when they bought something while Jimmy was gone. Pretty soon it worked into a full-time position. The little boys would come from school to the peanut warehouse, and we always had something for them to do, until they felt they were part of the business.

When Jimmy ran for the state Senate we didn't campaign very much. We did some, but it was a very quick election because they had reapportioned the Senate in order to comply with the one-man-one-vote rule. Then when Jimmy ran for governor in 1966, of course, the whole family got out and worked, all of the boys. (Amy was not born until the next year, 1967.) We all felt like we had run for governor together.

When Jimmy was elected governor in 1970 and we got to the governor's mansion, it was the first time we had been together for a long time because for two years we had been campaigning in all different directions. So it was wonderful to have that, to be all together at home. We lived on the second floor of the governor's mansion.

When we all campaigned for president, we had the same situation except that all of my children didn't live in the White House. But we all felt that Jimmy could not have been elected if we hadn't helped him. The whole experience drew us together as a family.

When you are in the White House or in the governor's mansion—more so the White House than the governor's mansion—the family members are all in the same situation when they go out. People want to look at you, to shake hands, to call you to sign autographs, take photographs. So we treasured those times when we could just be upstairs on the second or third floor of the White House and be normal people.

It's very hard to lead a normal life if you don't have some place you can go. I didn't want my office on the second or the third floors of the White House—that had been a general rule, I think—because I wanted it just to be home so that I didn't have to dress to go out of the bedroom, and so that the children could bring their friends and it would just be home. That's the way it was: my office was in the east wing. Jimmy's was in the west wing, of course. The first lady's staff is in the east wing.

This doesn't happen with all families, but I think politics drew our family together. I have known wives, when Jimmy was in the state Senate for instance, who never, never could participate, who didn't like it at all. Families were torn. But ours was never that way, and I think it was because we had all felt a part of the process.

It's hard, and it was harder for Amy. It was not hard for her while we were in the White House, but it was harder for her to leave Washington than it was for the others. Because she was thirteen, all of her friends were there, and she really was torn when she had to leave all of her friends.

I think Amy grew out of it and came through the experience with a good perspective. Amy knew nothing but a political life when we came to the White House. I remember at the governor's mansion sitting in my office on the second floor where we lived; I was working one day, and she came in. It was a Saturday, and her father was going to take her to the zoo. She was three years old, and she wanted a pencil that would fit in her pocketbook. I said, "Amy, what do you want a pencil for?" And she said, "To sign autographs." The first time I signed an autograph I was overwhelmed.

One day somebody asked Amy how it felt to live in the White House and she said, "Natural." We moved to the governor's mansion right after her third birthday. It has an 18-acre lot with a fence around it. I think the White House has 18 and 1/2 acres with a fence around it. In the governor's mansion we lived on the second floor with tourists downstairs everyday. At the White House we lived on the second floor with the tourists downstairs. So it was "natural" for her.

I think the only one of our children who was really distressed was Jeffrey, our youngest son, who was probably sixteen when Jimmy was elected governor. He was distressed at school because he was at that age—the two other boys were old enough to be a little bit secure—but Jeffrey didn't ever know whether people liked him because he was the governor's son or because he was Jeffrey. He had a tough time accommodating. He went out to Seattle and worked on a barge for a year while Jimmy was governor just to get away from people knowing he was the governor's son. He said it was so he could have some real friends that he knew liked him because he was Jeffrey. So he was the one that was hurt the most, I think.

QUESTION: In dealing and becoming associated with the spouses of various heads of state, was it possible to get beyond the purely formal relationship with them?

MRS. CARTER: Yes, it was, and that was one of the more interesting things to me. I enjoyed getting to know people like Mrs. Jim Callaghan, the wife of the former prime minister of Great Britain. I also became close to Jehan Sadat.

When we first got to the White House, before a state dinner we would go out onto the South Lawn of the White House and greet the head of state and his wife. The President, Jimmy, would welcome him, and then he would respond. Then we would go inside. We worked on that to get it just right. I had it drilled into me that I was supposed to keep the other first lady on my right; that was the highest position. We went inside to the receiving line; it was the Army that directed these arrivals. They were White House social aides, and they put the first lady on my *left*. I kept whispering, "This is wrong. This is wrong." And then one social aide said, "Mrs. Carter, it's all right; this is a left-hand receiving line." Well, I had been so nervous about protocol, whether I was going to do everything right or not. After that I decided that protocol is just being friendly. Southern hospitality is protocol.

When you relax with these first ladies you realize they are just human beings, and they were wonderful. They were so warm, and I learned a lot from them. We became close friends. Jehan Sadat is one of my very close friends. She has been to Plains to see us, and we visit together when we go to Egypt. She teaches in the United States now and has been doing so since the first year after Anwar Sadat died. She had a tough time over there, because after he died she was not very important in the eyes of the government that succeeded him. She had to stay in mourning for a year, and then she left and until last year only went back home for the memorial service for President Sadat in October, when she would see her family. Sometimes they would visit her in the United States, but now her country is accepting her back into society and she is staying over there more and more.

You do get to be friends with them. One time Jim Callaghan and Audrey were visiting their daughter who lived in Washington. They came to see us in the afternoon just to call, and we sat out on the Truman balcony and talked; they kept staying and kept staying, and it got to be dinner time. The staff was gone because it was a Saturday. One thing I never could get used to was having someone else cook for me. When we got to the governor's mansion I had to direct the staff. I got so distressed. I just got to where I longed to be in the kitchen; so I would go in to cook something, even though the pots were too big. (The staff cooked for twenty-five every day.)

The day the Callaghans were with us, Mary, the maid, was there. Mary was one of the prisoners who had helped us in the governor's mansion. She was a trustee, but she was not guilty of the crime she was in prison for. She was black and seventeen years old when she was charged with murder; she saw her assigned lawyer for the first time in the court room. He told her to plead guilty and he would get her off with life. She plead guilty and got life and was totally innocent.

Mary was Amy's maid. She stayed with Amy in the governor's mansion, and she could do anything. She could entertain guests; she could cook; she could do anything.

This particular Saturday, Mary wanted to cook dinner. (Every Saturday we let the staff go so that we could have Saturday night and Sunday.) Mary had cooked country-cured ham, collard greens, baked sweet potatoes, and corn bread. It was a real southern meal, and so finally I whispered to Jimmy that we had to invite the Callaghans for dinner because they just weren't leaving. So we invited them for dinner, and they loved it. You do get to be close with people who are in similar situations.

QUESTION: Do I remember correctly that you sat in on Cabinet meetings? Was that at your request or your husband's request, and what is your feeling about that?

MRS. CARTER: First, I cannot imagine anybody being in the White House and being asked to sit in on Cabinet meetings and not doing it. We had been there for over a year. It was in February of 1978 when I started going to Cabinet meetings. The reason that I went, that Jimmy asked me to come, was because there is almost no way to get a true picture of what is happening from the news. There may be a minute and a half on television about an issue or the newspaper will have a small write-up. The issues are so complicated, particularly the issues that come to the president's or the governor's desk. If they were easy they would have been solved somewhere else down the line. So they are the most difficult issues.

Every day when Jimmy got off the elevator I was there to say, "Why did you do this? What is happening about this?" and so forth. So finally—I think in exasperation—he said, "Why don't you come to the Cabinet meetings, and then you will know why we make these decisions."

What people don't understand about Cabinet meetings is that the Cabinet sits around the table; they have their names on chairs, and nobody but the Cabinet sits in these chairs. Around the walls are a lot of other people: secretaries, people whom Cabinet officers have asked to come in to report on some project or problem or issue, and lesser government officials. I would come in the door and sit by Max Cleland, who was the head of the Veteran's Administration; he was in a wheelchair and he always stayed by the door.

I went every Tuesday that I could. That year Jimmy was having Cabinet meetings every week, but I think they got less frequent before he left office. I would go and sit as much as I could, and I took notes. Sometimes if I didn't understand something, when Jimmy got home I would ask him about it.

I thought it was important for me to know generally what was going on. I never knew details. I thought it was important, because I had campaigned all over the country telling people what my husband was going to do; also, when I went out I had press conferences, and the reporters would ask me what he was doing. I needed to know. I got monthly briefings on Latin America from the national security adviser for Latin America. I got regular briefings from the assistant to the President for problems of the elderly. I got briefings on women's issues. Every month Zbigniew Brzezinski, the national security adviser, would brief all of the staff in the movie theatre at the White House on the relationship between our country and different countries in the world and what problems were going on there.

All of this was good because it gave me a general idea of what was happening. It gave me satisfaction to know what Jimmy was doing and why he was doing things, but it also gave me a clearer picture so that I could tell people when I went out. I got a lot of criticism for it, but I would do it over again and would do it sooner next time.

NARRATOR: Jody Powell and a number of others who have come have said that the reaction to the 1979 "malaise" speech would have been better if it had not been linked with the Cabinet firings. We've heard so much about first ladies being concerned about their husbands either staying too long or not staying long enough with staff members. Did you ever get into that area either in connection with the firings or anything else?

MRS. CARTER: I didn't particularly agree with him on just firing three or four people. I had been after him forever to get rid of Joe Califano.

I don't guess this is confidential, but anyway Califano was a leak to the *Washington Post*. We didn't know it for a while, but I remember one day I was supposed to speak at the World Health Organization in Geneva and he was going with me. We would be on the same airplane. I wrote down all of the things I didn't like that he was doing and showed it to Jimmy and said, "Can I tell him?" Jimmy said, "I don't care if you tell him." I told him exactly what I thought about all of the things he was doing. He was doing some good things, but it was the way he was doing them that just frustrated me so much. I think his intentions were good. But then we found that he was our leak direct to Ben Bradlee. Jimmy thought what he was doing was good, too, but he didn't like the way he went about it.

MR. YOUNG: My question is what, as you try to put yourself in the position of an historian looking back on this time, would you advise the future historian or the student to look at and to try to understand, the single most important thing they should know as they try to look back on the Carter presidency and understand it?

MRS. CARTER: I think they could look at the human rights issue. When we were doing the exhibits for the presidential library in Atlanta the young historian who did the movie about earlier presidents you see when you go in told me one day that Jimmy Carter would be next because he changed the way that we conduct foreign policy with his emphasis on human rights. Although we've gone backwards a little bit, the movement is too strong to stop, and it's going to be the way we conduct foreign policy in our country. So I think that would be one of the important issues to look at.

MR. YOUNG: In terms of the policies.

MRS. CARTER: Yes.

MR. YOUNG: One of the things that is an unusual aspect of the Carter presidency is that he was the first outsider to be elected since Woodrow Wilson. There haven't been all that many in history as you are no doubt more aware than most of us are. This is somebody who came to Washington not having had any experience in Washington much as Wilson came. Wilson had been a governor. Jimmy Carter had been a governor. This is such an unusual historical occurrence and it was so conscious a part, I think, of the message to the people that was communicated in the campaign about this fresh face in Washington. I wonder what your reflections are on that, how it was to be the first since Wilson, the outsider, and the first also from the deep south for many years to be elected.

MRS. CARTER: I thought you were asking me about policy in the last question. When Jimmy started planning to run for president, he might have spoken about it before, but it was probably 1974 before I took it seriously. We had studied the statistics, the demographics, and he thought he could win. Because a Democrat has to have some of the south to win, and if you look at the demographics you can almost tell the states. You can't tell the swing states but you have to have some of the south because you won't get some of the west and so forth. He thought he could carry the south and if the regular democratic states went democratic then he could win. We felt we could do it.

When he had campaigned for governor he got into the race in 1966 late. Our leading candidate, Ernie Vandever had dropped out with a heart attack, and nobody knew us. I think it was June before he announced an election was up early in August. So the family was forced to get out and campaign. It was not something that we just decided that we would go and help him; we knew that if he was going to win at all, we had to go in different directions because he was not known outside of the senatorial district at all. So I traveled with Jeffrey, our youngest son, who was fourteen. Jack and Chip both had their own schedules and we would go into a community and the main thing we wanted to do was get Jimmy's name on the front page of the paper. Nobody had ever campaigned that way in Georgia except Lester Maddox and he did it himself; his family didn't go out. So people had never seen the family of a gubernatorial candidate, and we could always get our picture on the front page. And that name recognition was what we needed at that point.

So that's how I started campaigning. When he ran for president we thought that we could do it the same way. But it was patterned after that gubernatorial race. We lost in 1966 and then he won in 1970. We all got out and campaigned then. It was exciting because you would go places and I'd say, "I'm Mrs. Carter; my husband is running for president." They would say, "President of what?" "President of the United States." "You've got to be kidding." Nobody would believe it, but it was fun. We had the same reaction as when we were running for governor because nobody, I think, had campaigned that way for president before. Everybody wanted to meet you and see you and you could always get the headlines. But you also learn so much. That's how I got interested in the issues. Because people would ask me Jimmy's stand on a certain issue and I would come home and ask him and he would tell me so that I could go back and tell people.

I was in 105 towns in Iowa. When we first started campaigning, some farmer and his wife would have a coffee in their house and maybe six people would come. If you have an hour scheduled there you can learn an awful lot about farming or the situation as it is. Later, when you got the big crowds you didn't learn much. You would just go in, make your speech and leave. But those early days, to Jimmy too, I think, were so important because we learned the issues in the country. We also learned that everybody is the same. They all want to make a living. They want better things for their children than they had for themselves. People are just interested in the same things. They are proud of their schools and their churches and their communities. That was a revelation to us, that people are the same. I didn't know whether when I went out of Georgia I would have a tough time or not, but I didn't. Of course there are local issues that are different and we tried not to get involved in any of that.

The Perspective of the First Lady

When we got to Washington, the campaign had been beneficial to Jimmy and I think to the whole family, and being an outsider we thought had its advantages and disadvantages. The advantages were that it's like young people starting out in anything; they never know that something can't be done. They have fresh ideas and means for doing things. I think that's the way Jimmy was when he went into office. He was willing to try. He always was a history buff. He had always studied history. We have a huge library of books on the presidency and the presidents. But he had some fresh ideas from being governor of Georgia such as zero-base budgeting and those kinds of things that he did.

The disadvantage is that the press doesn't know whether you know what you are doing or not. They are very cynical and skeptical. Also, one of the mistakes that we made—but if we went back we would do it the same way I'm sure because that's just the way Jimmy is—was that we didn't get involved in the social life in Washington. He felt he was there to run the government and not to go out and party every night. The power structure in Washington didn't like that. But if he went back he would do it the same way. We had not done that in Atlanta. It's so hard. In Washington when we first got there we received tons of invitations. You could go to two or three places every single day. Which do you accept and which not? Then if you start accepting some, you've got to accept others, and he didn't think that was necessary. That didn't go over too well with the power structure in Washington.

So there were advantages and disadvantages. Being from the south—there is a stigma against the south, there is no doubt about that. You wonder why, because so many of the press people were from the south originally. But if you are an outsider and if you are from the south, you have to prove yourself to them. How many times was it said that if Jimmy Carter doesn't get this energy legislation passed or whatever it is done, this will be the end of his presidency. Then you would do it and then you'd start all over. The next thing you started to do would be the end of his presidency and you had to prove yourself over and over if they didn't know you. The reason was they hadn't seen anybody like Jimmy, who operated the way he did. I used to fuss at him, even when he was governor because instead of choosing something that he knew he could do but which would not be sufficient, he would look at an overall program and study what needed to be done if you could do it and he always thought that it was better to get 95 percent of something than it was to get just an awful 5 percent of what you really wanted. But nobody does that. Most people get something so they can have a victory. It didn't matter to him. It didn't matter to him when he was governor and it didn't matter to him when he was president because he has always been a planner. We started the West Central Georgia Planning Commission in our district of Georgia. Jimmy was the head of that. He likes to plan things out, map out what needs to be done and try to do it.

You probably know that he made a list of foreign policy achievements he wanted to make and I used to say, "Why do you do this in the first term?" The Panama Canal treaties, for instance, "Why do you do it?" He said, "It needs to be done." I would say, "You can do that in the second term." He would say, "Suppose I don't have a second term?" And he was right. If he had taken my advice he would have gone down in history as a president who did nothing.

When he was in Washington I don't think he cared if the picture out there was that he wasn't doing what he ought to do, because he was confident that he was doing what was right and best. You realize you are going to get criticisms, and the issues are so complicated it's hard to explain them to people, but he knew what he wanted to do. He thought he was doing the right thing and he didn't worry about it. I worried about it. He didn't. I worried about it when we looked at the polls, but he never did. It didn't deter him. He didn't change his way of governing.

QUESTION: You mentioned as a problem in your book that presidents can get isolated and you talked about entourage problems. What kind of things were you able to tell the president that he couldn't get from other sources?

MRS. CARTER: I suppose he could have gotten them from other sources but I did things like go to a house in New Hampshire where young people were paying home heating bills that were so high. I could listen to them and come back and tell Jimmy what they said, and the same with problems of the underprivileged, the elderly, and the poor. I could tour the schools and the inner city. It's one thing to talk about it, it's another thing to be out there and see it. You can sit down and plan great school programs and say we need this and we need that, but until you go into a school in the inner city and see that two-thirds of the people just go to be counted in the morning because whether or not they pass depends on their ADA (average daily attendance) or on the teacher. There are such problems with some of them that the teacher didn't care whether they were in school or not. She was better off just teaching those who stayed. I saw those kinds of situations. I could come back and tell him that those things were happening.

I think there is a difference in having that kind of first hand information rather than just reading about it and going on.

It makes an impact. It made an impact on me when I would see things like that, problems with the minorities, urban living and problems of the elderly. You could also visit good programs. It was St. Louis, I believe, that had such a good program for the elderly. I could come back and tell him about it and give him some ideas about some things that might be done.

We didn't have the kind of relationship where Jimmy came and said, "What do I do about this?" Never in his life has he ever asked me that. But we used to sit out on the Truman balcony almost every afternoon and talk about the day and if I had been somewhere I could tell him what I did and what I saw and he would tell me what he did and what he saw. If I could somehow help him with some information that might help him make a decision, that was the kind of influence I had on him. I never did day, "Well, do it this way." Most of the times I would say, "Let's not do it this way."

MR. THOMPSON: When he didn't follow your advice, was it on grounds of practicality or was it a question of your vision versus his vision?

MRS. CARTER: No, he always made the decision about what he was going to do. He listened to a lot of people. But he listened to me, too. He would always listen to me. But he didn't always see things the way I did. I could have had some input.

One thing, for instance, one day at Camp David—he might have told you this—I was making a speech not long ago and somebody asked me to tell them one instance when I influenced Jimmy's decision and I told them the same thing I've told you, that we didn't have that kind of relationship where I said, "Do this." He would never do it if I said, "Do this." But he was in the audience, and I didn't know it. It was a YPO (Young Presidents Organization) meeting, and I was speaking to this group and he was in the back. I didn't see him, I didn't know he was there, and after it was over he said, "I can tell you one thing you did." He said, "Don't you remember when we were at Camp David walking around one day and I was having so much trouble with Begin and Sadat and you said, 'If we just could bring them here I know in this peaceful place . . .'" You probably heard him say that. So that was one of my suggestions that turned out well.

MR. YOUNG: That's quite a big one I would think.

MRS. CARTER: So that was my idea originally.

MR. THOMPSON: Is there any liability involved in having a first lady who is politically attuned and whose antennae are up on political questions? Does the public react negatively against that, do you think?

MRS. CARTER: I think they do react negatively. I received all kinds of bad press about it at the White House, about the size of my staff—I had eighteen on my staff. But I had to depend largely on volunteers. There is just no end to what you can do in that position. As I said, you can help with almost any issue.

The media had the habit of picturing Jimmy, particularly in the last year with the hostages, as a weak president and he was anything but a weak president. People who know him know that he was quite clear about what he wanted. He knew what he was going to do and nothing swayed him, including the criticism from the press about getting out of the White House. None of that ever swayed him at all. He was very strong. Another thing people didn't realize is that not to do something in a situation, such as with the hostages, takes a lot of strength. You have to be very strong to resist all that pressure to do something dramatic. This is particularly true when you know, as Jimmy and I both knew, that if he did something, if he bombed Teheran, as I said in my book, he would have been re-elected because people wanted to see him tough. They didn't know how much strength it takes to resist all of that terrible pressure; you cannot imagine the pressure it put on him to do something. He always said, "It would kill the hostages in the first place. It might teach the Ayatollah something, but in the process all of the hostages would be killed if you bombed Teheran or did something like that." So he sent the Ayatollah a message telling him that if he harmed one of them he would mine the harbors or he would do these things, and he never harmed one of them. Jimmy knew that we couldn't tell people what he was doing. So he sat there looking like a weak president. That's when the word was passed around that I was going to Cabinet meetings and making decisions; it was dumb and we knew it was dumb so it didn't matter. It didn't matter to Jimmy. I would get upset about it but he was so firm in his convictions and is so strong that that kind of thing just didn't bother him.

My mother would call and ask, "Oh, what are you doing? The press would say Jimmy was or we all were battered down in the White House and everything was going on and we didn't have control." I said, "Mother, don't worry." It's a lot easier to be in the eye of the storm than it is to be on the outside watching. Because we were there just working hard to do what we thought was right and the people that loved you and cared about you were the ones that were really worried.

QUESTION: Would you care to comment on your experiences with the Habitat for Humanity housing program?

MRS. CARTER: Habitat for Humanity is a program that we have been involved in since we got home. The international headquarters is in Americus, Georgia, which is ten miles from Plains. That's how we got involved with it. People come from all over the world for orientation in Americus and learn how to go back home and start a Habitat project.

Habitat is a program that builds decent homes in decent communities for God's people in need. It is not a give-away program. People who get the houses have to pay for them. We charge the new owners cost with no interest and give them 25 years to pay; that way they are able to afford a house when they never would ever be able to otherwise. The Bible says, "If you lend a poor man money, you don't charge him interest." Millard Fuller, who founded Habitat, says, "We go by the economics of the Bible."

The price is not minimal, but comparatively speaking it is because almost all the labor is donated, and so are many of the supplies for the houses. One day I went into a house in Charlotte, North Carolina, that had a yellow commode and a turquoise sink in the bathroom, but they had painted the room so that it looked fine. I guess some company had had some spare bathroom fixtures and had given them to Habitat.

When we moved back to Plains in 1981 there were programs in about 40 cities in the United States. Now we have, at last count, 326 communities in the United States, with over 70 programs in 26 countries overseas. It has just exploded. It's one of the most wonderful programs that I've ever been involved in.

Habitat does not go out and ask people to start a program. People come to Habitat or hear about it and then inquire; then they come to Americus for orientation, and Habitat teaches them how to organize the program. We get a lot more credit for our efforts with Habitat than we deserve, because we work in the summer one week on a work camp, but it has been highly visible. With all the things we are doing now, that's the one thing people know about. Jimmy has been on the board, and I've been on the board of advisers. Generally, if I am making a speech in a community, I will see if there is a Habitat project there and visit it, because we always need volunteers and we always need money. It's a wonderful program.

QUESTION: Mrs. Roosevelt's career stretched on so long after her husband's death, I think because of the deep interest she showed in issues when she was in the White House. Did you have experiences that you feel create a desire on your part to introduce new and leadership-oriented ways for women in our society?

MRS. CARTER: I am involved with women's issues now. We have the Carter Presidential Center in Atlanta. The presidential library is there, and we have two lakes that are joined by nineteen feet of waterfalls; it is really beautiful.

Across the lakes are three round buildings, "pods" we call them. The first one is the Carter Center of Emory University. It's a school of Emory like the Law School or the Medical School, and we have nine fellows who teach at Emory and are Carter fellows; they work year-round in that area. The Center sponsors studies of peace in the Middle East, African studies, U.S.-Soviet relations, arms control, democracy in Latin America, human rights, and conflict resolution. We have a heavy emphasis on health because our executive director is Bill Foege, who was the head of the Centers for Disease Control in Atlanta for ten years before he came to be with us. He has the reputation of being the leading expert in the world on preventive health care.

The next pod is one in which we have programs that try to put into action what we learn from the studies. We don't want just to be another center that does studies and puts them on the shelf. As a result we have agricultural programs, teaching farmers to increase their food production in many African countries and some Asian countries, Bangladesh for instance. We have health programs in many countries. These are very important to women. The women in these countries do most of the agricultural work and raise the children. Until the status of women is elevated there can be no change in the quality of life for people in the developing nations.

We have two philanthropists who finance these programs overseas. One man has banks in 72 countries in the world. He puts a certain portion of his profits back into the countries, at least 10 percent. In his home country of Pakistan, he puts 100 percent of the profits from his bank back into that country. He has the funds, and we have the expertise.

Because Jimmy was President we can call on anybody to help us with our program. We only send two or three people into a country. Jimmy signs a contract with the head of state, and they have to furnish the personnel. They have to agree, for instance, in the agricultural programs to let the farmers sell their produce at or about market price. In the past they have not been able to sell anything they made at a profit, so they just grow enough food grain to support their families. There was no incentive to do more. This arrangement is a big step forward for some of these socialist countries.

My main interest in the White House was in mental health. I have a grant from Gannett Foundation and am on the Gannett board. Gannett Communications Corporation publishes *USA Today* and over a hundred other newspapers and owns some television stations and so forth. I have a grant from the Foundation to do a study every year on some mental health issues. So I've kept my interest in that alive.

The college in my home county has started a Rosalynn Carter Institute for Human Development, and I'm working there. We are now getting together all of the care-givers, mostly women, in our whole surrounding area and bringing them together to help them with their problems. The first time was several years ago. It is exciting to see them share experiences with one another. There is so much "burnout" (as they call it) with people who care for others all the time. They very seldom are around people who smile and are happy. We are trying to start a model in our area because there is no program like this in the United States.

Last year we had a conference on women and the Constitution. We studied the influence of women on the Constitution from the early days to now, and the impact of the Constitution on women.

Now we are developing a secondary school curriculum on these women whom we learned about. We want to get them into our history books. I am teaching. I am distinguished lecturer at Agnes Scott College in Atlanta. We are having a symposium for the next two days on the transmission of values to women. I've been writing. I have to give my personal perspective on the transmission of values to women. I'll be talking about my mother, my grandmother, and how things have changed by the time we get to Amy, and what is in the future.

So I am busy. We travel so much to support our programs in these African and Asian countries. We have a program in China. One of our financial supporters has banks in China, and he wanted to do something there.

Deng Xiaoping wanted Jimmy to help teach the Chinese how to care for handicapped people. So we are developing now and are already establishing programs for teachers in China who work with children in special education classes. AT&T has developed a process whereby we can have teachers at the Carter Center teach the teachers in China via satellite. We have a few people there, but we are going through the first satellite program tomorrow night.

Deng Xiaoping's son was thrown out of a window during the Cultural Revolution and has been in a wheelchair most of his life. In China when somebody loses a leg or arm, they are a kind of outcast or they are taken care of by the family, but nobody really pays any attention to them. We learned in pursuing this that there was a man in Atlanta who lost a leg in the Civil War. He came back to Atlanta and whittled one for himself, and then he whittled some for friends and finally developed a factory, a process to do them on a large scale. This is now one of the largest businesses for manufacturing prostheses in the United States. We sent a man from this company over to China. (As I said, we only send two or three people into these countries.) Now they are building a factory in China that can produce the latest in prostheses.

It is exciting. Not long ago we were working only on legs and arms, and I had not thought about anything else. So I went to visit one of the programs in China, and this little girl—just a tiny little girl, she must not have been over four or five years old—was clinging to her mother's skirt and she had a sad look on her face. She had lost an eye; her mother said she had a tumor and had to have it removed. So I toured the building and came back down to the second floor, and this little girl was sitting there with a mirror. She had had an artificial eye put in. She had a grin from ear to ear. That makes you feel good. She was a totally changed child by the time I got from the top of the building back down.

We also started a similar program in Kenya. President Moi in Kenya found out about the China program and wanted us to start one in his country.

In all of these Third World countries there is a network of agricultural workers and health workers. The agriculture workers have been sent to the international experiment stations by foundations, by our country, and by European countries. These workers are supposed to learn how to go back home and teach the farmers how to improve their crops. They go back home, but there is no program for them in the government, no way for them to teach what they've learned. Some of them are teaching in schools and some working in drugstores or other places. The network of health people have been to the Centers for Disease Control in Atlanta. Dr. Norman Borlaug, who won the Nobel Peace Prize for the green revolution in India, oversees all of our agricultural programs. We also have Dr. Foege, who for ten years before he came to us had trained people from these countries in six-week training programs at the centers for Disease Control. He said it was always frustrating to them, because when they go back home they are supposed to know how to take care of everybody's medical program.

We asked for those people who have been either to the Centers for Disease Control for health programs or to the experiment stations for our agriculture programs. We not only ask for them; we get their records and see who made the best grades in the studies in these places and who did the best work.

We ask for them, and without exception the heads of state will give them to us.

We went into Ghana three years ago, and asked for two hundred agricultural workers. We sent three people in, some of the same scientists who worked with Dr. Borlaug in India. The first year we had fewer than a hundred farmers who agreed to plant half of their acreage (usually just an acre or two) using the seed that we told them to use, a little bit of fertilizer, and no mechanization. Some planted by sticking a stick in the ground and dropping a seed in. They planted half like we told them and the other half like they generally did. Two or three farmers in a community tried it, and their plot became kind of a little demonstration plot, a little experiment station. The first year we had fewer than a hundred. Last year we had 1,600. This year we have 16,000. Next year we are going to have 75,000 farmers. It will be nationwide. When we go to Ghana now, instead of trying to encourage the farmers, we are helping them with regional warehousing and export markets. Ghana is going to be self-sufficient in food production by 1990, and it is catching on all over. Now we've got so many people coming to us that there is no way we can do all they need done.

We also have the Child Survival Task Force at the Carter Center, which is an umbrella organization for UNICEF, the World Health Organization, World Bank, UN Development Program, and some foundations, working to immunize all the world's children by 1990 and teach mothers the oral rehydration therapy that is a cure for diarrhea. Bill Foege says this is the greatest medical discovery of the decade. You can mix a fourth of teaspoon of salt with a teaspoon of sugar, dissolve it in a glass of water, and it will alleviate diarrhea. I have seen babies who were so close to death from dehydration from diarrhea—and that's what most babies die of in the Third World—that you had to administer this solution with an eyedropper; but in twelve hours the child would be playing.

It's incredible, but it is not the panacea you think it would be, because we have to teach the mothers to give babies liquid when they have diarrhea. It's almost impossible to get them to do that. Also, they have to use clean water, which is a problem for them. We are working in some countries to eliminate guinea worm, and we've gotten the World Health Organization to choose that as a second disease to be eliminated. Smallpox was the first, and Bill Foege was the one who led the work to eliminate smallpox from the world. Guinea worm is a horrible disease that comes from unclean water, a little micro-organism that grows in the water; a person swallows it, and the worm grows in the body, and it is terribly painful when it emerges from the body. It totally incapacitates farms at planting season and at gathering season.

We go into these African villages. When we first started the guinea worm program, we went into one village that had about 750 people. Two-thirds of them had guinea worm, from babies on up to the elderly. They think the gods send it. People say that there are references to it in the Bible.

Most of our people who have worked with this are from the Centers for Disease Control; one man, for instance, worked on guinea worm for twelve years at the Centers for Disease Control, and now he is able to take leave and work for us in the country to try to do something about it. So we have these kinds of programs overseas. It's an exciting life.

NARRATOR: Mrs. Carter, there is a room full of press and media people waiting just one floor up, and we made a pact with them that at 12:45 p.m. you would add to your busy schedule by talking for a few minutes to them. Then at 1:00 p.m. there are a group of scholars who hope to meet with you. So perhaps we should adjourn for the moment, but we very much hope that there may be a chance in the future to visit with you again.

CHAPTER 14

THE PERSPECTIVE OF THE VICE PRESIDENT

VICE PRESIDENT WALTER F. MONDALE

NARRATOR: Compared with almost any of his predecessors, Walter Mondale had a closer and more trusting relationship with President Carter and assumed an important set of responsibilities. A graduate of the University of Minnesota Law School, Mondale first practiced law and then became attorney general of the state of Minnesota. From 1964 to 1977, he was U.S. senator from Minnesota and a protege of Hubert Humphrey. In 1977, he resumed the practice of law with Winston and Strawn, but in 1984 he was tapped as Democratic nominee for the presidency. He is the author of *The Accountability of Power*.

QUESTION: When and how did your association with President Carter begin? What were your first impressions of him? How did your impressions change, if they did, and why?

VICE PRESIDENT MONDALE: I met then Governor Carter on a few occasions, once in the Senate, I believe, and another time, I forget when. My first serious meeting with him, in fact, was in the summer of 1976 when Joan and I went down to be interviewed by him in Plains, Georgia. My first impression after these meetings was that he was a very able man, smart, with a lot of drive and ambition, and a person whose values drove his life. I don't mean to say he wasn't political because he was, but I think he tried to get the best deal he could for his values. He appeared to be, and I later saw that he in fact was, a Christian in the best sense of the word. As I got to know him better, as I spent more and more hours with him, and as the pressure built, those first impressions were the ones that persevered. He never, ever embarrassed me or my wife; he always let us have our dignity, and I think that was a first for the office that I held.

QUESTION: How would you describe Carter's style of leadership and the main sources of his strength? Did he have weaknesses as a political leader? How would you assess his relations as President with Congress? With White House staff? With you?

VICE PRESIDENT MONDALE: I think his main source of strength came from his faith, his values, his closeness to Rosalynn and his family, and a sense of confidence that he could get most things done. I say most things done because he did not have much confidence in his ability to communicate, at least on a mass basis, through television or radio or an auditorium speech. He had a lot more confidence that he could persuade in a more personal setting, and in fact he was more effective there. His style of leadership was one of seeking to master all the facts and details so that he could deal as an equal with his subordinates with the authority that flowed from such knowledge. He worked a driven, disciplined twelve- to sixteen-hour day, did his work way into the night, and was always ready for every meeting.

He administered his office in what we called the "spokes-on-a-wheel" style, by which almost anybody in the administration, any old friend, or any member of the Congress could come to him directly. I believe that is one of the great weaknesses. Try as hard as he could, there just wasn't time enough to handle the presidency with the mass of people expecting direct access.

I felt that his insecurity about the public education role of the president showed. He tended to speak to the public in the language of an engineer, and he recoiled against using emotion, poetry, and the rest. I believe that because of that, his appeal to the general public was not a strong one, and in many ways he was unable to convince the public that he was not somebody weak, uncertain, timid—which he wasn't at all.

I would say he had good relations with the leadership in the Congress. Tip O'Neill liked him a great deal; I think Tom Foley liked him, as did Jim Wright. I don't know about Bob Byrd, but I think Danny Inouye and others of the Senate respected Carter because they knew him.

On the other hand, Carter was not a buddy. He did not approach it that way. No backslapping, and he did not want to deal with the Congress from a bargaining-type psychology where they would give something and he'd give something, they'd get a deal and go out and get it done. He was more apt to define what he, as President, wanted done and then expect and hope that the

Congress would respond. The result was that many of these congressmen did not feel that there was anything to be gained from cooperating, and thus we did not get the support in the Congress that we should have had. However, having said that, I think we got more through the Congress than the public perceived to be the case. And part of that was, once again, due to Carter's tireless efforts to prod and move the Congress.

I would say he was widely respected by the White House staff. Certainly that staff was a lot stronger than its public reputation, and they respected Carter and were very loyal to him. I think they had less confidence in his political judgment in the setting of priorities or in his persuasive ability, but that did not diminish their respect for him. It was just one of the weaknesses that the President had as they saw it.

My relations with the President have been widely reported. I think it was the most successful presidential-vice presidential relationship maybe in the history of my beleaguered office, and I shall forever be grateful for that. The recent study, *A Heartbeat Away*, came to that same conclusion.

QUESTION: How did he use his Cabinet and how did he deal with Cabinet members? How important were Cabinet meetings at the beginning and end of this administration? How did the Carter White House work with heads of departments and agencies?

VICE PRESIDENT MONDALE: Carter used the Cabinet members on a one-to-one basis. The Cabinet meetings themselves may have been of more help to him than I perceived them to be. I think it was the President's availability to each of his Cabinet members that built a respectful relationship between a particular Cabinet member and the President.

Here again, I think the structure of presidential decision-making permitted Cabinet officers who wanted to go their own way, who looked on their Cabinet position and their department as a personal fiefdom, to go ahead as they wished. Since the President was busy with many things—couldn't keep up, as a matter of fact—and since authority was not lodged in a chief of staff to implement the President's will, many Cabinet officers were able to deal contemptuously with the White House. It isn't that the President didn't become aware of that and didn't punish some of those Cabinet officers, but it was a long time in coming and I think we suffered a great deal from that.

I think the Carter White House worked quite well with the departments and the agencies, and we started working better as the years went on. At first the President was very anxious that these Cabinet officers and agency heads feel totally independent and free from White House staff. He went out of his way to tell them that they didn't have to listen to anyone except him, that if they had any personal grievances or hopes or aspirations, he wanted them to come directly to him, the President. The result was that the staff, such as Hamilton Jordan and Stu Eisenstadt, and Jack Watson and the others who had to deal with these Cabinet officers and agency heads, found them often reluctant or resistant to accept orders unless they were personally issued by the President to them. So I would say that that was an area of less than perfect effectiveness.

QUESTION: Who were his closest advisers? How did they relate to one another? How did Carter use them? What are your evaluations of his advisers? What were your relations with them?

VICE PRESIDENT MONDALE: Who were his closest advisers? A long list: Rosalynn Carter, his key staff that he brought with him from Georgia—I'm sure I'll forget some, but Jody Powell, Ham Jordan, Stu Eisenstadt and Burt Lance—and then friends that would come in and out like old Charlie Kirbo, whom he respected a lot. He had an affection for people who had stuck with him early. When he first started running he was ridiculed as a candidate for president, and those who came with him early and never left his side, who took him seriously when everyone else was laughing, they had his heart and he wouldn't let anybody touch a hair on their heads. We had some fine people there who weren't really too good in their jobs, but because of that factor Carter supported them. Sometimes we paid quite a price for that. I think he figured that they would be loyal and he didn't know whether the others would be loyal to him when times got tough. He, however, listened to a broad range of people who cannot be so defined. I would like to think I was one of them, certainly Cy Vance, Zbigniew Brzezinski, Harold Brown, Cecil Andrus and, depending on the subject that came up, people like Bob Bergland and Stan Turner. The list is too long. I think he tried to keep an open ear. He listened carefully to all of his people and was respectful to all of them.

I would say the staff related very well to each other. Even in the toughest of times there was very little finger pointing within the White House. Now with respect to others, for example, Cy Vance and Zbig Brzezinski were fighting all the time, and a couple of the Cabinet officers got away on their own programs and resented any interference and they were able to get away with it, I think, for the reasons cited above. So that relationship maybe was as good as it ever is (I think we cannot idealize this), but it was not as good as it should have been.

I thought many of his advisers were superb. I got along well, I thought, with all of them. I thought Stu Eisenstadt was about as good as anybody I've ever seen in that position. I thought Jody Powell was a very able news secretary. I think Ham Jordan had some weaknesses, but his personal judgment, his strategic judgment, and his courage in standing up to the President made him an indispensable part of the administration. It was a tragedy that Burt Lance's personal problems, unrelated to government, by the way, destroyed him as a source of daily advice because he was able, more than most of them, to get Carter to consider the political dimensions of a problem. Carter came in there with a kind of Baptist antagonism as to how the real world would respond to his concept of what his faith indicated should be done. To him on most days, those who argued politics were really coming in on the cheap and he would often lament, oppose, and show anger toward those who would do so. I learned to package my recommendations differently, although I often just hit him directly with what I thought were the political realities of what was going on.

Carter was strangely antipolitical for a person who had gone so far and proved himself so effective in the political arena. I've often thought that if that had been different we would have easily won reelection. Carter was so good, so smart, so disciplined that if we had had that political knack and an approach to problems which would allow us to hold the country together, it would have made a big difference.

I remember early in the administration when they decided to attack all the water problems in the west at once, and somebody, hoping to destroy us, issued a "hit list" of some 70 or 100 water projects, most of which were in the West. Our reaction was one of, "Well, we are going to review them." We mumbled around and basically Carter wanted to take a look at every one of them and whack them. Well, this comes so close to life itself in the West, that by the time we got that issue down the road a few months we were dead in the West. It was called the "war on the West," and as I predicted, the fact that we tried to do so much at once automatically put in place a coalition that guaranteed we would not get anything done. History shows that a water policy worked out in cooperation with the governors is essential, but it takes time, cooperation, coordination, and all the rest. That was an example of the way he would approach problems.

I guess I've gotten off the point here; my relation with his advisers, I think, were excellent in most cases.

QUESTION: How did he organize the White House? What were the strengths and weaknesses of his system? How did his mode of organization affect or limit relations with President Carter?

How did this organization of the White House compare with others you've known?

VICE PRESIDENT MONDALE: He did not use a chief-of-staff system, a pyramidal system. He used this "spokes-on-a-wheel" system where people came directly to him. I thought it overwhelmed the system and didn't allow him to spend as much time as he should on the big problems, trying to generalize and summarize. It was somewhat like a quarterback running all the plays to the center of the line. We needed him back there with a clear head calling the signals.

QUESTION: How would you describe his relations with the press and the public in general and on key issues such as human rights, SALT II, the Panama Canal, the Middle East, the environment, energy and the budget? Did this affect your relations with Carter?

VICE PRESIDENT MONDALE: I thought that President Carter's relationship with the press and the public was one of the tragedies of his administration. He was far more open than Reagan; he was far more responsive to questions. He tried as best he could to educate the public, but he just wasn't very good at it, and because of that he didn't have a lot of confidence in himself. Because of that there was a sense of uncertainty, even anxiety occasionally. He would have high moments like the night he defended Billy Carter. But it was a heavy burden. You can work as you want, and he did, but if you can't keep the public with you, you just lose the essential power of the presidency, and that's what happened to us toward the end.

The other thing is that he seemed to have that engineer's method of describing things. If you asked about the car, he'd want to tell you how to build an engine. He figured that if he told you the details, the central and sometimes very technical arguments, then honest minds would be driven by the power of the calculation. Of course it doesn't work that way.

How did this work out in specific cases? Well, in human rights I think there is a lot of support for it. As a matter of fact, the public support for human rights finally forced Reagan back on essentially the right road. I think the polls showed that he carried the day on that. Unfortunately I think we sounded pious and preachy, maybe a little impractical, but I think that was one of the strong points of the Carter administration.

Certainly the negotiation of SALT II was a victory, but the invasion of Afghanistan kicked that all into a cocked hat, and there wasn't much we could do about it.

The Panama Canal was a great victory but also a Pyrrhic victory because we spent so much of our early goodwill and trust on that highly divisive issue, that by the time we were over that we were badly weakened. It became a *cause celebre* for the right wing, and they organized around it. As important as that issue is and as proud as I am of what we did on it, because we were right and we succeeded where about seven presidents had failed, nevertheless I think it was at a cost that was very, very high.

The Middle East: that's one of the great conundrums. Probably Carter did more to find peace—not probably but certainly—than any president since the history of the reestablished state of Israel. And yet through hundreds of little mosquito bites, we were unable to gain the defense of the constituency that should have been the most grateful. That had serious political repercussions in certain states in the union.

Unbelievably, after the official signing of the Egyptian-Israeli treaty in Washington on that wonderful day, I thought the polls would soar, and they didn't move an inch. Here was one of the great victories of the human spirit in modern history and something for which Carter was clearly to be credited—not by himself but he certainly was the leader there. That showed you the condition that we were in with the public. If Reagan had done one-fifteenth of that he would have had 100 percent approval in the polls.

Carter was a great, committed, honest, gutsy environmentalist, no question about it, and the environmental leaders knew that and appreciated it, but they picked on him if he made any compromise whatsoever. The support we should have had from rank-and-file environmentalists I don't think really developed as strongly as it should.

Energy: Once again the basic outlines of the oil and gas legislation were shaped by Carter, adopted in the early days of his presidency, and proved to be very sound. As a matter of fact that was one of the reasons that we got some reprieve. I used to say that under Carter we always front-loaded pain and back-loaded pleasure. We did what we had to do. We paid a heavy price for it and the country benefitted, and so did Ronald Reagan.

On the budget, we were far from perfect, but we were infinitely more responsible than either our predecessor or our successors. He told the truth and he tried hard under difficult circumstances. I'm not sure the public accepted that definition at all.

None of this adversely affected my relations with Carter. We became closer as the years went by. It seemed that the tougher things became, the more we came to trust each other. Joan and I will never forget how kind and decent the Carters were to us at all times, and that relationship remains the same today.

QUESTION: What was Carter's view of the office of the presidency?

VICE PRESIDENT MONDALE: Well, I've tried to answer that question. I think Carter wanted to be remembered as a president motivated by his values, by his faith, and by his personal abilities and his capacity to persuade and to move a nation. I think contrary to public perception he was a man with a lot more depth and more understanding, than was believed to be the case. We accomplished a great deal in those four years, but I think the failure to handle the public education role in a different, more effective way robbed us of a lot of the credit that would have been ours.

I think the President felt that the fact that he was the President would automatically cause the system, that is, the Congress and the courts, the governors, and our friends, to be more responsive than they proved to be, that there was something about being the commander-in-chief and the President that would give him the advantage in public argument. In fact, he learned to his great chagrin that after the first few hundred days there was no such presumption, and I think he felt that there was a lack of respect for him. He felt that other presidents had not been treated this way. He never said it that way to me, but I always had the impression that he felt the way I've just described.

When all is said and done, President Carter told the truth, obeyed the law, and kept the peace, and I don't believe that's bad. I think history is going to deal very kindly with President Carter.

QUESTION: How would you assess the record of the Carter presidency? How would you compare it with other presidencies?

VICE PRESIDENT MONDALE: I've tried to answer that by implication. Every president brings strengths and weaknesses to the job, and we remember a president's weaknesses in the short term. I think his strengths become more important as history is able to write the record without partisan or personal implications.

I've often said that Carter and Reagan reminded me of the opposite sides of the same coin. Carter was superb in his discipline, his ability, his understanding, his intellectual honesty, and the courage and directness with which he sought to do what the country needed to do. But he was tragically weak in the public education role of the presidency. Reagan was abysmal in terms of the merits and substance of the presidency. Every book written now by some seven aides of his—this is not me talking—have all said that he was uninvolved, uninformed, and just not there; it was an empty White House—a "Ghost Ship". But he had the Hollywood knack of mesmerizing the American people. And guess who won and who lost?

QUESTION: How do you think future historians will judge the Carter presidency? How do you judge it?

VICE PRESIDENT MONDALE: I've already tried to answer that question. I think that they will look at what we did on energy, on the environment, on education, on human rights, on arms control, on the Panama Canal, the Middle East certainly with Camp David, the Egyptian-Israeli Peace Treaty, and the strengthening of NATO. Another thing we didn't get credit for were the choices made at the Defense Department by Harold Brown and his scientific director. These choices were very, very sound, and history has confirmed every one of their judgments. Since then we've wasted billions on nonsense like the B-1, and we resisted the "Star Wars" baloney, and so on. I think history will give us credit for that.

There was a civility, a decency, to President Carter that will wear well with time. And I'm proud to have been a part of that administration.

NARRATOR: Thank you, Mr. Vice President.